Gender Nonconformity and the Law

Gender Nonconformity and the Law

KIMBERLY A. YURACKO

Yale

UNIVERSITY PRESS

New Haven and London

For Michael, Sacha, and Katja

Yale University Press books may be purchased in quantity for educational, business, or promotional use. For information, please e-mail sales.press@yale. edu (U.S. office) or sales@yaleup.co.uk (U.K. office).

Set in Janson type by IDS Infotech Ltd. Chandigarh, India.
Printed in the United States of America.

Library of Congress Control Number: 2015942777
ISBN 978-0-300-12585-6 (cloth : alk. paper)

A catalogue record for this book is available from the British Library.

This paper meets the requirements of ANSI/NISO Z39.48-1992 (Permanence of Paper).

10 9 8 7 6 5 4 3 2 1

Contents

Acknowledgments

This book has been a long time in the making. It is the product of my thinking and writing about sex discrimination in employment over the past decade. It has been a very interesting journey, as so much has changed in the law over that time. Indeed, the case law and the social opinions it reflects have in many regards changed much faster than I ever predicted. Given the length of my journey toward completion of this book, I have many people to thank. Mark Kelman has been a teacher, mentor, and friend to me for over twenty years now. He is the best reader I have ever encountered. I am deeply indebted to him not only for improving this work but for actually sparking my interest so many years ago in studying discrimination and pursuing an academic path, a path that has been richly engaging and rewarding for me ever since. I also owe a great debt to the late Susan Moller Okin, who, like Mark Kelman, played a formative role in my intellectual development and my career path.

ACKNOWLEDGMENTS

I have benefited from comments and suggestions on many parts of this manuscript from Ron Allen, Michael Barsa, Cynthia Bowman, David Dana, Shari Diamond, and Andrew Koppelman. I am grateful for the time they have invested in this work and for their encouragement. I would also like to thank Melissa Goldman for her outstanding and careful research support, as well as my library liaisons Marcia Lehr and Jesse Bowman. Finally, I am grateful for the institutional support I have received while writing this book from Dean Dan Rodriguez and the Northwestern Summer Research Fund, as well as for the generous support I have received from the Judd and Mary Morris Leighton endowed chair.

My greatest debt of gratitude goes to my husband, Michael Barsa, and our children, Sacha and Katja. Their creativity, playfulness, and joy are like sparks of magic that fill my days with fun and laughter. It is for them that I am most extraordinarily grateful.

Introduction

The Aggressive Woman: Ann is a senior manager at a large accounting firm. Ann works hard. She is successful at winning new contracts for the firm and at advising clients. Yet when she is considered for promotion, she is denied admittance to the partnership. Some partners find her too aggressive and unladylike. To improve her chance of promotion the following year, she is advised to dress more femininely, wear makeup and jewelry, and have her hair styled. Ann sues for sex discrimination. She wins.[1]

The Effeminate Man: Antonio works as a food server at a restaurant chain. For several years, he is subjected to a steady stream of insults and name-calling from some of his male coworkers. They refer to him using female pronouns and mock him for carrying his tray like a woman. Antonio complains about the harassment to no avail. He sues for sex discrimination. He wins.[2]

The Transsexual: Philecia is a transsexual police officer who has been diagnosed with gender identity disorder. As part of her transition from male to female, Philecia begins living off duty as a woman. While still presenting as male at work, Philecia does display some feminine characteristics on the job.

1

She has a French manicure and arched eyebrows, and sometimes she comes to work wearing makeup. Philecia is denied a promotion to sergeant. In justifying the denial, one supervisor explains that she is not sufficiently masculine; she is criticized by several others for lacking "command presence." Philecia sues for sex discrimination. She wins.[3]

The Garden-Variety Gender Bender: Darlene works as a bartender at a casino. In order to protect its image, the casino has rigid and detailed grooming codes for female and male employees. The code for female employees requires them to wear makeup, have their hair styled, and wear nail polish. The code for male employees prohibits them from wearing makeup. Darlene objects to the requirement that she wear makeup. She does not object to any other gendered aspect of the grooming code and she does not have gender identity disorder. She refuses to wear makeup and is fired. Darlene sues for sex discrimination. She loses.[4]

Why do courts increasingly protect workers from discrimination based on their gender presentation in addition to their biological sex? Why do some employees receive more protection from gender stereotypes than others? In particular, why are transsexuals winning their challenges to sex-based gender conformity demands while garden-variety gender benders are not? This book looks for answers to these questions by examining the rich body of recent case law in which gender-nonconforming workers seek protection for their atypical expressions of masculinity or femininity.

This body of case law is particularly important because it is the area of sex discrimination law that has evolved most quickly and changed most dramatically in the past twenty-five years. Moreover, the changes, at least at the federal level, have been entirely the result of judge-made law rather than statutory change. Judges have been interpreting the prohibition on sex discrimination contained in Title VII of the Civil Rights Act of 1964 in ways unforeseen at the time of the act's passage. Perhaps because of the rapidity of change, and perhaps because of the conceptual difficulties these cases raise, the decisions themselves are dramatically undertheorized and poorly explained. There has not yet been an effort by courts or scholars to provide an overarching analytical framework to help understand and bring coherence to this body of case law. This book attempts to build such a framework by identifying the values, principles, and priorities that have been driving, often without explicit articulation, this fast-moving area of the law.

This body of case law is also important, however, because of the light it sheds on the social purposes and goals of sex discrimination law more generally. This is the area of sex discrimination law in which courts struggle most overtly with changing social norms. Indeed, it is the only area of sex discrimination law in which courts sometimes permit employers to treat women and men in the same position differently. The cases raise starkly, as a result, a core question of sex discrimination jurisprudence—the extent to which antidiscrimination law requires only access and the extent to which it requires more sweeping challenges to social gender norms, mores, preferences, and expectations. Dress, appearance, and grooming cases challenge the last realm in which employers are permitted to treat women and men in the same position differently. Courts struggle overtly in these cases to respond to and act upon social gender norms in the name of furthering the law's antidiscrimination mission. As a result, gender nonconformity cases provide particularly rich and fertile insight into the scope of sex discrimination law's protection and the reasons for its sometimes seemingly haphazard expansion.

When the Civil Rights Act was passed in 1964, its target was clear. It aimed to eliminate the categorical workplace exclusion of women and minorities. At the time, African Americans were routinely excluded from jobs and even from whole industries.[5] Women, too, were confined to "pink collar" jobs and often barred from the more prestigious and profitable positions reserved for men.[6] Title VII sought to, and did, end this kind of categorical group-based discrimination.[7]

In the decades that followed, however, discrimination became much more subtle and complex. No longer were women or minorities categorically excluded from jobs. Inclusion did, though, require that they "fit" the corporate mold. An employer might be happy to hire female lawyers, for example, as long as they did not appear too "butch" or masculine. An employer might be happy to hire black ticket agents as long as they did not wear their hair in "cornrows." Those who expressed their gender or race in disfavored ways continued to be excluded.

Workplace "fit" demands have been labeled "second generation" discrimination and have become a focal point of antidiscrimination litigation and scholarship. Feminist scholars argue that such fit demands require employees to embrace traditional conceptions of masculinity and femininity and punish employees whose gender expression deviates from that typically associated with their biological sex. Race scholars have made similar arguments contending that workplace fit demands punish workers whose racial expression deviates from white middle-class norms. Both types of fit demands, scholars argue, should be treated as actionable under Title VII's prohibition on sex and race discrimination.

The U.S. Supreme Court paved the way for such protection in the sex context in the 1989 case of *Price Waterhouse v. Hopkins*, in which the Court declared that sex stereotyping was a prohibited form of discrimination in employment. The Court's pronouncement came in a case where a woman was denied promotion to the partnership of a large accounting firm despite outstanding professional reviews by clients and tremendous success in winning new business contracts. Evidence suggested that she was denied promotion, at least in part, because she was viewed as inadequately feminine and ladylike. While the Supreme Court had previously held that it was an actionable form of sex discrimination to penalize a female employee based on stereotypical assumptions about how women actually behave, this was the first time the Court made clear that it was also a form of sex discrimination to penalize a woman based on stereotypes about how women *should* behave.

The Court's seemingly simple declaration has been the most important development in sex discrimination jurisprudence since the passage of Title VII, and it has been responsible for dramatic expansions in how courts have interpreted the act's coverage. The prohibition on sex stereotyping has led to protection for men who are harassed by their coworkers because they are perceived as inappropriately feminine in how they walk, talk, stand, and move their bodies. It has also led to protection for transsexuals—once excluded from the act's protection altogether—from workplace disadvantage as they transition in their outward appearance from one gender to the other.

Yet not all gender nonconformists have gained protection. Garden-variety gender benders—those who object to some but not all of the conventions associated with their biological sex—remain outside the law's protection and continue to be subject to their employers' gender conformity demands. Employers remain free to adopt and enforce sex-based grooming codes requiring, for example, that men refrain from wearing earrings or that they keep their hair short.

The result is a body of case law that is on a trajectory while still being in something of a muddle. The trajectory is in the direction of greater and more expansive protection for the ways in which people experience and express their gender. The muddle is due to the fact that the trajectory is imperfect. Some workers continue to be denied protection for their gender nonconforming conduct, and it is difficult to identify a single guiding principle or rule to explain who wins and who loses. The cases look contradictory and even incoherent.

To the extent, for example, that one reads the gender nonconformity protection as reflecting a commitment to formal neutrality, then protection for the aggressive woman may make sense, but permitting sex-based grooming codes and penalizing garden-variety gender benders looks irrational. To the extent that one reads gender nonconformity protection as reflecting a narrower commitment to eliminate only those gender performance demands that are directly at odds with job requirements, then failure to protect garden-variety gender benders may become more understandable, but protection of the effeminate man and the transsexual becomes perplexing. Finally, to the extent that one reads gender nonconformity protection as shielding workers only from performance demands that burden their core gender identity, then protection for the transsexual becomes understandable, but protection of the aggressive woman from feminine workplace demands is rendered mysterious.

My goals in this book are twofold. First, I seek to explain the muddle. Antidiscrimination law has always reflected a mosaic of principles and values rather than a single commitment or requirement. It is the search for a single guiding antidiscrimination principle that makes this area of sex discrimination law look particularly inconsistent and incoherent. I strive in the coming chapters to identify the range of different values and principles underlying contemporary sex discrimination jurisprudence generally and to reveal the work that these different principles are doing in driving courts' quickly changing response to gender nonconformists.

Second, I seek to raise a note of caution about the trajectory. The most recent expansion of protection for gender nonconformists is due to an increasing medicalization of gender in the courts. Protection for transsexuals, in particular, has depended in large part upon courts' acceptance of testimony by medical experts affirming the fixed, stable, and immutable nature of gender identification in those who suffer from gender identity disorder. Such evidence, however, serves to essentialize the gender experience not only of transsexuals but of women and men generally, defining masculinity and femininity for everyone in terms of fixed, stable, and highly traditional forms of gender performance. Paradoxically, then, the current trajectory of expansion may be bringing new protections for individual gender nonconformists at the expense of a subtle hardening of gender expectations for everyone.

At its core, this book is more a work of doctrinal deconstruction than of moral philosophy. It seeks to explain not when discrimination is wrong in some abstract moral sense but when discrimination is wrong as a matter of law in the United States in the early decades of the new millennium. Moreover, it challenges existing law not on theoretical grounds but on the grounds of the law's concrete implications for workplace freedom, sex equality, and gender fluidity.

Chapter 1 of the book offers an overview of the trajectory and muddle of contemporary federal sex discrimination case law dealing with the claims of gender nonconformists. It highlights the Supreme Court's seminal decision in *Price Waterhouse v. Hopkins* in which the Court famously declared that sex stereotyping was a prohibited form of sex discrimination, and shows how courts have used that decision to dramatically expand the scope of Title VII's sex discrimination protection—first to men perceived as effeminate and then to transsexuals. Nevertheless, as the chapter shows, despite such expansions in coverage, courts remain steadfastly unwilling to protect garden-variety gender benders from particular sex-based dress and grooming demands that such workers find offensive.

The remaining chapters examine the values and principles that underlie antidiscrimination law generally and show the work that these values and principles are doing in the evolving case law involving gender nonconformists. Chapter 2 focuses on the popular equation of nondiscrimination with neutrality. The idea that like must be treated alike, combined with a conviction that women and men are alike in most relevant respects, lies at the core of Title VII's antidiscrimination prohibition and has been responsible for dramatic changes in women's workplace opportunities. Nonetheless, neutrality has limits—both conceptually and practically—as an antidiscrimination mandate in sex cases, and a commitment to neutral treatment of the sexes cannot wholly explain courts' recent protection of gender nonconformists.

Chapter 3 focuses on Title VII's antisubordination goals, which aim to improve the social status of women as a group. Despite the breadth and complexity of such goals, they have been operationalized by courts into a few discrete and concrete tests. I show both the power and the limits of such tests to explain forms of protection that cannot be explained by courts' constrained commitment to neutrality.

Chapter 4 considers the importance of status versus conduct in antidiscrimination law and courts' willingness to prohibit discrimination based on status but not on conduct. Some gender nonconformists have been able to tap into historical concerns about status-based harms in order to win expanded protection for conduct that could otherwise be legally prohibited. Medical evidence regarding gender identity disorder has played a critical role in such cases and in the victories increasingly won by transsexuals. Yet the search for status-based harms has given dangerous incentives to even progressive courts and plaintiffs to rely on and endorse traditional, even reactionary, accounts of gender as fixed, binary, and biologically rooted.

Chapter 5 suggests that sex discrimination jurisprudence reflects not only discrete, identifiable principles but also more substantive and complex judicial judgments about human flourishing. Such views are distinctly illiberal and controversial. Indeed, they are perfectionist, evincing a substantive conception of the good life and of the activities and capabilities that are, and those that are not, compatible with it. Although judges rarely state their perfectionist commitments explicitly, it is possible to tease them out from certain decisions. Recognizing such commitments is a critical piece in understanding courts' response to gendered dress, appearance, and behavior requirements in the workplace. In particular, an implicit prioritization of intellectual development and distrust of sexuality underlie and help to explain courts' willingness to protect women from hypersexualized conformity demands. Recognizing such perfectionist principles provides a richer and more accurate picture of the case law than relying on more traditional antidiscrimination principles alone.

Chapter 6 considers and rejects an argument being made by some recent scholars—namely, that a new judicial commitment to freedom of gender expression is behind recent protections for gender nonconformists. Despite suggestive rhetoric in some cases, no such principled commitment exists. Courts are not in fact committed to free gender expression in the workplace and do not view gender freedom as part of the law's antidiscrimination mandate. Indeed, far from being a core antidiscrimination value, liberty of expression is actually antithetical to such protection. Sex discrimination doctrine depends on and demands a definition of gender, yet such a definition necessarily excludes idiosyncratic or unconventional expressions.

Finally, in chapter 7, the book considers why there has not been any parallel development or expansion in courts' protection of racial minorities from workplace conformity demands that implicate racially loaded social norms regarding dress, appearance, and behavior. The chapter takes an albeit brief comparative look at recent race discrimination jurisprudence, focusing on cases that parallel in some respects those being brought by gender nonconformists in the sex context. These cases involve claims that certain workplace rules and practices penalize employees for expressing their race in a particular way. The chapter considers why such claims uniformly lose and why the values and commitments that have led to such dramatic change in the sex context have not produced similar results in the race context.

Antidiscrimination law reflects society's most basic commitments to fairness, inclusion, and opportunity. In recent years, courts' interpretations of what the nation's central sex discrimination prohibition demands have changed sharply, yet the reasons given for these changes have been superficial and inconsistent. This book urges not a reversal of the current trend of expanding protection but a moment of pause—a pause to consider more closely, systematically, and carefully the values and beliefs driving the current expansion—in order to ensure that both judicial outcomes and, importantly, judicial reasoning continue to reflect and promote our most fundamental commitments.

CHAPTER ONE

The Case Law
Expanding Protection

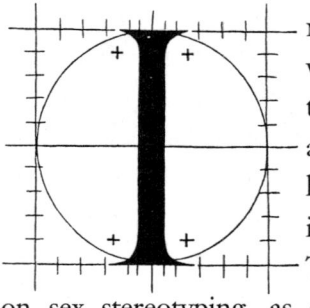NCREASINGLY, Title VII protects workers not only from discrimination based on their biological sex but also from discrimination based on how they express their gender—that is, their masculinity or femininity. The Supreme Court's prohibition on sex stereotyping, as articulated in *Price Waterhouse v. Hopkins*, provided the impetus for such expansion, leading to protection for men perceived as effeminate as well as for transsexuals. Yet some types of conduct remain unprotected. Cases involving garden-variety gender benders highlight the limits of this expansion and show the imperviousness of sex-specific grooming codes to the sex stereotyping prohibition. This chapter presents a roadmap of the key cases marking the scope of antidiscrimination protection for gender nonconformists. The subsequent chapters will excavate beneath the rhetoric of

these and other important cases to expose the values, principles, and concerns that drive them.

THE AGGRESSIVE WOMAN

Ann Hopkins was a senior manager in Price Waterhouse's Office of Government Services in Washington, D.C. She had been very effective in this role. She worked well with clients and had been particularly successful in winning new contracts for the firm. Indeed, the district court noted that "[n]one of the other partnership candidates at Price Waterhouse that year had a comparable record in terms of successfully securing major contracts for the partnership."[1] Hopkins was also exceptionally hard working, having billed more hours than any of the other candidates under consideration that year.[2] She had been at the D.C. office for five years when, in 1982, the partners in her office proposed her for the partnership. Hopkins was one of eighty-eight employees proposed for partnership that year and the only woman. In total, Price Waterhouse had at the time 662 partners, of whom seven were women.

The road to partnership is a long one, with several points of review along the way. The process begins when partners at each office choose whether to propose a senior manager from their office for consideration. To nominate a candidate, partners in that manager's office write a recommendation and a detailed description of the candidate's qualifications. These proposals are then distributed to the firm's partners, who are invited to submit evaluations of the candidate. Partners may use either a long- or a short-form evaluation, depending on their degree of contact with the candidate. Both forms ask partners to rank the candidate in different categories and also to provide a recommendation regarding admittance to the partnership, along with explanatory comments.

These evaluations then go to the firm's Admissions Committee, which reviews and summarizes them before making its recommendation to the Senior Partner and Policy Board, the group elected by the partners to manage the firm. The Admissions Committee recommends that the candidate be admitted to the partnership, denied admittance, or held for further consideration the following year. The Policy Board then decides which candidates to include on the ballot, which is submitted to the entire partnership. Candidates not included on the ballot are told of the board's reasons for rejecting their candidacy or holding it for possible consideration the following year.

In Hopkins's case the comments submitted to the Admissions Committee indicated that she had problems dealing with staff members. She was criticized for being "overly aggressive, unduly harsh, difficult to work with and impatient."[3] Other comments touched on her sex as well as her qualifications. One commentator said " 'she may have overcompensated for being a woman.' "[4] Another said she should take a " 'course at charm school.' "[5] One supporter opined, " 'Many male partners are worse than Ann (language and tough personality),' " and said that people were focusing on her profanity " 'because it is a lady using foul language.' "[6] Another supporter said " 'she had matured from a tough-talking, somewhat masculine hard-nosed mgr. to an authoritative, formidable, but much more appealing lady partner candidate.' "[7]

The Admissions Committee recommended that Hopkins's candidacy should be held until a later year, and the Policy Board concurred.[8] The head partner of her office, who was also one of her strongest supporters, was responsible for telling Hopkins of the Policy Board's decision and giving her advice for improving her chances in the future. He advised her "to walk more femininely, talk more femininely, dress more femininely, wear make-up, have her hair styled, and wear jewelry."[9] The following year the partners in Hopkins's office refused to propose her again for the partnership. Hopkins resigned and sued for sex discrimination.

At a bench trial before the district court, Hopkins introduced testimony from expert witness Dr. Susan Fiske, who testified that while she could not determine whether any particular comment was the result of sex stereotypes or the degree to which such stereotypes had influenced the ultimate decision, the comments from male partners showed that sex stereotyping had played a role in the decision-making process. In particular, Fiske testified that "[o]ne common form of stereotyping is that women engaged in assertive behavior are judged more critically because aggressive conduct is viewed as a masculine characteristic."[10]

The district court found that Hopkins's promotion process had been infected by sex stereotypes and that Price Waterhouse had done nothing to purge them from the process despite clear evidence of their presence. The court concluded, "Price Waterhouse's failure to take the steps necessary to alert partners to the possibility that their judgments may be biased, to discourage stereotyping, and to investigate and discard, where appropriate, comments that suggest a double standard constitutes a violation of Title VII in this instance."[11] The court further explained that given that Hopkins had shown that sex stereotyping played a role in her promotion decision, Price Waterhouse could avoid liability only if it could show by clear and convincing evidence that it would have made the same decision absent discrimination. This, the court ruled, Price Waterhouse had not done.[12] The district court granted a judgment in favor of Hopkins and awarded her attorney's fees but refused to award her back pay or require Price Waterhouse to make her a partner, because it held that she had resigned her position voluntarily rather than being constructively discharged.

Both Price Waterhouse and Hopkins appealed the district court's decision. On appeal, the D.C. Circuit Court of Appeals found there was "ample support in the record for the District Court's finding that the partnership selection process at Price Waterhouse was impermissibly infected by stereotypical attitudes toward female candidates."[13] It further found that the district court had properly found Price Waterhouse liable for discrimination because the firm could not demonstrate by clear and convincing evidence that impermissible considerations were not the determining factor in the partnership decision. The court of appeals did, however, reverse the district court on the question of whether Hopkins had been constructively discharged, holding that Price Waterhouse's decision to deny her admittance to the partnership along with her office's failure to renominate her the following year "would have been viewed by any reasonable senior manager in her position as a career-ending action. Accordingly, it amounted to a constructive discharge."[14]

When the case reached the Supreme Court, the main question at issue was whether Price Waterhouse could avoid liability if it could show that it would have placed Hopkins's candidacy on hold even absent discrimination and, if so, what Price Waterhouse's burden of proof was in this regard. The Court held that Price Waterhouse could avoid liability entirely if it could show by a preponderance of the evidence that that it would have made the same decision absent discrimination. Congress, however, overturned this part of the decision with the Civil Rights Act of 1991. The 1991 act provided that an employer would be liable for a violation of Title VII if sex was a motivating factor for an employment practice, even if an employer would have made the same decision absent the criteria; the plaintiff's remedies in such a case would simply be limited to declaratory relief and attorney's fees.[15]

Of more lasting effect was the Supreme Court's strong pronouncement that sex stereotyping was a form of discrimination prohibited by Title VII. "As for the legal relevance of sex stereotyping," the Court explained, "we are beyond the day when an employer could evaluate employees by assuming or insisting that they matched the stereotype associated with their group," for " '[i]n forbidding employers to discriminate against individuals because of their sex, Congress intended to strike at the entire spectrum of disparate treatment of men and women resulting from sex stereotypes.' "[16]

After the Supreme Court's decision, Hopkins's case wound its way back down to the district court and the court of appeals. Ultimately, Hopkins won elevation to the partnership at Price Waterhouse and also back pay.[17] Yet while Hopkins's own saga was finally ending, the real impact of her case, and in particular of the Court's broad sex stereotyping prohibition, was just beginning.

The first wave of cases to take advantage of the Supreme Court's sex stereotyping prohibition were brought by men harassed because of their perceived effeminacy and often also their perceived homosexuality. Rather than arguing that discrimination based on sexual orientation violated Title VII, an argument that had consistently lost, such plaintiffs argued that they were being penalized for violating gender stereotypes, in violation of Title VII's prohibition on sex stereotyping.

One of the earliest such cases was *Doe v. City of Belleville*.[18] The plaintiffs were two sixteen-year-old brothers, J. and H. Doe, who took summer jobs with the city of Belleville as gardeners in the local cemetery. Immediately after beginning work, the boys were subjected to relentless harassment from their male coworkers. H. Doe was the prime target. He was derided for looking and acting too feminine and was even threatened with rape. On one occasion, H. Doe's primary tormentor did in fact grab his testicles in an effort purportedly to " 'finally find out' " if H. was male or female.[19] H. and J. quit their jobs and sued, alleging that they had been sexually harassed and constructively discharged.

The district court granted summary judgment for the city on all of the plaintiff's claims, concluding that the harassment H. and J. suffered was based on their perceived homosexuality rather than on their sex. As such, the conduct was not actionable. The court of appeals, however, reversed. Relying on the

Supreme Court's prohibition on sex stereotyping, the court of appeals concluded that the plaintiffs had presented sufficient evidence to show that the harassment they suffered was discrimination because of sex under Title VII. The court explained that "the fact that H. Doe apparently was signaled out for this abuse because the way in which he projected the sexual aspect of his personality (and by that we mean his gender) did not conform to his coworkers' view of appropriate masculine behavior" provided proof that the discrimination at issue was because of sex.[20] The court continued that just as it was actionable sex discrimination in *Price Waterhouse* to penalize a woman based on a perception that she was too "masculine," so too "a man who is harassed because his voice is soft, his physique is slight, his hair is long, or because in some other respect he exhibits his masculinity in a way that does not meet his coworkers' idea of how men are to appear and behave, is harassed 'because of' his sex."[21]

The Seventh Circuit Court of Appeals also held that the harassment that H. Doe experienced was because of sex simply because of its sexual nature. According to the court: "In view of the overt references to H's gender and the repeated allusions to sexual assault, it would appear unnecessary to require any further proof that H's gender had something to do with this harassment; the acts speak for themselves in that regard."[22]

The Seventh Circuit's decision in *Belleville* was subsequently vacated by the Supreme Court for further consideration in light of the Court's decision in *Oncale v. Sundowner Offshore Services*.[23] In *Oncale*, the Supreme Court resolved the circuit split that existed at the time regarding whether same-sex harassment could be discrimination under Title VII. The Court made clear that it could, yet the Court rejected the argument made in *Belleville* that the sexually explicit nature of conduct alone was sufficient proof. The Court noted instead that it had "never held that workplace harassment, even harassment between men and women is automatically discrimination because of sex merely because the words used have sexual content or connotations."[24] The Court did, however, outline three ways in which a plaintiff could show that same-sex harassment was because of sex. First, one could show that the harassment was sexual in nature and that the harasser was homosexual. The idea was that had the victim been of the other sex, the harasser would not have been sexually attracted and the harassment would not have occurred. Second, a plaintiff could show that the harassment was of such a sex-specific and derogatory nature as to make clear that the harasser was motivated by a general hostility to men (or women) in the workplace. Finally, the Court explained that a plaintiff could show that same-sex harassment was because of sex by showing that the harasser treated male and female employees differently in a mixed-sex workplace.[25]

While the Court did not explicitly refer to evidence of sex stereotyping as another way a plaintiff in a same-sex harassment case could demonstrate that harassment was because of sex, neither did it directly challenge or retract the framework.[26] As a result, the sex stereotyping logic has become the dominant tool by which men harassed by other men, and, to a much lesser extent, women harassed by other women, have sought to prove that the harassment was actionable sex discrimination.[27]

Even more dramatic than the expansion of Title VII to protect men harassed because of their perceived effeminacy has been courts' recent use of the sex stereotyping prohibition to protect transsexuals from discrimination. Such protection marks a direct reversal of course from earlier cases, in which transsexuals were explicitly denied protection under Title VII. As the Seventh Circuit bluntly explained in *Ulane v. Eastern Airlines:* "The phrase in Title VII prohibiting discrimination based on sex, in its plain meaning, implies that it is unlawful to discriminate against women because they are women and against men because they are men. The words of Title VII do not outlaw discrimination against a person who has a sexual identity disorder."[28]

The first circuit court to provide such protection to transsexuals was the Sixth Circuit in its 2004 decision in *Smith v. City of Salem.*[29] In *Smith*, the court relied on the Supreme Court's sex stereotyping prohibition from *Price Waterhouse* to hold that a preoperative male-to-female transsexual who alleged that he was penalized for expressing feminine attributes at work could state a cause of action for sex discrimination.

Jimmie Smith worked as a lieutenant in the Salem Fire Department in Salem, Ohio. He was a biological male who had been diagnosed with gender identity disorder (GID). Shortly after Smith began expressing a more feminine appearance at work, in accordance with international protocols for treating GID, his coworkers began to comment on his appearance and his inadequate masculinity. After Smith told his supervisor about his GID and his intention to transition from male to female, the chief of the fire department held a meeting to find a basis for terminating Smith's employment.

As a result of the meeting, Smith was required to undergo three separate psychological evaluations with doctors of the city's choosing. Shortly thereafter he was suspended for twenty-four hours on the basis of a purported policy infraction. He sued in federal court, arguing that it was a form of sex discrimination to penalize him for his failure to conform to stereotypes about how a man should behave. The Sixth Circuit agreed, relying on the Supreme Court's prohibition on sex stereotyping in *Price Waterhouse* to reverse the district court's dismissal of his claims.[30] As the Sixth Circuit explained: "After *Price Waterhouse*, an employer who discriminates against women because, for instance, they do not wear dresses or makeup, is engaging in sex discrimination because the discrimination would not occur but for the victim's sex. It follows that employers who discriminate against men because they do wear dresses and makeup, or otherwise act femininely, are also engaging in sex discrimination because the discrimination would not occur but for the victim's sex."[31]

The Sixth Circuit's decision in *Smith* was followed one year later by the court's ruling in *Barnes v. City of Cincinnati*.[32] Philecia Barnes was a preoperative male-to-female transsexual who worked as a police officer in the Cincinnati Police Department. Barnes lived as a man while on duty but often lived as a woman while off duty. Despite presenting as male at work, he did retain some of the feminine expressions of his off-duty persona. He "had a French manicure, had arched eyebrows and came to work with makeup or lipstick on his face on some occasions."[33]

Barnes applied for promotion to sergeant, passed the initial exam, and was subjected to a probationary period with intensive and frequent evaluations. During the course of his probation, one supervisor told Barnes that he did not appear masculine enough. Another supervisor told him that he had heard rumors that Barnes was going to fail probation because he had not been acting masculine enough. Several supervisors also found him lacking in "command presence." Barnes did fail his probationary period and subsequently sued the department for sex discrimination.

A jury heard Barnes's case and ruled in his favor on his sex discrimination claim. On appeal the Sixth Circuit affirmed. Relying on its prior ruling in *Smith* for support, the Sixth Circuit explained that a jury could have reasonably concluded that Barnes was discriminated against because of his failure to conform to masculine gender norms. The Sixth Circuit has not been alone in its use of the sex stereotyping prohibition to protect transsexual workers. The Ninth Circuit as well as several district courts have recognized similar protection for transsexual workers.[34]

THE GARDEN-VARIETY GENDER BENDER

In the years following *Price Waterhouse*, the sex stereotyping prohibition seemed on a collision course with employer grooming codes. If employers were not permitted to penalize transsexual workers for challenging sex-based gender norms, how could they penalize nontranssexual workers for challenging sex-based grooming codes? Yet in *Jespersen v. Harrah's Operating Company*, the Ninth Circuit made clear that the sex stereotyping prohibition did not extend protection to all gender-nonconforming workers. Notably, it did not extend protection to those I call garden-variety gender benders—women and men who seek to challenge some, but not all, of the formal gender conventions associated with their sex.[35] Such workers could still be subject to sex-specific grooming codes. The *Jespersen* case reinvigorated a line of decisions dating back to Title VII's inception holding sex-based grooming codes immune to challenge as a form of sex discrimination, and also made clear that the prohibition on sex stereotyping was not a mandate for total gender freedom in the workplace.

Darlene Jespersen had worked as a bartender at Harrah's Casino for twenty years when she was terminated for refusing to comply with the company's sex-specific makeup requirement. The requirement was part of a new "Personal Best" program that imposed grooming and appearance requirements on all bartenders. While the program dressed bartenders of both sexes in the same uniform of black pants, white shirt, black vest, and black bow tie, it also required female bartenders to wear makeup but prohibited male bartenders from doing so. Specifically, female bartenders were required to wear "face powder, blush and mascara . . . applied neatly in complimentary colors" with "lip color . . . worn at all times."[36]

Jespersen argued that the makeup requirement " 'forced her to be feminine' and to become 'dolled up' like a sexual object."[37] Moreover, she argued, it actually interfered with her ability to do her job. In her position as a bartender, she sometimes had to deal with unruly, intoxicated customers, and the makeup requirement, she contended, undermined her credibility in dealing with such situations. Relying on

Price Waterhouse's pronouncement against sex stereotyping, she challenged the makeup requirement as a form of illegal sex discrimination.

Yet Jespersen lost at every level of review. The district court granted summary judgment for Harrah's, holding that the company's Personal Best program did not constitute sex discrimination, because it imposed equal burdens on both sexes. The panel of the Ninth Circuit that originally heard Jespersen's appeal agreed, although it strained to explain why the prohibition on sex stereotyping did not prohibit Harrah's imposition of a makeup requirement on Jespersen. The prohibition against sex stereotyping applied to sexual harassment cases but not to grooming code cases, the panel maintained, while offering no explanation or justification for such a cabined view, which seemed particularly odd given that *Price Waterhouse* itself was not a sexual harassment case.[38]

The Ninth Circuit reheard the case en banc and again affirmed the district court, though it did no better at explaining why the sex stereotyping prohibition stopped short of sex-based grooming codes. Indeed, if anything the en banc court's opinion was even more mysterious. Unlike the panel opinion, the en banc decision made clear that appearance standards, including makeup requirements, may be subject to the sex stereotyping prohibition, but it held that in this case "Jespersen has failed to create any triable issue of fact that the challenged policy was part of a policy motivated by sex stereotyping."[39] "There is no evidence in this record" the court explained, "to indicate that the policy was adopted to make women bartenders conform to a commonly-accepted stereotypical image of what women should wear."[40] Judge Pregerson in dissent objected to the court's conclusion. According to Pregerson, "[t]he inescapable message is that women's undoctored faces compare unfavorably to men's, not because of a physical difference between men's and women's faces, but because of a cultural assumption—and gender-based stereotype—that women's faces are incomplete, unattractive, or unprofessional without full makeup."[41]

While the court's reasoning was muddled, its fear was clear. If it were to protect Jespersen from having to comply with the makeup requirement, "we would come perilously close to holding that every grooming, apparel, or appearance requirement that an individual finds personally offensive, or in conflict with his or her own self-image, can create a triable issue of sex discrimination."[42] The prohibition on sex discrimination, according to the court, simply could not go that far. The workplace was not to become a place of unfettered gender freedom.

CONCLUSION

In recent years, the idea that Title VII prohibits sex stereotyping has been used as a kind of trope—invoked when courts seek to strike down a conformity demand and overlooked or glossed over when they seek to uphold it. The result, as the above cases show, is a rhetoric that is powerful but also, at times, empty or contradictory. In the following chapters, I begin to look behind the rhetoric to excavate the values and principles that are in fact driving the dramatic recent changes in sex discrimination law. I seek to explain to what extent the new protections for gender nonconformists stem from deepened commitments to traditional antidiscrimination values

like neutrality and antisubordination, to what extent they reflect more controversial values like a distrust of sexuality, and
to what extent the changes reflect deeply ingrained, and perhaps unconscious, beliefs about the ways in which people experience their gender.

CHAPTER TWO

Neutrality

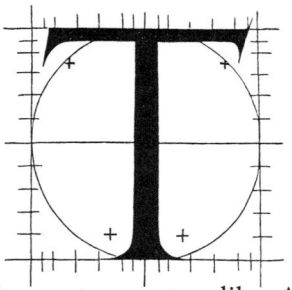HE value that most clearly and firmly grounds American antidiscrimination law is "neutrality"— the idea that like must be treated alike.[1] Women and men must be treated alike in the workplace because they are fundamentally, and in most respects, alike. Antidiscrimination law's demand for neutrality ended employers' dual-track hiring processes and gave women a road out of the pink-collar ghetto. Yet the demand for neutrality is not always simple. Indeed, in cases implicating strongly held gender norms, determining when like are (or are not) being treated alike may be truly vexing. Gender norms can make technically similar conduct by women and men look different and have very different meanings. As a result, it is sometimes difficult to determine when women and men are in fact similarly situated and deserving of similar

treatment. It is because of such socially pervasive and meaningful gender norms that courts' commitment to neutrality has never been absolute. In this chapter, I recognize the tremendous changes brought about by courts' commitment to sex-based neutrality in the work world, while highlighting the limits of courts' commitment. Moreover, I explain why recent protections for gender nonconformists, often attributed by scholars to an increasingly strict judicial demand for neutrality, have been misunderstood. Courts' commitment to neutrality in the workplace remains far too partial to explain courts' expanding protection for gender nonconformists. Yet, rather than criticize courts for being more pragmatic than pure in their demand for sex-blind neutrality, I conclude that complete sex-blind neutrality would in fact be normatively unappealing.

NEUTRALITY AS NONDISCRIMINATION

Much has been made of the fact that "sex" was introduced into the Civil Rights Act of 1964 only one day before its passage in the House in an apparent attempt to derail the bill.[2] Congressman Howard Smith of Virginia, a principal opponent of the bill, offered the amendment during a debate on the House floor. Despite his repeated claims that he was "serious" about the amendment, Smith mocked his cause and seemed to reveal his true motives by reading a letter of "support" that trivialized women's need for antidiscrimination protection. The letter complained about the difficulty women had in finding husbands and argued that Congress should take immediate steps to protect a woman's " 'right' to a nice husband and family." The letter, Smith proclaimed, revealed that women had "real grievance[s]" that justified Congressional action.[3]

Not surprisingly, given this introduction, the amendment was viewed with suspicion by supporters of the act and even by some supporters of women's rights. Representative Emanual Celler of New York, the floor manager of the bill, for example, called the amendment "illogical, ill timed, ill placed, and improper."[4] Representative Edith Green of Oregon, who had written the just recently passed Equal Pay Act of 1963, opposed the amendment arguing that "it will clutter up the bill and it may later . . . be used to help destroy this section of the bill by some of the very people who today support it."[5] Indeed, she reminded the House that some of those who appeared most strongly in support of women's rights with this amendment were the staunchest opponents of the Equal Pay Act just months earlier.[6] As she noted in her testimony: "I remember when we were working on the equal pay bill that, if I correctly understand the mood of the House, those gentlemen of the House who are most strong in their support of women's rights this afternoon, probably gave us the most opposition when we considered the bill which would grant equal pay for equal work just a very few months ago."[7]

Certainly, there was genuine support for the amendment, including that voiced by the five female representatives who spoke in its favor. These supporters viewed the amendment as necessary to eliminate barriers to women's workplace participation and to put them on equal footing with men in their search for jobs. Representative Katharine St. George of New York, for example, stressed that women did not want or need special privileges and argued that one important purpose of the amendment would be to overturn protective legislation that served only to exclude women from higher-paying jobs.[8] Representative Edna Kelly of New York explained that her "support and sponsorship of this amendment and of this bill is an endeavor to have all persons, men and women, possess the same rights and same opportunities."[9] The amendment passed in the House after a mere two hours of discussion,[10] and it received even less discussion in the Senate.[11] Revealingly, "all nine members of Congress who joined Mrs. Green in voicing opposition to the sex amendment voted for the Civil Rights Bill as a whole. Conversely, only one of the eleven male members who spoke in favor of the amendment voted for the Civil Rights Bill as amended."[12]

Although legislative intent was sparse, the dominant interpretation of Title VII's sex discrimination prohibition in the years following the act was as a demand for formal sex-blind neutrality in employment. Women and men needed to face the same hiring requirements and job conditions regardless of their sex. Discrimination existed when similarly situated women and men were treated differently. As the Supreme Court declared in *Phillips v. Martin Marietta Corp.*, "Section 703(a) of the Civil Rights Act of 1964 requires that persons of like qualifications be given employment opportunities irrespective of their sex."[13]

The effect of this equation of nondiscrimination with neutrality, as at least some proponents of the act had hoped, was to eliminate various forms of protective legislation that curtailed women's workplace participation and to place women on more equal footing with men in the work world. In

Bowe v. Colgate-Palmolive Co., for example, the Seventh Circuit held that it was a form of sex discrimination to allow male employees as part of a seniority system to bid for jobs plant-wide while restricting female employees to jobs that did not require lifting more than thirty-five pounds.[14] Nondiscrimination, the court held, required that employees of both sexes have access to the same jobs on the same terms. The company could retain its thirty-five-pound lifting limit as a requirement for certain jobs, but the jobs needed to be open to all employees.[15] Similarly, in *Rosenfeld v. Southern Pacific Co.*, the district court held that an employer's refusal to consider women for positions with certain hour and weight-lifting requirements violated Title VII, as did the California state law pursuant to which the employer had required women's exclusion.[16] Antidiscrimination law demanded, the court explained, that women be evaluated for positions on the same terms as men.

This leveling of the playing field encouraged women to enter the labor market in greater numbers.[17] Indeed, between 1965 and 1979, women's labor market participation rates increased by more than 11 percent, even as the rate of men's labor force participation declined.[18] Increases in participation rates for married women were even more steep.[19] Neutrality demands changed the look and composition of the work world.

NEUTRALITY'S LEGAL LIMITS

Yet neutrality has its limits. Gender norms significantly complicate workplace neutrality demands and make it particularly difficult in cases dealing with dress or behavior expectations to determine when female and male workers are in fact similarly situated and hence deserving of similar treatment. Complete sex-blind neutrality requires a rejection of gender norms, and courts have never been willing to go this far.

Neutrality requires that women and men who are similarly situated be treated the same. The question for determining whether treatment is nonneutral becomes in effect: is a woman being penalized for possessing a trait that a man is not penalized for possessing, and vice versa. The problem is that in a gendered society, women and men can never possess the same trait in precisely the same way. Determining when "similarly situated" women and men are being treated differently, and hence nonneutrally, becomes a game of indeterminate nominalism whose outcome depends on how one names the relevant trait at issue and frames the cross-sex comparison.

The problematic nature of cross-sex neutrality is most clear in cases where specific biological traits are at issue. In such cases, determining whether an employer is behaving nonneutrally by comparing its treatment of women and men with precisely the same trait is not possible. Findings of nonneutrality and discrimination must, therefore, depend on approximate cross-sex comparisons, which are themselves indeterminate and socially loaded.

Consider, for example, an employer who happily hires both women and men but refuses to hire women with high-pitched voices. The employer has no problem hiring or promoting women; the employer simply finds female high-pitched voices grating and so refuses to hire women with such voices. In order to determine whether a woman with a high-pitched voice is being discriminated against in the sense of being treated nonneutrally, it is necessary to compare her treatment to that of a man with the same trait. Men, though, will not possess the very same trait. Some men may possess high-pitched male voices, but none will possess a high-pitched female voice.[20] It is not possible, therefore, to assess the high-voiced woman's sex discrimination claim by looking to the employer's treatment of men with the very same attribute.

In practice, one must loosen the comparison, and it is this process of loosening that reveals the indeterminacy of neutrality as a conception of nondiscrimination in the sex context. One might, for example, name the trait for which the woman was fired as a voice that was unusually high-pitched and then compare her treatment to that of men who also had unusually high-pitched voices. It is not at all clear, however, that framing the cross-sex comparison in this way makes sense. Unusually high-pitched female voices really are different from unusually high-pitched male voices in both tone and effect, and it may be that only the former give the employer a headache. Renaming the trait at issue as a voice that is unusually or unexpectedly high-pitched for the speaker may enable a cross-sex comparison, but it may also fundamentally distort the trait for which the woman is being disadvantaged.

Difficulties determining what neutrality demands have been most obvious and acute in courts' analysis of sex discrimination claims based on pregnancy. Pregnancy, like the high-pitched female voice, has no identical cross-sex parallel. As a result, under a rigid, yet theoretically pure, neutrality requirement, pregnancy discrimination would never constitute sex discrimination. Because a pregnant woman could never show that she was being treated differently from or worse than a pregnant man, she could never prove nonneutral treatment and hence discrimination because of her sex.

This was in fact the conception of neutrality the Supreme Court adopted, and the conclusion it reached, in *Geduldig v. Aiello*[21] and *General Electric Co. v. Gilbert.*[22] *Geduldig* involved a Fourteenth Amendment challenge to a California state disability insurance program that denied benefits for pregnancy-related needs.[23] The Court held that the program did not violate the Equal Protection Clause, because it did not penalize women for possessing a trait for which men were not penalized. In effect, according to the Court, the program did not discriminate on the basis of sex, because it did not distinguish between pregnant women and pregnant men. Instead, the program simply distinguished between "pregnant women and nonpregnant persons."[24]

Two years later, in *Gilbert*, the Court equated nondiscrimination with the same formal conception of neutrality.[25] *Gilbert* involved a Title VII challenge to an employer's disability plan that, while otherwise comprehensive, excluded coverage for disabilities arising from pregnancy. Following *Geduldig*, the Court held that the exclusion of pregnancy-related disabilities from coverage did not violate Title VII, because the employer was not treating female employees worse than similarly situated male employees.[26] Rather than denying women something that was granted to men, the plan denied pregnancy-related benefits to all employees regardless of their sex. The Court explained that "pregnancy-related disabilities constitute an *additional* risk, unique to women, and the failure to compensate them for this risk does not destroy the presumed parity of the benefits, accruing to men and women alike, which results from the facially evenhanded *inclusion* of risks." According to the Supreme Court, pregnant women were treated neutrally, and nondiscriminatorily, because they were not treated worse than pregnant men.[27]

Congress responded to *Gilbert* and *Geduldig* by passing the Pregnancy Discrimination Act, in which it told courts that the appropriate comparison in pregnancy discrimination cases was between the treatment of pregnant women and that of nonpregnant persons similar in terms of their "ability or inability to work."[28] In a sense, Congress renamed the trait at issue from pregnancy per se to the more generalized trait of physical disability and then reframed the cross-sex comparison in terms of this non-sex-specific trait. According to Congress, pregnant women were treated neutrally only when they were treated the same as men with similar, though obviously not identical, physical limitations.

Yet framing questions in the pregnancy context remain. Circuit courts are divided as to whether the precise comparison should be to employees similarly situated in their ability or inability to work regardless of the source of their injuries or to only those similarly abled employees suffering from nonoccupational injuries.[29] Breastfeeding poses similar problems for a formal neutrality analysis. It is perhaps not surprising, then, that no court has held that discrimination against a woman for breastfeeding at work constitutes sex discrimination under Title VII.[30]

Related nominalism issues arise in cases involving discrimination based on sexual orientation. When a woman is fired for engaging in a sexual relationship with a woman, how one names the trait for which she is being adversely treated determines whether her treatment is deemed neutral or discriminatory. If one names the trait at issue as having sex with women, then the appropriate opposite-sex parallel might be a man who has sex with women. If the woman who has sex with women is treated adversely while the man who has sex with women is not, then the neutrality mandate may have been violated and sex discrimination exists. If, however, one names the trait at issue as engaging in same-sex or homosexual relations, then the opposite-sex parallel would be a man who has sex with men. If men who engage in homosexual conduct are also treated adversely by the employer, the neutrality mandate has not been violated and sex discrimination does not exist. Here again, while attractive in principle, neutrality becomes fraught in practice. How one names the initial trait at issue is conceptually ambiguous, politically loaded, and outcome determinative.

Cases involving transsexuals raise the issue most starkly. Imagine a preoperative male-to-female transsexual who is terminated for wearing skirts and feminine blouses to work. Is the appropriate comparator for purposes of trait neutrality analysis a woman wearing conventionally feminine clothes? Or, is the preoperative male-to-female transsexual better compared to a woman wearing conventionally male clothes or to a female-to-male transsexual wearing male clothes? Several courts have struggled with precisely this problem. In *Oiler v. Winn-Dixie, Louisiana, Inc.*, for example, the court held that the male plaintiff, who was fired for dressing as a woman while off duty, was not doing the same thing as and need not be treated the same as a woman who wore similar clothing while not at work. As the court explained: "This is not a situation where the plaintiff failed to conform to a gender stereotype. Plaintiff was not discharged because he did not act sufficiently masculine or because he exhibited traits normally valued in a female employee, but disparaged in a male employee.... The plaintiff was terminated because he is a man with a sexual or gender identity disorder who, in order to publicly disguise himself as a woman, wears women's clothing, shoes, underwear, breast prostheses, wigs, make-up, and nail polish, pretends to be a woman, and publicly identifies himself as a woman named 'Donna.' "[31] In *James v. Ranch Mart Hardware*, the court similarly held that the treatment of a male-to-female transsexual should be compared not to that received by a woman but instead to that received by a female-to-male transsexual.[32]

Neutrality problems are not, however, limited to a narrow range of cases involving sex-specific biological attributes, sexual orientation, or gender identity disorder. They pervade dress, appearance, and grooming cases as well precisely because the strength of gender norms in such cases makes nominalism choices so difficult. Consider, for example, a hypothetical employer who is generally willing to hire women but refuses to hire women who wear sexy clothes to work.[33] There is no exact male equivalent to the female trait of sexy dressing, and attempts to choose an appropriate cross-sex approximation are puzzling. One could identify the trait in a narrow and literal way as, for example, wearing clothes such as low-cut blouses or tight skirts. By naming the trait in this way, the woman is the victim of sex discrimination only if she is treated worse than a man who wears the same types of clothing to work. Framing the issue in this way is, of course, unlikely to result in a finding of sex discrimination.

It is far from clear, however, that this narrowly literalistic framing of the cross-sex comparison is appropriate. The proper comparator for the sexy-dressing woman may not be a man dressed in the very same clothing. A man dressed in a low-cut blouse and tight skirt might be objectionable to the employer, but it is probably not because he is sexy. If the employer is really objecting to a female employee exuding sexuality at work, it arguably does not bolster or refute this woman's claim of nonneutral treatment to show that the employer also objects to hiring men in drag. Sexily dressed women and men in drag arguably do not possess the same trait, or even a close approximation thereof. Similarly, consider a woman and man who both wear high-heeled shoes to work. High heels mean something very different on a woman from what they mean on a man. For women, high heels fit comfortably within a set of gender-appropriate behavior. They denote sexiness, dressiness, and physical display. Wearing high heels as a man is entirely different. It is not part of a set of gender-appropriate behavior; it is commonly perceived as neither sexy nor dressy but simply deviant and strange.[34]

Alternatively, one could frame the cross-sex comparison for the employer who does not like sexy-dressing women by looking at the way the employer treats men dressed in sex-specific sexy clothing. Of course, deciding what constitutes sexy dressing for men is itself not obvious, and is probably open to disagreement.[35] Is the parallel to a woman in short skirts and low-cut blouses a man in an open-chested shirt and tight pants? Or, because of the significantly different social

and symbolic meanings of women and men in skimpy clothing, are tight and revealing clothes considered sexy in women
but inappropriate and nonsexy in men?

Finally, one could instead compare the employer's treatment of sexy-dressing women with its treatment of men who
violate appropriate workplace norms. At this level of abstraction, however, a neutrality demand becomes toothless and
unable to challenge employers' endorsement of any gender
stereotypes. The problem is not only that there is no exact
cross-sex trait parallel but also that there is no good, and certainly no uncontroversial, approximation.

Naming and framing issues of this sort dominated the
court's analysis in the case of *Craft v. Metromedia, Inc.*[36] A television station in Kansas City, Missouri, hired Christine Craft
as a TV coanchor. Immediately after she started the job, the
station became concerned about her appearance. Public opinion surveys performed by a media consultant found that
viewers had an "overwhelmingly negative" response to Craft's
appearance. After continually poor survey results, the station
reassigned Craft from coanchor to reporter. She refused to
accept the assignment and sued for sex discrimination, arguing that she was being held to more stringent appearance
standards than were male newscasters. The district court
ruled in favor of Metromedia on Craft's Title VII sex discrimination claim, and the Eighth Circuit affirmed.[37]

As with the previous examples, analyzing Craft's discrimination claim under a neutrality rubric is difficult. It is not
clear how to characterize the trait for which she was fired nor
how to identify appropriate male employees with whom to
compare her treatment. Was Craft demoted for possessing

particular traits (for example, having short hair or wearing oxford shirts) such that her treatment should be compared to that of male newscasters possessing the same traits? Interpreting the trait for which Craft was demoted in such a narrow way does not, however, really capture what the station found problematic about her appearance. The station clearly was concerned that she have an overall appearance that was pleasing and attractive to viewers. It was not committed to or concerned about her having any particular aesthetic attributes. Indeed, judging from the many different people hired by the station to advise her about her wardrobe and appearance, it appears that the station did not have a clear idea about what physical and clothing attributes would please mercurial viewer tastes.

Alternatively, was Craft demoted for having an overall appearance that was unattractive to viewers such that her treatment should be compared to that of male newscasters whose appearance was also unattractive to viewers? This was essentially the comparison that both the district court and the circuit court made. The district court concluded: "Defendant's standards of appearance for its on-air personnel can in no way be considered discriminatory per se. Both men and women were required to maintain a professional, businesslike appearance consistent with community standards."[38] The court of appeals agreed that the station's enforcement of socially gendered appearance standards for its newscasters was consistent and nondiscriminatory. According to the court:

> While there may have been some emphasis on the feminine stereotype of "softness" and bows and ruffles and on the fashionableness of female anchors, the evidence suggests such

concerns were incidental to a true focus on consistency of appearance, proper coordination of colors and textures, the effects of studio lighting on clothing and makeup, and the greater degree of conservatism thought necessary in the Kansas City market. The "dos" and "don'ts" for female anchors addressed the need to avoid, for example, tight sweaters or overly "sexy" clothing and extreme "high fashion" or "sporty" outfits while the male "dos" and "don'ts" similarly cautioned against "frivolous" colors and "extreme" textures and styles as damaging to the "authority" of newscasters. These criteria do not implicate the primary thrust of Title VII, which is to prompt employers to "discard outmoded sex stereotypes posing distinct employment disadvantages for one sex."[39]

Interpreting the neutrality demand at this high level of abstraction, however, simply reifies socially gendered conceptions of beauty and fails to find discrimination any time an employer consistently enforces sex-specific gender norms.

In fact, Craft did not object to being held to a different gender-specific standard of grooming and appearance. She simply argued that these standards were more stringent and more strictly enforced for women than for men.[40] Once one accepts the legitimacy or necessity of sex-specific appearance scales, however, there is no way to identify a good opposite-sex parallel to Craft's level of attractiveness so as to determine whether men with similar levels of attractiveness were treated differently. Neutrality, under such conditions, is both conceptually and practically fraught.

In a sexist society, virtually nothing done by men and women has precisely the same meaning. Traits are not understood or viewed as isolated technical attributes. They are necessarily viewed in relation to all of the other traits an individual possesses and through a systematically gendered lens.

As a result, the indeterminacy of the neutrality mandate is not limited to exceptional sex cases. The impossibility of cross-sex trait parallelism and the naming and framing problems that stem from it are systemic across a wide range of cases in more subtle ways.

Traits such as competitiveness or active leadership, for example, are perceived very differently when possessed by women or men. Consider one study in which participants were told to evaluate job candidates for a computer lab manager position at a university. Participants viewed videotapes and read "life philosophy" essays from female and male candidates.[41] Researchers found that female candidates with essays that emphasized "agentic" qualities such as competitiveness were rated "less socially skilled and likeable than an identically presented man."[42] Another study found that the same leadership activities of women and men resulted in very different affective responses from those dealing with them.[43] Women engaging in group leadership activities received more displeased responses and fewer pleased responses from group members than did men engaging in the same behavior and making the same suggestions and arguments.[44] Anger expression has also been shown to affect professional women and men differently. A study in which participants viewed videos of actors pretending to be professionals interviewing for a job found that "professional women who expressed anger were consistently accorded lower status and lower wages, and were seen as less competent, than angry men."[45] In other words, even when technical trait symmetries are possible, in the sense that women and men can physically do precisely the same thing, traits will mean very different things when possessed by a woman or by a man. Determining whether women and men are being treated neutrally or nonneutrally under conditions of such perceptual distortion is in effect impossible.

Price Waterhouse v. Hopkins[46] itself provides a good example. It is simply not the case that Ann Hopkins was fired for exhibiting the same traits that men exhibited. Social meanings are real. Aggressiveness in women is "bitchy" in a way that aggressiveness in men is not. Competitiveness in women is threatening in a way that competitiveness in men is not. Vulgarity in women is shocking and disturbing in a way that vulgarity in men is not. Even if Hopkins had engaged in behavior technically identical to that of her male colleagues, her behavior would not have been socially the same. Determining whether she was the victim of sex discrimination under a neutrality mandate depends on how one chooses to name the behavior for which she was fired and to frame the cross-sex comparison.

In order to be operational in those cases in which technical trait parity is possible, sex-blind neutrality requires a rejection of gender norms. Neutrality must be defined in a literal and formalistic way without regard to the actual social meaning of the traits and attributes at issue. To use Professor Mary Anne Case's colorful example, if women are free to wear "frilly pink dresses" at work, then men must be free to do so as well,[47] despite the fact that a frilly pink dress signals conservatism in a woman and transgression in a man. This is precisely the reading that some scholars have given to *Price Waterhouse*.[48]

Courts, however, have never taken their commitment to neutrality this far. The Ninth Circuit's decision in *Jespersen v.*

Harrah's Operating Co. provides the most high-profile recent example of neutrality's legal limits. Far from rejecting gender norms, the Ninth Circuit did not even seem to notice them. It both upheld the requirement that women but not men wear makeup and proclaimed, without explanation, that the requirement did not reflect sex stereotypes at all. Yet in *Jespersen* the Ninth Circuit was merely reaffirming a limit on neutrality that had been drawn by courts over the preceding four decades. Antidiscrimination law did not require formal neutrality between women and men with regard to dress and grooming norms, even in those cases where technical trait parallelism was possible. Courts have consistently held that men with long hair need not be treated the same as women with long hair and that men with earrings need not be treated the same as women with earrings. Courts viewed such burdens, when they were recognized by courts as such at all, as too insignificant to warrant antidiscrimination protection. Any principled commitment to neutrality was outweighed in such cases by the perceived value of protecting comfortable gender conventions.

Indeed, even when courts have protected workers from sex-specific conformity demands, a commitment to neutrality does not seem to be the reason. Consider, for example, courts' increasing willingness to protect individuals diagnosed with gender identity disorder from sex-based dress and grooming demands. Under a principle of formal neutrality, it is impossible to distinguish between a man who wants to wear a dress or earrings because he suffers from gender identity disorder and one who wants to do so because of a personal proclivity. Yet this is precisely the distinction that courts make when they permit a man diagnosed with gender identity disorder to transgress sex-based grooming codes but refuse to permit nontranssexual men to do so.

Similarly, it seems unlikely that protection for effeminate men stems from a commitment to formal neutrality when such cases have far less clear cross-sex comparators than do those involving nontranssexual cross-dressers in which courts regularly deny protection to nonconformists. It is not at all clear, for example, that a man who is harassed for walking like a woman or acting like a woman is in any real way walking or acting like a woman. Certainly it would be difficult to conclude that he is walking in precisely the same way as a female coworker. If neutrality toward men and women doing the same thing were driving the protection, it would be very strange for courts to provide protection in the effeminate men and masculine women cases but not in the dress and grooming code cases in which the cross-sex comparators are more apparent and the neutrality demands more clear. Yet, again, this is precisely the distinction that courts currently make.

Such distinctions help to demarcate neutrality's limits as an antidiscrimination commitment. They also suggest that a principle other than neutrality is driving recent expansions of protection to gender nonconformists.

NEUTRALITY'S NORMATIVE LIMITS

Courts' unwillingness to reject social gender norms or to demand sex-blind neutrality with regard to all traits and attributes is not surprising. Gender norms are both pervasive and, often, comforting. Moreover, in some instances denying that such norms exist and demanding formally neutral treatment may actually look discriminatory. Formally, nonneutral treatment in such instances may look more equal and fair. In short, sex-neutral rules do not always look nondiscriminatory, and nonneutral rules do not always look discriminatory. Moreover, equating nondiscrimination with rigid neutrality is likely to encourage an androgyny in the workplace that, while being unnecessary for substantive equality, has serious costs for individual liberty. Both issues suggest a normative disconnect between sex equality and rigid neutrality.

To highlight the disconnect, consider three scenarios.

The Aggressive Woman. As the *Price Waterhouse* case illustrated,[49] aggressive women are viewed differently and more negatively than aggressive men. Aggressive men are commonly perceived as authoritative and competent, while aggressive women are commonly perceived as "bitchy," shrill, and overbearing. A woman whose employment is terminated or who is denied a promotion for engaging in the same aggressive behavior that male coworkers engage in without adverse effect might argue that formal neutrality requires that she be treated the same as similarly behaving men despite the different social meanings attached to her behavior.

The Cross-Dressing Man. Men in traditionally female clothing and makeup are viewed more negatively than are women in the same attire. Women wearing traditionally female clothing are viewed as social conformists, while men wearing women's clothes are viewed as gender nonconformists and, sometimes, as social deviants. A man denied or terminated from employment because of his cross-dressing might argue that the neutrality mandate precludes his employer from penalizing him for engaging in the same behavior—for example, wearing skirts, high heels, and makeup—that female employees engage in without adverse action.

The Buzz-Cut Woman. A buzz haircut on a woman has a significantly different meaning from a buzz haircut on a man. Shannon Faulkner made this point when she fought to gain admittance to the Citadel without also being forced to get the "knob" haircut traditional to male cadets. As Faulkner argued, while the meaning of the buzz cut on a man is an acceptable masculinity, on a woman it denotes an unacceptable and strange masculinity at odds with appropriate gender norms. On a woman, a buzz cut would signal not straight-laced hyper-masculinity but socially and sexually deviant "outlaw" status.[50] The Citadel responded by simply equating nondiscrimination with neutrality. If nondiscrimination means treating women and men the same regardless of the different social meanings attached to particular traits, then the Citadel could not be engaging in sex discrimination by treating Faulkner the way it would treat any incoming male cadet who refused to get the knob haircut.[51]

If the relevant metric for nondiscrimination is neutrality, these cases are difficult to distinguish. The neutrality mandate, at least when applied in the way its advocates most often encourage, seems to protect the aggressive woman, the cross-dressing man, and the Citadel. One might believe, however, that as a substantive matter, by rejecting gender norms the Citadel hindered rather than encouraged sex equality.[52] This was the argument made by Faulkner and the Department of Justice. As Faulkner's lawyer argued: "The principle of formal equality . . . ignored the social meaning of the haircut, a code for masculinity that marks a cadet as male. . . . Stripped of her hair, Shannon would be doubly excluded: she would not look like a male cadet, but neither would she look like a real woman. She would be a gender outlaw—neither male nor female. Doubtless many male cadets would label her a 'dyke,' a butch lesbian whose sexual desire for women makes her not a 'real woman.' "[53]

Similarly, the Department of Justice argued that the Citadel "was proceeding 'under the guise of gender-neutral grooming policies [that] implement rules which altogether denigrate Ms. Faulkner's identity as a woman.' "[54] The district court rejected these norm-based arguments and adopted instead the idea that nondiscrimination requires formal neutrality when it refused to enjoin the Citadel from requiring Faulkner to get the knob haircut.[55] As the district court essentially asked, if neutrality is the appropriate definition of nondiscrimination, then how can it be discrimination to impose a sex-neutral trait requirement?

One might, of course, argue that it is one thing for courts to require sex neutrality when it is being sought by a plaintiff who wants to possess a gender-atypical trait, but it is something quite distinct to allow employers to impose a sex-neutral, but gender-bending, requirement on an unwilling plaintiff who does not want to challenge traditional gender norms. In other words, to say that the Citadel must permit Faulkner to get a knob haircut if she had wanted one is different from saying that the Citadel may require Faulkner to get a haircut even if she does not want one. Imagine that Faulkner had wanted to get a knob haircut and the Citadel had tried to stop her by arguing that on women the haircut signified a strange outlaw status that was not in keeping with the mission and message of the Citadel. In this scenario, arguments about the social meaning of hair probably seem less persuasive, and arguments in favor of formal neutrality more persuasive, than they did in the actual case. The distinction is certainly meaningful. It suggests, however, that what it means not to discriminate on the basis of sex is significantly more complicated than a simple requirement of employer neutrality.

Neutrality advocates might respond that although nondiscrimination always requires sex-neutral requirements, not every neutral requirement will be acceptable; some will be impermissibly burdensome or unfairly costly for individuals of one sex or the other.[56] Neutrality, they might argue, is, in a sense, a necessary, but not a sufficient, condition for nondiscrimination.

Even this claim is too strong, however. Neutrality and the nonenforcement of gender norms are not always necessary for nondiscrimination, and nonneutrality does not always constitute sex discrimination. Certainly, many gender norms—such as that equating female aggressiveness with "bitchiness"—are incompatible with women's full, effective participation in the work world. Not all gender norms, however, are created equal. Employers may recognize some norms without impeding sex equality in the workplace. An employer may, for example, require male employees to have hair no longer than the tops of their collars while imposing no such requirement on female employees. The gender norm at issue—that serious, professional men have short hair—does not reinforce messages of male dominance or of female weakness, sexual availability, or incompetence. Enforcing the norm that men should have short hair does not limit the range of job possibilities available to men or diminish their perceived competence for such jobs. Permitting women a wider range of acceptable hairstyles enables them to mimic a professional male hairstyle or choose a more traditionally feminine style. Similarly, an employer may permit women to wear skirts without permitting men to do so. Again, men are not disadvantaged in the work world by being forced to mimic the clothing style of the ideal male worker, and women, too, are not harmed by being given the choice of mimicking the ideal male clothing style or choosing a more traditionally feminine style.

Allowing employers to act on the gender norm that makes men in dresses seem deviant does not impede the ability of men (or women) to participate fully and effectively in the work world. Certainly, some men will feel constrained by the sex-specific trait requirements, but the requirements themselves do not inhibit the substantive sex equality that is Title VII's goal. Moreover, as a practical matter, it is unlikely that gender-bending men will be less constrained under a formal neutrality regime than they will be under one allowing for limited instances of sex-specific workplace rules.

One possible result of a neutrality mandate, the one for which advocates hope, is that employers will expand the range of permissible traits and attributes open to employees of both sexes, allowing both women and men to gender bend or not gender bend, depending on their own preferences.[57] An employer might, for example, have a grooming code that allows for two possible haircuts, one shoulder-length "bob," generally more appealing to women, and one crew cut, generally more appealing to men. Both women and men would be free to choose either cut. This is not, however, the only, or perhaps even the most likely, response to the trait equality requirement. If employers are uncomfortable with gender-bending behavior—either because of their own sensibilities or because they think it will offend their customers—they may choose instead to narrow the range of trait options available to their employees to only those that the employer will find acceptable when possessed by either sex.[58] The options, in other words, will converge toward an androgynous mean. The employer who does not want to employ men in bob haircuts will simply not make this an option under its dress code, even if it does not mind women wearing them. The result is not more options for men to gender bend but fewer traditionally gender-conforming options for women.

CONCLUSION

Neutrality is, without doubt, a core value of American anti-discrimination law. It is a foundational premise that women should have access to the same jobs on the same terms as men. At a high level of generality, Title VII has enforced this mandate, ending formal sex segregation and opening the floodgates for women to participate fully in the work world. Yet as I have shown in this chapter, at a more micro level our jurisprudential commitment to sex-based neutrality has always been limited and, indeed, often been superseded by competing commitments. I have sought to explore why this is so by highlighting the conceptual and normative limitations of neutrality in sex discrimination cases. Salient gender norms make determining the meaning of neutrality difficult and often contested. They also make formally neutral treatment itself in some cases look unfair and contrary to the goal of equal opportunity for women and men in the workplace. Neutrality is for these reasons not an absolute mandate but a more partial or pragmatic goal. It is a value and commitment, but one that works in concert with other antidiscrimination values and in the context of a deeply gendered society. In particular, a commitment to neutrality does little to help explain the most recent expansions of sex discrimination law in which courts have been providing critical forms of protection to some, but not all, gender nonconformists. This is perhaps not surprising, since it is in precisely these cases that neutrality demands are most indeterminate and controversial. In the coming chapters, I consider what other values and commitments may be at work in these cases.

CHAPTER THREE

Antisubordination

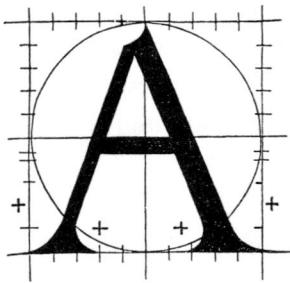s the last chapter made clear, neutrality may be a core antidiscrimination concept, but its practical mandate is not absolute. Nor is it exclusive. American antidiscrimination law is committed to more than simply the neutral treatment of individual workers without regard to sex or race. It is committed as well to dismantling the caste-like hierarchies based on sex and race that have been entrenched by pervasive historical discrimination.[1] It is concerned, in other words, not only about individuals but also about groups and overcoming entrenched group disadvantage. In the context of gender nonconformity cases, antisubordination values have driven courts not only to require that women be given access to jobs but also to require that certain jobs be redefined, and social norms shifted, so as to make their success more likely.

Title VII claims fall into two categories: those that allege disparate impact and those that allege disparate treatment. The disparate impact framework, crafted by the Supreme Court from whole cloth in *Griggs v. Duke Power Company*, is the most direct reflection of the Civil Rights Act's antisubordination ideals.[2] In *Griggs*, African American employees challenged the company's requirement of a high school diploma and passing score on a general intelligence test for workers seeking entry to any but the lowest-paid jobs. The requirements, although neutrally applied, disproportionately excluded black workers from more highly paid positions. Despite Duke Power Company's history of pre–Civil Rights Act discrimination against black workers, the Fourth Circuit held that Duke Power had adopted the diploma and test requirement "without any 'intention to discriminate against Negro employees.' "[3] Nonetheless, the Supreme Court made clear that neither good intentions nor neutrality were sufficient to shield a company from liability where practices reinforced racial hierarchy. "[P]ractices, procedures, or tests neutral on their face, and even neutral in terms of intent, cannot be maintained if they operate to 'freeze' the status quo of prior discriminatory employment practices."[4] Title VII, the Court explained, prohibited facially neutral policies that operated to disadvantage African Americans when the employer could not demonstrate that the requirements were job related and consistent with business necessity.[5]

Title VII's antisubordination mission is less central to the disparate treatment framework, which focuses on protecting individual plaintiffs from intentional discrimination. Nonetheless, here too antisubordination goals shape the act's sex discrimination coverage both overtly and covertly. In particular, courts' willingness to permit nonneutral treatment of women and men in deference to socially salient gender norms is tempered by courts' concerns about group equality and relative access. Within the disparate treatment framework, courts have expressly identified two tests that focus on and target harms to the group rather than focusing solely on the individual. The first is the unequal burdens test, which calls upon courts to strike down sex-specific dress and grooming demands that disproportionately burden one sex. The second is the double-bind test, which calls upon courts to reject sex-specific dress, grooming, or behavior demands if they make it more difficult for workers of one sex to succeed professionally. Less explicit is a third test, focused on equality of group opportunities, which courts have used to strike down sex-based hiring that threatens to distort too greatly the job opportunities available to one sex as compared with the other. As formally expressed, these tests focus quite abstractly on relative group advantage rather than on historical patterns of group disadvantage. As applied, however, the tests target narrowly and strategically those social practices and gender norms that most inhibit women's workplace success.

UNEQUAL BURDENS

Courts first articulated the unequal burdens test in the 1970s to provide some check on sex-specific dress and grooming requirements that seemed to disadvantage women. Many of the early cases successfully challenged sex-specific employment demands in the airline industry. In *Laffey v. Northwest Airlines,* for example, the district court struck down an airline's requirement that female flight attendants wear only contact lenses, while male flight attendants could wear either contacts or eyeglasses.[6] In *Gerdom v. Continental Airlines*, the Ninth Circuit struck down an airline's policy imposing weight requirements on female "flight hostesses" but not on male employees in comparable positions.[7] Likewise, in *Frank v. United Airlines*, the Ninth Circuit struck down United Airlines' sex-based weight requirements limiting male flight attendants to maximum weights that corresponded to large body frames but limiting female flight attendants to maximum weights that corresponded to medium body frames.[8] In all three cases, the courts emphasized that the burdens imposed on female workers were disproportionate and unequal to those imposed on male workers.[9]

As formally expressed, the unequal burdens test would seem to demand the elimination of any and all gender conformity demands that burden one sex more than the other. In order to assess the burdens imposed by sex-based grooming codes, courts have suggested that the requirements should be looked at in total rather than item by item, and that burdensomeness should be assessed in terms of the time and money required for women and men to comply with their respective requirements.[10]

Courts have not in fact applied the unequal burdens test so strictly or formally. Instead, they have regularly found sex-specific grooming requirements nondiscriminatory even when their burdens are unequal according to the courts' own terms. It is difficult to believe, for example, that grooming codes that require men to keep their hair short while imposing no hair length or style requirement on women do not impose an unequal burden on male employees.[11] It is similarly difficult to believe that a no-beard requirement for men, when not matched by any kind of general shaving or facial grooming requirement for women, does not impose an unequal burden. Nonetheless, courts routinely uphold such differential grooming requirements against claims of discrimination.[12]

Indeed, courts regularly uphold conformity demands that impose unequal burdens on male and female workers as long as the demands mimic conventional, role-appropriate gender norms. *Craft v. Metromedia, Inc.,*[13] and *Jespersen v. Harrah's* both provide clear examples. Television news anchor Christine Craft, in challenging as discriminatory her station's intense oversight of her makeup and wardrobe, presented evidence showing that "only females were subject to daily scrutiny of their appearance or were ever required to change clothes at the station before going on the air."[14] In addition, she presented testimony from the image consultant that the station had hired to work with her who explained that "she had told Craft not to wear the same outfit more than once every three to four weeks because people would start calling in about it; males, however . . . could wear an outfit every week and a suit even twice within the same week if combined with a different tie."[15]

Yet despite these unequal burdens on women and men, the court held that the television station's clothing and grooming requirements for anchors did not discriminate on the basis of sex. In reaching this conclusion, the court emphasized that the station was simply enforcing appropriate gender norms for television news anchors.[16] Accordingly, the court of appeals held that the district court did not err "when it concluded that KMBC's appearance standards were shaped only by neutral professional and technical considerations."[17]

When Darlene Jespersen challenged her employer's requirement that female, but not male, bartenders wear makeup, the Ninth Circuit ruled that she had not established a record showing that the grooming requirements imposed on women were more burdensome than those imposed on men, even though such a disparity seemed clear from the face of the requirements.[18] As Judge Kozinski noted in his dissent, "It is true that Jespersen failed to present evidence about what it costs to buy makeup and how long it takes to apply it, but is there any doubt that putting on makeup costs money and takes time? Harrah's policy requires women to apply face powder, blush, mascara and lipstick. You don't need an expert witness to figure out that such items don't grow on trees."[19]

Yet the majority seemed predisposed to reject a claim of sex discrimination regardless of any evidence Jespersen might have presented demonstrating the differential time and money demands of the grooming codes at issue in the case. The Personal Best requirements, the court emphasized, simply matched conventionally gendered grooming requirements for bartenders and hence seemed definitionally to not "unreasonably burden one gender more than the other." As the court explained: " 'Where, as here, such [grooming and appearance] policies are reasonable and are imposed in an even-handed manner on all employees, slight differences in the appearance requirements for males and females have only a negligible effect on employment opportunities.' Under established equal burdens analysis, when an employer's grooming and appearance policy does not unreasonably burden one gender more than the other, that policy will not violate Title VII."[20]

As more narrowly conceived, the unequal burdens test is triggered only when workplace conformity demands are not justified by conventional, role-appropriate, gender norms. This narrower test explains why courts have been unwilling to strike down short-hair and no-beard requirements for men despite the seemingly disproportionate burdens they imposed: such requirements were viewed by courts as simply enforcing conventionally gendered professional norms.[21] It also explains why courts have been willing to strike down sex-specific weight and eyeglasses rules for flight attendants. Rules requiring female flight attendants to be relatively thinner than male attendants and to refrain from wearing glasses go beyond both conventional gender norms and the more professional, less sexualized, role norms for flight attendants being imposed on airlines by the courts.[22]

The narrower test also helps make sense of *Carroll v. Talman Federal Savings & Loan Association of Chicago*[23] and *O'Donnell v. Burlington Coat Factory Warehouse*,[24] two early cases often referred to as exemplars of the unequal burdens test.[25] In both cases, employers imposed sex-specific dress codes on workers. In *Carroll*, female employees were required to wear a uniform that consisted of five basic items: "a color-coordinated skirt or slacks and a choice of a jacket, tunic or vest."[26] Male employees were not required to wear a formal uniform but were required to wear "customary business attire" consisting of a "suit, a sport jacket and pants, or even a leisure suit, as long as it is worn with a shirt and tie."[27] In

O'Donnell, female sales clerks were required to wear smocks, while male sales clerks were required to wear a shirt and tie.[28]

The plaintiffs' challenge, in both cases, was not to the employer's enforcement of conventional gender norms but to the employer's different treatment of female and male employees in ways that were not demanded by these norms. The female employees in *Carroll*, for example, did not object to wearing female clothing, they objected to being constrained in their choices within this category in a way that male employees were not. Similarly, the female employees in *O'Donnell* did not object to dressing like women, they objected to wearing a nongendered smock when their male colleagues were not so similarly required.

The courts, too, in both cases viewed the grooming codes at issue as going beyond conventional gender requirements. In *Carroll*, for example, the court explained:

> So long as they find some justification in commonly accepted social norms and are reasonably related to the employer's business needs, such regulations are not necessarily violations of Title VII even though the standards prescribed differ somewhat for men and women. However, the situation is different where, as here, two sets of employees performing the same functions are subjected on the basis of sex to two entirely separate dress codes one including a variety of normal business attire and the other requiring a clearly identifiable uniform.[29]

Similarly, in *O'Donnell* the court emphasized that, unlike sex-based hair-length requirements, the sex-specific smock requirement "finds no justification in accepted social norms."[30]

On one level, these cases look like simple anticlassification cases—reflecting a concern about differentiation rather than subordination. By this view, the problem was that the employers marked female employees as different, not that they imposed disproportionate burdens on them. Indeed, although the court in *Carroll* did note that the uniform requirement subjected female employees to additional economic costs not borne by male employees,[31] the *O'Donnell* court stated explicitly that no similar cost disparity existed in that case, suggesting again that differentiation, rather than disproportionate costs, prompted the courts' findings of illegality.[32]

Nonetheless, in both cases the courts associated differentiation, when not rendered invisible by conventional gender norms, with stigmatization of women workers. It was stigma—rather than inequality in terms of time or money—that constituted women's unequal burden. In *Carroll*, for example, the court explained that "when some employees are uniformed and others are not there is a natural tendency to assume that the uniformed women have a lesser professional status than their male colleagues attired in normal business clothes."[33] Similarly, in *O'Donnell* the court explained: "[I]t is demeaning for one sex to wear a uniform when members of the other sex holding the same positions are allowed to wear professional business attire."[34] In fact, contrary to what both courts said, the disadvantage to be remedied probably would have been the same had it been the male employees who were required to wear uniforms and smocks instead of the female workers. Workplace sex differentiation not explained by conventional gender norms is likely to stigmatize female workers regardless of how the actual requirements go. Conversely, if the differentiation had been between people born in Idaho and those born in Oregon, it would probably not have "stigmatized" either group. The stigma seems to come from making group identity salient in a context where one group is already assumed to be inferior.

One would expect, for example, a similar finding of discrimination had Christine Craft been required to read the news off pink paper while her male coanchor read off blue paper, or had Darlene Jespersen been required to serve her drinks in pink glasses while male bartenders served theirs in blue glasses. The compliance costs for female workers would not be any higher than for male workers. Nonetheless, the differentiation itself, unjustified by conventional professional gender norms, would stigmatize and thereby burden female workers.

In practice, then, the unequal burdens test is less about equalizing the concrete burdens imposed on women and men and more about minimizing the stigmatic burden that some sex-based distinctions impose on female workers. The test calls upon courts to distinguish between sex-based distinctions that degrade or oppress by highlighting women's difference and those distinctions that are normalized, neutralized—and indeed rendered virtually invisible—by widely shared gender norms. Doing so does not call for a frontal attack on gender norms. It does, however, require courts to engage in a process of sorting, sifting, and shifting gender norms based on their social meaning. Workplace requirements based on outdated or controversial gender norms are most likely to be viewed as oppressive. The unequal burdens test serves, then, as an antisubordination-motivated check on sex-based distinctions that would otherwise fall within the neutrality principle's safe harbor for dress and grooming codes. The test strikes down such distinctions when context or changing social norms render them noticeably stigmatic.

DOUBLE BINDS

The unequal burdens test is not, however, the only antisubordination-oriented test explicitly at work within the disparate treatment framework. In *Price Waterhouse v. Hopkins*, the Supreme Court articulated a double-bind test. The double-bind test addresses a subset of sex stereotyping cases in which there is a conflict between gender and professional demands.

Price Waterhouse had created a double bind for Ann Hopkins by demanding that she be demure and ladylike, when successful performance of her job required more traditionally male attributes such as assertiveness and competitiveness. By refusing to allow Price Waterhouse to punish Hopkins for deviating from its feminine ideal, the Supreme Court shielded her from this double bind and facilitated her move up the corporate ladder. As the Court explained: "An employer who objects to aggressiveness in women but whose positions require this trait places women in an intolerable and impermissible Catch-22: out of a job if they behave aggressively and out of a job if they do not. Title VII lifts women out of this bind."[35]

Reading *Price Waterhouse* as prohibiting double binds, rather than as demanding formal sex-blind neutrality, eliminates much of the apparent inconsistency in the case law dealing with gender conformity demands. For example, courts upheld short-hair and no-earring requirements for male employees, both before and after *Price Waterhouse*, because in their view these gender conformity demands did not hinder women's (or men's) ability to succeed in the workplace.[36] Courts instead view the effect of such requirements as de minimis. Likewise, the Ninth Circuit refused to protect Darlene Jespersen from Harrah's requirement that she wear makeup—despite the Supreme Court's willingness to protect Ann Hopkins from requirements that she " 'walk more femininely, talk more femininely, dress more femininely, wear make-up, have her hair styled, and wear jewelry' "—because it concluded that the demand did not undermine Jespersen's success as a bartender.[37] "[T]he record contains nothing," the court explained, "to suggest the grooming standards would objectively inhibit a woman's ability to do the job."[38]

Although the Ninth Circuit did not explain why it found no double bind in the *Jespersen* case, the conclusion likely flowed from a tacit acceptance of the contemporary performance and display aspects of bartending. As legal scholars Dianne Avery and Marion Crain have documented, although bartending in the United States was an almost exclusively male profession until the 1970s, "within less than two decades, bartending was feminized more rapidly and extensively than any other predominantly male profession."[39] By 2004, women dominated the profession.[40] Along with feminization came sexualization of the job. Increasingly, Crain and Avery explain, bartending is dominated by sexy young women for whom acting as eye candy for male customers is as integral to the job as pouring drinks.[41] Given this recent feminization of bartending, the court might have believed that a makeup requirement would actually enhance, rather than impede, a woman's professional success.

Indeed, a study by psychologist Peter Glick and his colleagues suggests that the Ninth Circuit might even have been correct.[42] Glick tested the effect sexy self-presentations had on perceptions of competence of female workers in high-status, traditionally male occupations and in low-status, traditionally female occupations. Study participants rated the competence of a woman in a video who was described as either a receptionist or a manager. The woman in the video was dressed in either a deliberately sexy or a neutral manner.[43] Glick found that sexy dressing resulted in diminished ratings of competence for the female manager but not for the receptionist.[44] Sexy dressing, in other words, undermined perceptions of competence only for women in high-status occupations.

In its narrowest form, the double-bind principle would strike down only those gender conformity demands that directly conflicted with an employee's professional demands. Only conformity demands that actually made it impossible for a worker to satisfy her professional demands would be illegal. Imagine, for example, a construction worker required to perform her job duties while satisfying a grooming code like that imposed on Jespersen by Harrah's. It would be impossible for her to work on the construction site while keeping her hair styled and lipstick on at all times.

The double bind faced by Hopkins in *Price Waterhouse* approached, but did not quite reach, this per se level. Seven women had been able to satisfy both sets of demands and become partners at Price Waterhouse.[45] Still, the requirement that Hopkins behave in a traditionally feminine manner was at odds with professional role demands calling for aggressive and competitive behavior. Moreover, the seeming equation of female aggressiveness with bitchiness by several male partners made it virtually impossible for her to be viewed as both competent and collegial.

The double-bind principle may, however, also be conceived of more broadly. Rather than requiring a direct conflict between gender conformity demands and professional role demands, the double-bind principle may require only a tension between the two. The broader conception would call upon courts to strike down conformity demands that make it more difficult, even if not impossible, for female workers to also satisfy professional role demands. Such was certainly the case in *Price Waterhouse.* In this broad form, the double-bind principle resembles, and blends with, the unequal burdens test. A double bind reflects a disproportionate or unequal burden on female workers. The key difference between the double-bind test and the unequal burdens test is that the former requires that courts look at the relationship between the gender conformity demand and the employee's likely job success, while the latter looks at the gender conformity demand alone.

Broad double-bind concerns of the type raised by the Supreme Court in *Price Waterhouse* are particularly helpful in explaining courts' willingness to strike down gender conformity demands that sexually objectify female workers. Courts check such demands in a range of cases, but their reasons for doing so are poorly articulated. A broad double-bind principle provides a unifying thread.

Courts check sexualization demands in cases in which women are harassed as a result of their objectification. Rather than simply hold employers liable for the harassment, courts routinely deny them the power to objectify their female employees in the first place. In *EEOC v. Sage Realty*, for example, Margaret Hasselman, a lobby attendant in a New York City office building, was required to wear a Bicentennial uniform, which was a red, white, and blue poncho-like outfit.[46] The uniform was largely open on the sides, but Hasselman was not permitted to wear a shirt under the uniform and could only wear blue dance pants on her legs. The uniform revealed her thighs, portions of her buttocks, and both sides of her body. When wearing the uniform, Hasselman was subjected to a steady stream of sexual comments and gestures by people entering and leaving the building. She sued her employer for sexual harassment and won.[47] Yet the court not only found Sage liable for failing to stop the harassment, it also ruled that Hasselman could not be required to wear a sexually revealing uniform.[48] The court would not, in effect, permit Sage to explicitly sexualize the position of lobby hostess.[49]

Courts also check such demands in cases in which only female workers are held to a sexualized ideal. Consider again the airline cases in which courts struck down dress and appearance requirements for female flight attendants. While these are often thought of as unequal burdens cases, broad double-bind concerns may also explain the courts' decision to intervene and strike sex-specific grooming codes in these cases (but not in so many others). In *Gerdom v. Continental Airlines*, *Frank v. United Airlines*, and *Laffey v. Northwest Airlines*, the challenged grooming codes were part of a larger effort by the airlines to make women's bodies and sexuality part of the goods for sale. In *Gerdom*, for example, Continental openly asserted that its weight standards for female flight attendants were implemented "to enhance its business image by assuring passengers were served by attractive women."[50] "The purpose of the weight program was . . . to create the public image of an airline which offered passengers service by thin, attractive women, whom executives referred to as Continental's 'girls.' "[51] The weight requirements at issue in *Frank* were a holdover from earlier days when United employed only women as flight attendants and required them, in addition to being slim, to refrain from marrying or having children, to satisfy general appearance criteria, and to retire by the age of thirty-five.[52] Similarly, the no-eyeglasses rule at issue in *Laffey* had been part of a larger grooming and behavior code at Northwest that required female flight attendants to meet restrictive height and weight requirements, refrain from marrying, and retire at the age of thirty-two.[53]

Finally, courts check sexualization demands in cases in which employers seek to add sexual titillation as a job requirement for otherwise mainstream nonsexualized jobs. Perhaps the most famous case of this sort is *Wilson v. Southwest Airlines.* In 1971, Southwest, then a fledgling airline trying to carve out a market niche, decided, upon the advice of an advertising agency, to conceptualize and market itself as a company selling not only air travel but also heterosexual male titillation. In accordance with Southwest's conceptualization of itself as the "love airline," it hired only women for the high-customer-contact positions of ticket agent and flight attendant. The court, however, rejected Southwest's attempts to sexualize its business and dismissed its argument that sex was a bona fide occupational qualification for the positions at issue. Sexual objectification, the court held, was not a legitimate job requirement for Southwest flight attendants.[54] As a result, the court forced Southwest to hire men as well as women to the newly desexualized positions.[55]

The result was the same in the similar, though less high-profile, case of *Guardian Capital v. N.Y. State Division of Human Rights*.[56] Guardian Capital operated a Ramada Inn that contained a dining establishment called the Cabaret. In July 1972, Guardian Capital sought to change the Cabaret from a standard restaurant to one selling heterosexual male sexual titillation along with food. To this end, Guardian Capital fired its male waiters and replaced them with female food servers dressed in "alluring costumes."[57] A male waiter who had been laid off sued for sex discrimination. As was the case in *Southwest*, the New York Appellate Division refused to allow the defendant restaurant to sex-up its business by firing its male waiters and replacing them with scantily clad female waitresses.[58]

It is true that a per se double-bind principle cannot explain these cases. It is not impossible for female flight attendants, waitresses, and lobby attendants to perform the technical functions of their jobs while looking sexy—particularly if the employer prevents actual harassment. A broader and more expansive double-bind principle, however, can help explain them. Satisfying sexual-objectification demands may make satisfying nonsexualized job demands more difficult for female workers in two ways. First, sexualization demands may distract women from the nonsexualized aspects of their jobs and diminish the energy they have left to devote to them.[59] Second, sexualization demands may distract customers and coworkers and diminish their perceptions of the competence of female workers.[60] Both dangers are discussed in more detail in the chapter on perfectionism.

Courts may protect female workers from sexualization demands precisely because they place women in a double bind, making it more difficult for them to satisfy the other demands of their jobs. Certainly, courts do not seek to eliminate female sexuality, or the female body as gaze object, from all jobs. They recognize that women's bodies and appearance may be an important part of the experience being sold in many service-sector jobs.[61] Nonetheless, broad double-bind concerns may help explain why courts are particularly suspicious of sexual-objectification demands for female employees and why they use Title VII to keep sex out of many jobs and minimized in others.

GROUP EQUALITY

Concerns about the sheer number of job opportunities available to women as opposed to men also seem at work, further pushing courts to limit the extent to which employers can engender jobs and exclude workers based on sex. Title VII permits employers to engage in sex-based hiring where sex is a "bona fide occupational qualification [BFOQ] reasonably necessary to the normal operation of that particular business or enterprise." This defense to what would otherwise be a clear violation of Title VII has been interpreted narrowly. Courts explain their BFOQ decisions by saying that sex discrimination is permitted when sex is necessary to preserve the "essence of the business."[62] In fact, there is no consistent or coherent account of business essence that can make sense of courts' decisions in BFOQ cases.[63] What does seem to be at work in these cases, however, is a judicial concern about group-based equality of opportunity. Such a concern does not demand that women and men should be equally successful in their quests for jobs; it simply demands that they should have the same opportunities to compete for the vast majority of public-sphere jobs on the same non-sex-based terms. The goal seems to be to ensure that women as a group face basically the same number, type, and range of job options as do men as a group. The effect again is to limit the gender norms and preferences that can be enforced or acceded to in the workplace.

In practice, sex-based BFOQ defenses are raised primarily in two types of cases: privacy cases and sexual-titillation cases. In the former, employers argue that they must discriminate on the basis of sex in hiring in order to protect their customers or other employees from personal or intimate contact with employees of the opposite sex. In the latter, employers argue that they must discriminate in order to provide customers with the type of sexual arousal their businesses promise.

Both types of cases fall along a continuum. At the far end of the privacy continuum are the strongest BFOQ claims, those most likely to succeed. These claims typically involve jobs requiring actual physical contact with or inspection of others' naked bodies. Courts have upheld sex discrimination in such situations based on the intimate nature of the services being provided. For example, courts have allowed sex discrimination in hiring labor-room nurses, personal caregivers, nurses' aides, and certain other types of hospital staff.[64] The middle of the BFOQ privacy continuum involves jobs that require an employee to see—but not touch—patients or customers in various states of undress. In these situations too, courts have generally upheld sex discrimination in hiring based on a similar intimacy rationale.[65] The other end of the privacy continuum is composed of cases in which an employee's duties might cause a client or coworker embarrassment or discomfort when performed by an individual of the opposite sex, but the duties do not necessarily involve touching or seeing a client's or coworker's naked body. These cases raise the weakest BFOQ claims, though the claims are still sometimes successful.[66]

Sexual-titillation cases too fall along a continuum. At one end are cases involving jobs in which a particular body is needed and used physically for the sexual gratification of another person. Prostitution and, arguably, lap dancing, rest at this end of the sexual-titillation continuum. Though I know of no challenges to the sex-based hiring of prostitutes (where legal) or lap dancers, it seems likely that courts would permit such sex-based hiring as a BFOQ.[67] The middle of the sexual-titillation continuum consists of those cases in which the good for sale is not the use of another's body for sexual gratification but the use of another person as a sexual-gaze object. As in the cases described above, in these cases sexual titillation is the exclusive good for sale, but the means of producing the arousal differ. Cases involving the sex-based hiring of strippers and *Playboy* Centerfolds fall into this category. Again, courts and commentators have assumed that sex is a BFOQ for these positions.[68] The other end of the sexual-titillation continuum consists of cases in which employers seek to sell sexual arousal, generally through the provision of gaze objects, plus or along with some other nonsexual good or service. In these "plus-sex" businesses, the nonsexual good or service can be anything from food to safe air transport. Attempts to discriminate on the basis of sex in hiring for plus-sex businesses are virtually always unsuccessful.[69]

In privacy cases courts worry explicitly about whether the exclusion of persons of one sex from a particular job will affect the general range of employment opportunities available to that sex compared with the range available to individuals of the other sex. In response to this concern, courts have created a type of balancing test that weighs the importance of the privacy interests at stake against the effect that sex-based hiring would have on the range of job opportunities available to the excluded sex. In *EEOC v. Hi 40 Corp.*, for example, defendant Physicians Weight Loss Centers argued that sex was a BFOQ for the position of weight-loss counselor because its overwhelmingly female clientele did not feel comfortable having their bodies measured by men or receiving counseling from them.[70] In concluding that sex discrimination was impermissible in the hiring of weight-loss counselors, the district court focused explicitly on the harmful consequences that discrimination in this context would have on the job opportunities of men as a group. The court noted that in considering whether sex discrimination was permissible in cases where customer privacy was at issue, the court had to balance the privacy interests of the customers against the impact of exclusion on members of the disfavored sex. If the effects of exclusion on the employment opportunities of the potentially excluded sex were minimal, the court explained, then the discriminatory hiring would be permitted. Conversely, if the effects of exclusion were severe, then a "minimal intrusion on the privacy of customers must be tolerated," and sex-based hiring would not be permitted.[71]

Similarly, in *Hardin v. Stynchcomb*, the Eleventh Circuit rejected the argument of the county sheriff's department that sex was a BFOQ for positions in the male section of the county jail.[72] The policy of assigning new deputies to the county jail for at least their first six months severely limited women's law-enforcement opportunities, since the sheriff would consider hiring female deputy sheriffs only when positions were available in the smaller female section of the jail. The court noted that the sheriff's assignment policy "all but eliminate[d] the opportunity of women to gain employment with the Sheriff's Department" and held that the defendants had to prove that "because of the nature of the operation of the business they could not rearrange job responsibilities in a way that would eliminate the clash between the privacy interests of the inmates and the employment opportunities of female deputy sheriffs."[73] The court concluded that defendants had failed to make this showing.

Courts are most likely to permit sex-based hiring because of privacy concerns in those cases in which both women and men face similarly constrained job options, thus creating a kind of parity of exclusion. In other words, sex-based hiring for privacy reasons is most likely in precisely those cases in which group-equality concerns are weakest. In *Jones v. Hinds General Hospital*, for example, the hospital sought to engage in sex-based hiring and firing in order to have female nurses available to perform certain sensitive procedures on women, and male orderlies available to perform sensitive procedures on men.[74] In *Norwood v. Dale Maintenance Systems, Inc.*, the employer sought to engage in sex-based hiring for daytime washroom attendants to ensure that women's washrooms would always be cleaned by a female attendant and men's washrooms would always be cleaned by a male attendant.[75] Although in both cases individuals were denied particular employment opportunities because of their sex, in neither case did the discrimination serve to exclude individuals of one sex disproportionately from a particular type of employment opportunity.

Group-equality concerns also help explain why courts have been so unwilling to permit employers to make sexual titillation an element of mainstream jobs and to allow employers to create new categories of plus-sex jobs—jobs that explicitly combine sexual and nonsexual requirements. Such jobs never result in the kind of parity of exclusion that exists in some privacy-based cases. The sexuality being commodified is, virtually always, female. Indeed, all of the cases in which employers have sought to discriminate on the basis of sex in order to sell sexual titillation along with some other good or service have sought to sell female sexuality to male customers and to discriminate against men in hiring. This is not a coincidence: there is a much greater demand for the commodification and sale of female sexuality than there is for the commodification and sale of male sexuality. Therefore, if courts were to permit employers to define jobs freely as requiring sexual titillation, the result would, in all likelihood, be a massive asymmetry of exclusion. Employers would be able to redefine a wide range of service-sector jobs as plus-sex jobs from which men would be excluded. While there would also be some plus-sex jobs aimed at sexually arousing straight women or gay men from which women would be excluded, the exclusion would be uneven. It is not surprising, then, given such group-equality harms, that courts rigidly police the boundaries between sex and nonsex jobs and do not permit employers to sexualize mainstream jobs.

There is, however, something odd about attributing courts' protection of women from workplace sexual-titillation demands to concerns about men's equal opportunity in the workplace. Certainly such concerns may be real, but Title VII was, after all, concerned about ensuring equal opportunities for women, not men. There may, however, also be a more subtle group-equality concern motivating the courts—one that is more clearly antisubordinationist in its orientation.

It may be that courts are concerned about a slippery slope. Once employers are permitted to make hiring decisions based on their desire to sell female sexual-gaze objects along with other goods and services, it becomes difficult to see why employers should not also be permitted to make hiring decisions based on their desire to sell not only a gendered type of sexuality but also a gendered type of allure or aura or even a particular kind of business ambience inextricably linked with workers of one sex or the other. Moreover, it is likely that the jobs linked directly or indirectly to maleness, for which an employer may hire only men, will be of higher status and higher pay than the jobs linked directly to femaleness, for which an employer may hire only women. The result would be a sex-segregated job market in which women were, once again, formally relegated to the jobs with less pay and prestige.

Job qualifications may be thought of as falling along a continuum from technical qualifications to soft or subjective qualifications. Technical qualifications are those that are capable of discrete measurement or verification, for example, being able to type a certain number of words per minute, being able to lift boxes of a certain weight, being able to speak particular languages, or possessing a degree in a particular field. Although social conditions (and biological ones in the case of strength requirements) may make it more difficult for people of certain races or genders to obtain technical qualifications, the qualifications are themselves race and gender neutral.

Soft qualifications do not lend themselves to discrete measurement. They are usually assessed and deemed to exist as a result of subjective evaluations and include such things as being personable, friendly, cooperative, or authoritative. Soft qualifications can be either sex neutral or sex specific. Although it is probably the case that virtually all soft qualifications are more readily associated with individuals of one sex than the other, I consider them to be sex neutral if, as a theoretical matter, individuals of both sexes may be deemed to possess them. For example, women may be more likely to be labeled cooperative, but as a theoretical, practical, and perceptual matter men may also possess this qualification.

I reserve the term "sex-specific soft qualifications" for those qualifications that require the possessor to be of a particular sex. For example, female sex appeal may be a sex-specific soft qualification for serving food at a restaurant that is trying to sell heterosexual male sexual titillation along with food. Only women will possess the required soft qualification.

Similarly, only men will be qualified for jobs in which male sex appeal or male allure are required soft qualifications. Sex-specific soft qualifications might also include being able to create or enhance a particular type of workplace environment or ambience that is inextricably linked to one gender or another.

Currently, courts do not permit employers to make hiring decisions on the basis of sex-specific soft qualifications except in the very narrow range of cases in which the only good being sold is a particular type of sexuality. Courts also recognize the potential equal-opportunity problems caused by permitting soft qualifications, even when they are formally sex neutral, to be used in hiring decisions. Hiring based on soft qualifications can lead to unequal job opportunities for women and men both because it is easier to hide discriminatory animus behind a subjective evaluation of an applicant's soft qualifications than behind a more objective, concrete evaluation of an application's technical qualifications and because certain soft qualifications may be more readily perceived in and attributed to members of one sex.

The potential problems associated with permitting employers to hire based on soft qualifications are made clear in the race discrimination case of *Robbins v. White-Wilson Medical Clinic, Inc.*[76] Delores Robbins, a black woman, applied for a position as a record clerk at a medical clinic in Florida. She was interviewed for the position by the record-room supervisor and turned down. The supervisor eventually told Robbins that she had not been hired because she lacked a pleasant personality. Robbins sued for race discrimination. At trial, the clinic argued that a pleasant personality was a necessary qualification for the record clerk position and that Robbins's unpleasant personality was a legitimate nondiscriminatory reason for its failure to hire her. The district court agreed and concluded that Robbins had failed to prove that the reason was a pretext for race discrimination. Accordingly, the district court ruled in favor of the clinic.[77]

On appeal, the Fifth Circuit viewed the clinic's explanation of its failure to hire Robbins far more skeptically. The court noted that while a job applicant's unpleasant personality might indeed be a legitimate reason for failing to hire her, the determination of whether an applicant's personality was or was not pleasant could not be based on the applicant's race. Based on the testimony presented at trial, the court of appeals concluded that the supervisor whose interview of Robbins was the basis for the hiring decision equated pleasant personalities with white people and less pleasant personalities with black people. The critical testimony from the supervisor followed questions she received on cross examination about black employees who had been hired by the clinic after Robbins's rejection as part of an affirmative action program initiated by the clinic:

> Q. What about Donna Richardson? Is she presently in your department?
> A. Yes, and she's real jolly and fun to be with.
> Q. And how does she relate to the other people in the department?
> A. Well, she's more white than she is black. Does that answer your question?
> THE COURT: Well[,] I'm not sure I understand what you mean. Is her race black?
> A. Uh-huh.

THE COURT: But she's in your thinking, more white than she is black?

A. Yeah. She's, you know, she's—her father was military, right, so if you're military, well, you know, you're not a military man but if you've been in the military you're around a lot of black and white people. You go to school with a lot of whites, right, if you're in the military, especially overseas. My kids did.

THE COURT: But you make a distinction between white people and black people in your thinking, and she's more white than black?

A. Yes, she is.

THE COURT: What does that distinction mean between black people and white people, that she's more white?

A. Well, she's just, I think of her as being very normal, just, I mean, being just like—I feel like she's just a white person. I don't think of her—you're saying is she black or white. I'm saying as far as I'm concerned she's white.[78]

As a result, the court of appeals held in favor of Robbins on her race discrimination claim.

Despite the ease with which sex-neutral soft qualifications may mask conventional status discrimination, courts consider these qualifications legitimate criteria for many, if not most, hiring decisions. The Eleventh Circuit, for one, has emphasized that "subjective [hiring] reasons are not the red-headed stepchildren of proffered nondiscriminatory explanations for employment decisions. Subjective reasons can be just as valid as objective reasons."[79] The court explained that soft qualifications often target real skills and attributes critical to an employee's success, even though evaluation of an applicant's possession of such qualifications is necessarily subjective. Courts do, however, try to ensure that soft qualifications are applied and interpreted neutrally by requiring employers to state specifically the facts or observations that led the employer to conclude that a particular applicant did or did not possess the required qualifications.[80] In this way, courts permit employers to make hiring decisions based on sex-neutral soft qualifications but attempt to minimize the potential equal-opportunity problems they may cause.

If, however, courts were also to permit employers to make hiring decisions on the basis of *sex-specific* soft qualifications, group-equality problems would be impossible to mitigate. Yet once employers are freely allowed to make hiring decisions based on their desire to sell a particular type of sexuality, it is difficult to explain why they should not also be permitted to make hiring decisions based on other sex-specific soft qualifications, such as the ability to contribute to a particular type of all-male ambience.

Consider, for example, the argument made by Joe's Stone Crab in response to allegations that it discriminated against women in hiring food servers. Joe's Stone Crab is a Miami Beach landmark restaurant that has been in service since 1913.[81] In 1991, the Equal Employment Opportunity Commission (EEOC) filed a charge against Joe's, alleging that it discriminated against women in hiring food servers. From 1950 on, the serving staff at Joe's was almost exclusively male. Indeed, from 1986 through 1990, Joe's 108 food servers were all male. In response to the EEOC's disparate treatment claim, Joe's argued that it did not intentionally discriminate against women in hiring but instead hired so as to create a particular kind of Old World ambience associated with the highest-quality restaurants in Europe. This ambience, Joe's managers and experts made clear, was inextricably linked with male-only food servers.

After a bench trial, the district court found that Joe's "sought to emulate Old World traditions by creating an ambience in which tuxedo-clad men served its distinctive menu."[82] Despite this factual finding, the district court concluded that Joe's had not engaged in intentional discrimination against women.[83] In reaching this conclusion, the court necessarily accepted that a job candidate's ability to contribute to the particular ambience that Joe's sought to create was a legitimate soft qualification on which Joe's could base hiring decisions. The court of appeals did not agree. According to the Eleventh Circuit, Joe's practice of hiring food servers based, in part, on the sex-specific soft qualification of their ability to contribute to the restaurant's Old World ambience was an illegitimate form of intentional sex discrimination.[84]

As *Joe's Stone Crab* makes clear, there are various soft qualifications other than sexuality that may be exclusively, and even definitionally, associated with one sex and not the other. Once employers are permitted to make hiring decisions in order to create a particular type of sexually charged atmosphere, it becomes difficult to explain why employers should not also be permitted to make hiring decisions in order to create other kinds of environments that are associated with or require the exclusive presence of one sex. In other words, if a restaurant is permitted to hire only women because it wants to sell a sexualized atmosphere for heterosexual men, it is difficult to explain why Joe's and other restaurants should not also be permitted to make hiring decisions in order to sell an Old World male ambience to customers along with their food.

The slippery slope thus created poses serious group-based equality-of-opportunity dangers. As with hiring based on sexual titillation alone, the exclusion of women and men from jobs based on other sex-specific soft qualifications is unlikely to have even the rough symmetry of exclusion present in privacy cases, nor can the gendered nature of the exclusion be minimized as it can with sex-neutral soft qualifications. The danger is not only that women will be disproportionately excluded from certain jobs but also that they will be excluded from jobs that are the most desirable.

Given the historical roles of women and men in the workplace, positions associated with exclusively male environments are likely to be more lucrative and prestigious than those associated with exclusively female environments. In the restaurant world, for example, permitting employers to make hiring decisions in order to create an exclusively female or male dining atmosphere would lead, in all likelihood, to women's disproportionate exclusion from food-server positions in the most high-quality, high-prestige, and high-paying restaurants. Women would face a range of lower-paying and lower-prestige options. As Joe's former maître d' noted: "Traditionally, I mean, it's just some restaurants, when you walk in, you know there are going to be women waitresses, other restaurants you know it is going to be male waiters."[85]

Once sex-specific soft characteristics are deemed acceptable hiring criteria, it is unlikely that women's asymmetrical exclusion would be limited to food service. A law firm might, for example, want to sell a particularly "male" type of aggression or a distinctly "masculine" bravado along with its technical legal skills. Alternatively, a law firm might want to offer its customers the comfort of a traditional 1950s corporate environment in which men in suits make executive decisions and women in dresses provide secretarial services. If employers were permitted to make hiring decisions in order to sell female sexuality along with other goods and services, it is difficult to see why employers should not also be permitted to sell masculinity or a particular gendered kind of atmosphere along with other goods and services. This path, though, would lead to significant disparities in the employment opportunities of women and men.

Frederick Schauer, in his analysis of the structure and meaning of slippery slope arguments, explains that for every such argument, an equally logical slippery slope argument can be made in the opposite direction.[86] Schauer contends that which argument is the more persuasive will depend not on the logic of the arguments per se but on the empirical reality underlying them. The slippery slope argument opposite to the one I am making in this chapter might be framed as follows: If employers are not permitted to engage in sex-based hiring in order to sell a particular type of sexuality along with other goods and services, then they must also not be permitted to engage in sex-based hiring when they seek to sell only or primarily sexuality. The slippery slope in this direction would lead, for example, to forbidding *Playboy* from engaging in sex-based hiring of its centerfolds. There is good reason, however, to believe that the slope really is more slippery in the direction with which I am concerned than in the direction just described.

In our society, jobs have historically been labeled "women's jobs" or "men's jobs," and despite the legal move away from formally categorizing jobs in this way, many jobs are still thought of as distinctly gendered. Thus, the danger that allowing employers to make sex-based hiring decisions in order to sell female or male sexuality along with other goods will lead to a widespread explicit gendering of jobs is far more real than the danger that forbidding sex-based hiring for plus-sex jobs will lead to a prohibition on sex-based hiring of *Playboy* Centerfolds. Moreover, the danger resulting from the slope pointing in the direction I am concerned about is more severe than that resulting from the slope pointing in the opposite direction. Because of the harm gendered job classifications would do to women's and men's actual life opportunities as well as to society's ideological commitment to a more than purely formal conception of equal opportunity, the possibility that mainstream jobs will become explicitly gendered is more dangerous than the possibility that businesses in the sex industry will not be permitted to discriminate on the basis of sex in their hiring.

The slippery slope version of the equality-of-opportunity argument may better address the equal-opportunity concerns courts really have in sexual-titillation-based BFOQ cases. The concern with sexualizing the workplace is not simply that there will be a large number of jobs requiring female sexuality for which men cannot qualify. This is already the case in the sex industry. The true worry may be that, potentially, the work world will become divided (as it once was) into distinctly male and distinctly female jobs in a way fundamentally antithetical to the goals of Title VII.

One potential weakness of the slippery slope argument may be that the slope is not as slippery as I make it out to be.

One might argue that plausible distinctions can be drawn between the soft qualification of sexiness and other soft qualifications. That is, simply recognizing sexiness as a job requirement for plus-sex jobs does not necessarily mean that courts will be unable to prevent employers from also making a wide range of other soft qualifications be job requirements. One might argue that sexiness and sexual titillation are valid and distinct soft qualifications whose recognition does not force courts to also recognize all the other fuzzy soft qualifications that employers might name. This may be so; the slope may not in fact be so slippery. Nevertheless, group-based concerns about equality-of-opportunity harms of both the standard and the slippery slope variety help to explain and justify courts' BFOQ decisions in privacy and sexual-titillation cases.

CONCLUSION

Concerns about traditional group hierarchy and disadvantage permeate sex discrimination jurisprudence in ways that are both explicit and unspoken. Certainly courts have not interpreted Title VII's prohibition on sex discrimination to require substantive workplace equality between women and men (perhaps through quotas or, more modestly, affirmative action).[87] Nonetheless, concerns about relative group power in and access to the work world have led courts to challenge social norms and reconstruct job descriptions. The changes have been highly context dependent. Gender conformity demands may be struck down in one workplace while identical demands may be upheld in another because the broader implications of the demands play out differently in the different contexts—female bartenders may be required to wear make-up, but female professors probably could not be. Despite these limits, the impact of courts' antisubordination concerns has been sweeping, gaining women access to jobs throughout the economy and encouraging a critical take on social gender norms.

CHAPTER FOUR

Status

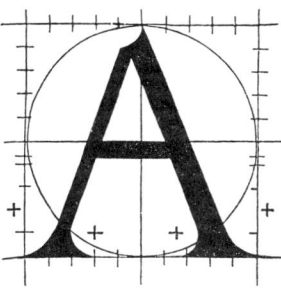MERICAN antidiscrimination law not only prizes neutrality and seeks to undermine group subordination, it also cares about the particular ways in which workers are burdened and constrained. Indeed, central to antidiscrimination jurisprudence is the distinction between status and conduct—with burdens on status being viewed as far more deserving of antidiscrimination protection than burdens on conduct.[1] While workers are expected to conform their conduct to employer dictates, expressions of status are given more protection. Understanding what courts mean by status and the extent to which they are willing to treat certain expressions of gender as status-like and immutable helps considerably in making sense of recent expansions in protection for gender nonconformists. It also suggests some cause for concern. While the idea

that antidiscrimination law should protect status rather than conduct may not be controversial, courts' willingness to treat discrete expressions of gender as status-like is not only socially contested, it is actually dangerous. The danger flows from courts' willingness to entrench and essentialize traditional conceptions of gender in the course of providing new protection for nontraditional plaintiffs. The result is that increased protection for individual gender nonconformists may come at the expense of more entrenched and rigid gender expectations for women and men generally.

THE MEANING OF STATUS

The traditional and narrowest conception of status is "ascriptive status." Ascriptive status is determined at birth, is not easily changed, and is independent of individual conduct.[2] Sex and race are paradigmatic types of ascriptive status. Both are assigned at birth based on legal and medical criteria, are highly stable, and are determined independently of any conduct on the part of the individual. Indeed, courts generally point to the ascriptive status of sex and race to explain why discrimination on these bases is prohibited.[3] Yet while a concern about harms based on ascriptive status can explain the ban on discrimination based on sex per se, it cannot help to explain why courts have interpreted this ban more broadly to encompass at least some gender conformity demands. This is because such demands do not penalize status of this kind. For example, when employers discriminate against men with effeminate mannerisms, they do so because of the employee's actual conduct, not because of a condition ascribed at birth. Indeed, even gender identity disorder (GID), the official psychological diagnosis for one whose internal sense of gender does not correspond with birth sex,[4] does not seem to be a purely ascriptive status. Although there are theories that GID may have its origin in prenatal brain development,[5] the condition cannot be identified at birth, for reasons that probably go beyond the inadequacy of current medical technology. Instead, diagnosis requires examination of a person's behavior.[6] Individuals are not diagnosed with GID—and certainly are not discriminated against because of it—without reference to their conduct. A narrow focus on protecting ascriptive status cannot, then, explain why courts protect men who are effeminate as well as those diagnosed with GID from being penalized for violating masculine conformity demands.[7]

Ascriptive status is not, however, the only definition of status that courts have used to justify protecting individuals from discrimination. In *Robinson v. California*, for example, the Supreme Court held that the state of California could not criminalize the "status" of being a drug addict,[8] yet the status at issue in the case was not ascriptive status. Although individuals are sometimes born addicted to drugs, drug addiction is more often the result of future conduct by the individual. The Supreme Court's decision thus suggests a broader definition of the kind of status that may deserve protection. In *Robinson*, the Court emphasized that addiction was a condition over which an individual had little control. More precisely, the Court focused on two types of lack of control: lack of responsibility for acquiring the condition, and lack of ability to change the condition.

The Court considered the first type when it noted that addiction is "an illness which may be contracted innocently or involuntarily."[9] An addict, the Court suggested, is not responsible for and could not control the condition of being addicted. Of course, as Professor Mark Kelman has argued, a finding of lack of responsibility for one's condition is often a function of the time frame examined.[10] One may not be able to control the fact that one becomes addicted to narcotics, but often one can control whether one takes such narcotics in the first place. Nonetheless, important to the Court's conception of status seems to be a sense that, at least in a narrow time frame, the individual is not responsible for the condition that defines his or her status. The Court considered the second type of lack of control when it compared persecution for being a drug addict with persecution for being "mentally ill, or a leper, or . . . afflicted by a venereal disease."[11] What was unfair about persecution in all cases, it seemed, was that the conditions were not ones that the individual could readily change or eliminate.

While gender conformity demands do not implicate ascriptive status, they do, at least at times, burden attributes that look status-like in this more expansive sense. Indeed, the broad conception of status, defined by a lack of individual control, rather than an absence of relevant conduct, seems central to understanding courts' emerging protection of transsexuals from requirements that they satisfy the grooming code of their biological sex.

GENDER AS STATUS

The Sixth Circuit in *Smith v. City of Salem* and *Barnes v. City of Cincinnati* was the first circuit court to use the sex stereotyping prohibition to find protection for transsexual workers under Title VII.[12] Other circuit and district courts have followed suit.[13] Such protection has depended upon the medicalization of GID and expert testimony regarding the pain one would experience as a result of this condition if one were forced to alter a particular gender expression. By focusing on the individual's pain, such testimony has helped establish a judicial perception of transsexualism as a condition beyond one's control.

The importance of such evidence was most pronounced in the case of *Doe v. Yunits*, which involved a claim of sex discrimination in education rather than employment. Doe was a fifteen-year-old student who had been diagnosed with GID. Although biologically male, Doe began wearing "girls' makeup, shirts, and fashion accessories to school."[14] When Doe arrived at school in girls' apparel, the principal would often send her home to change.[15] The following year, as an eighth grader, Doe was instructed to come by the principal's office every day so that the principal could approve her appearance; if it was deemed too feminine, she would again be sent home.[16] At the start of the next year, when Doe was to repeat eighth grade due to her many absences, the principal told her that she "would not be permitted to enroll if she wore any girls' clothing or accessories."[17] Doe sued for sex discrimination under the Massachusetts Constitution and also filed a motion for preliminary injunction. In interpreting the sex discrimination provision of the Massachusetts Constitution, the Massachusetts Superior Court found "persuasive" the plaintiff's reliance on the sex stereotyping prohibition articulated in *Price Waterhouse v. Hopkins*.[18]

The court concluded that Doe had shown a likelihood of success on her sex discrimination claim, and her pain seemed critical to the court's ruling. The court relied on expert medical testimony that showed that forcing Doe to come to school in boys' clothes would actually "endanger her psychiatric health."[19] Moreover, the medical evidence helped the court to distinguish *Doe v. Yunits* from *Harper v. Edgewood Board of Education*,[20] in which a court had upheld a school board's right to prevent two students from attending the prom in clothing of the opposite gender. In that case, the court had treated the students' efforts to gender bend as a matter of whimsy or teenage rebellion—an interest that was not very weighty—while emphasizing the school's important and substantial interest in maintaining order. As the *Yunits* court explained, in *Harper* "the court found the school's action permissible because it fostered community values and maintained discipline."[21] In contrast, in *Yunits*, the court emphasized, "Plaintiff . . . is not merely engaging in rebellious acts to demonstrate a willingness to violate community norms; plaintiff is expressing her personal identity."[22] It was these greater compliance costs in *Yunits* that seemed to tip the scales in the plaintiff's favor.

Medical evidence appeared to play a similar role in *Smith*, the case involving a male-to-female transsexual firefighter. Smith, the court emphasized, suffered from gender identity disorder. His female gender expression, through dress and grooming, was part of the accepted medical treatment of his condition.[23] As in *Yunits*, this information seemed important to the court because it reinforced that for Smith cross-dressing was not a voluntary choice but a medical necessity—one that could be avoided only with great pain and hardship.[24]

Similarly, in *Lie v. Sky Publishing Corporation*[25] the court relied on medical evidence to highlight the involuntary nature of the plaintiff's gender nonconformity. Lie, a preoperative male-to-female transsexual, sued for sex discrimination under state law after she was fired for wearing female clothes to work.[26] The trial court, in denying the defendant's motion for summary judgment, emphasized the plaintiff's evidence showing her lack of control over her gender expressions. The court explained: "The plaintiff avers that she is a biological male who has desired to live as a woman for a number of years, that she has been diagnosed with gender identity disorder, that she engages in psychotherapy, and that she takes hormones as part of her treatment. . . . Consequently, the plaintiff has alleged sufficient facts to establish she is a transsexual, not simply a man who prefers traditionally female attire."[27] Again, it was the plaintiff's lack of control over her own noncompliance that seemed to tip the scales in favor of protecting her from gender conformity demands.

THE FRAMEWORK FOR GENDER STATUS PROTECTION

Certainly employees do not always win simply by showing that a particular employment practice burdens a type of gender expression that is difficult for them to change. When employees can show that such status-like gender traits are at issue, however, a presumption of protection does seem to attach. To overcome the presumption, an employer must present a business justification for the gender conformity demand. Status-like expressions of gender are being protected, in other words, not absolutely but through a burden-shifting framework.

Such a framework helps explain the one type of case in which transsexuals continue to routinely lose—those involving transsexual workers' access to the bathroom associated with their gender rather than their biological sex. Courts permit employers to require employees to use the bathroom associated with their biological sex because they respect employers' claims that such physically based categorization is necessary to protect the personal privacy of other restroom users.

Consider, for example, *Etsitty v. Utah Transit Authority*.[28] Etsitty was a preoperative male-to-female transsexual who had been diagnosed with GID.[29] At the time Etsitty began working as a bus operator with the UTA, she presented herself as a man. Soon thereafter, however, she informed her employer that she was transsexual and would begin to appear as a female at work and to use female restrooms while on her route.[30] The UTA terminated her employment, explaining that it was unable to "accommodate her restroom needs."[31] Etsitty sued for sex discrimination and lost. The Tenth Circuit affirmed the lower court's grant of summary judgment for the defendants on the plaintiff's sex discrimination claim.

Certainly Etsitty's gender expression was difficult for her to change. In addition to being diagnosed with GID, Etsitty had begun the transition from male to female by taking female hormones.[32] Nonetheless, the court ruled against her on her sex discrimination claim. Although Etsitty had made out a "prima facie" case of sex stereotyping, the court concluded that the employer had a legitimate business justification for burdening the plaintiff's gender expression in this way.[33] Even though the UTA had not received any complaints about Etsitty's bathroom usage,[34] the UTA's "legitimate" concerns about potential liability from having a biological male use women's public restrooms justified its prohibition on her doing so.[35] The court explained: "The record also reveals UTA believed, and Etsitty has not demonstrated otherwise, that it was not possible to accommodate her bathroom usage because UTA drivers typically use public restrooms along their routes rather than restrooms at the UTA facility. UTA states it was concerned the use of women's public restrooms by a biological male could result in liability for UTA. This court agrees with the district court that such a motivation constitutes a legitimate, nondiscriminatory reason for Etsitty's termination under Title VII."[36] Although the court did not elaborate on the basis for the UTA's potential liability, the intimation is that the liability would stem from invasion of privacy claims brought by other restroom customers.

The court's reference in *Etsitty* to a "prima facie" case is strange but revealing. The language nominally tracks the burden-shifting framework from *McDonnell Douglas Corp. v. Green* that was designed to help courts identify the true reason behind the employer's adverse employment action. In *Etsitty*, however, there was no dispute over the reason for the employer's decision. It was clear that the employer had made a decision about bathroom usage because of Etsitty's sex. The *Etsitty* court's use of *McDonnell Douglas*–type language does suggest, however, that it was using a similar burden-shifting framework to determine liability, albeit with different underlying evidentiary assessments at stake. The employer won because its reason for making the sex-based decision overcame the presumption of impermissibility attached to the highly burdensome sex-based classification in that case. In terms of outcome, the *Etsitty* ruling is typical. Preoperative transsexual plaintiffs routinely lose sex discrimination cases in which they challenge their employers' bathroom assignments.[37]

Judicial concern about protecting immutable or status-like gender expressions—but not those that are mutable and conduct-like—also helps explain why transsexuals are winning their challenges to sex-based grooming requirements while nontranssexuals are not. Transsexuals are beginning to win because they are able to convince courts that, for them, sex-based grooming demands are painful. In contrast, non-transsexual gender benders lose precisely because courts view the burdensomeness for them of such conformity demands as trivial. In *Pecenka v. Fareway Stores, Inc.*,[38] for example, the Iowa Supreme Court upheld an employer's right to terminate a male employee for refusing to remove his ear stud, emphasizing that the requirement was one with which Pecenka could easily comply. "Wearing an ear stud is not an immutable characteristic," the court noted.[39] "Pecenka can remove his ear stud or cover it with a bandage."[40] Similarly, in *Austin v. Wal-Mart Stores, Inc.*, the district court upheld an employer's sex-specific requirement that male employees keep their hair above the collar, emphasizing that "hair length is not an immutable characteristic, for it may be changed at will."[41] "Discrimination based on factors of personal preference" the court explained, "do not necessarily restrict employment opportunities and are thus not forbidden."[42] In *Jespersen* as well, the court seemed to belittle the burdensomeness of the make-up requirement on Jespersen by emphasizing that compliance, or lack thereof, was simply a matter of personal choice. According to the court, Jespersen's desire not to wear makeup was based on her "subjective reaction"[43] and desire "to be true to herself and to the image that she wishes to project to the world."[44]

Concerns about status harms and compliance costs also help make sense of courts' protection of men harassed because of their perceived effeminacy. Typically, such men are harassed not because of a simple discrete trait that they can easily change and undo. Instead, they are harassed because of how they walk, talk, and stand—traits that are largely unconscious and difficult to alter. Moreover, employers in such cases do not claim a business need for the enforced masculinity. They typically seek to deny, not defend, the harassment. Consider, for example, the harassment suffered by Antonio Sanchez in *Nichols v. Azteca Restaurant Enterprises.*[45] Sanchez, a food server, was harassed for "walking and carrying his serving tray 'like a woman.' "[46] Yet whatever it was about Sanchez's movement that made his coworkers refer to him as "she" and "her"[47] was not susceptible to easy identification or quick fix. Indeed, the harassers themselves would probably have struggled to describe precisely what it was about Sanchez's movements that they found objectionable. Even if they could, it would have been extremely difficult for Sanchez to alter his walk and movements so as to eliminate the offending affect. Changing unconscious behavior is not like changing one's shirt. It is more like changing one's way of being in the world.

The harassment faced by sixteen-year-old H. Doe in *Doe v. City of Belleville, Illinois* was similar.[48] H. was subjected to repeated physical and verbal harassment focused on his inadequate masculinity.[49] Certainly, H.'s earring was a focal point of harassment.[50] Yet it is unlikely that the harassment would have ceased, or never have started, if H. had simply removed it.[51] The harassment was prompted not by a discrete, easily identifiable action on H.'s part but by the gestalt of how H. presented himself—the way in which he occupied and moved his body.[52] As was the case for Sanchez, identifying what exactly it was about H.'s self-presentation, much less getting H. to change it, would likely have been impossible.[53]

Interestingly, this same focus on gender as status actually permeated the Employment Non-Discrimination Act (ENDA) of 2007 and defined the scope of its protection.[54] In its most expansive form, ENDA prohibited discrimination based on "gender identity" and defined gender identity broadly to include "the gender-related identity, appearance or mannerisms or other gender-related characteristics of an individual, with or without regard to the individual's designated sex at birth."[55] Nonetheless, the act expressly permitted employers to retain gendered dress and grooming standards and provided an exception to such gender norm enforcement only for "an employee who has undergone gender transition prior to the time of employment, and any employee who has notified the employer that the employee has undergone or is undergoing gender transition after the time of employment."[56] Employers of individuals who had already committed to transitioning from one sex to the other would have been required to permit them to adhere to the dress and grooming standards associated with the sex to which the employee was transitioning.

Far from providing protection to garden-variety gender benders seeking to challenge the binary codes of traditional gender norms, ENDA would have provided protection only for the far narrower class of transsexuals—those whose biological sex had caused employers to mistake their true gender status. It was gender identity as binary status, rather than gender identity as individual expression, for which ENDA would have provided protection. Indeed, as Representative Barney Frank, a sponsor of the act, explained in subcommittee testimony, the act would protect "people who are born with the physical characteristics of one sex who strongly identify with the other. . . . This is something people are driven to." Those protected by the act, he emphasized, were not gender bending "by choice."[57] Because Representative Frank did not believe that a gender-identity-inclusive ENDA could pass the House, he ultimately split the protections against discrimination based on sexual orientation and gender identity into two separate bills. The gender identity antidiscrimination bill never received a vote from the Committee on Education and Labor.[58]

The fact that Congress, in drafting ENDA, like the courts in interpreting Title VII, treats the status-like nature of gender as the source of protection for gender nonconformists suggests that courts' distinction between transsexuals and garden-variety gender benders reflects a broadly shared community sentiment about how people experience gender and who is entitled to antidiscrimination protection. There are dangers associated with this view of gender, however, that go beyond the narrowness of protection for nonconformists to which it leads.

DANGERS OF STATUS EXPANSION

Certainly courts' willingness to treat some expressions of gender as more immutable and status-like than others, and to award antidiscrimination protection as a result, has had profound implications for Title VII's coverage and has brought important and much-needed protection to previously excluded individuals and groups. There are, however, risks in expanding Title VII's coverage by relying on the power and allure of the act's preoccupation with status harms. This expanding conception of gender status has not been fully recognized and acknowledged by courts and scholars and, hence, neither have its dangers.

Most obviously, the focus on status-like expressions of gender means that those whom I refer to as "garden-variety gender benders" will (continue to) lack antidiscrimination protection. Male workers who are generally comfortable with their masculinity will not be protected if they want to express their feminine side through dangling earrings or nail polish in violation of their employer's grooming code for men. Female workers who are generally comfortable with their femininity will not be protected if they want to express a more masculine side by rejecting such adornments in violation of their employer's grooming code for women. Such workers will be unable to convince courts that noncompliance reflects some essential gender core rather than more transient personal preference. Without new medical evidence to the contrary, courts will continue to view noncompliance for such casual gender benders as a matter of personal taste, and compliance as relatively painless.

What may be less clear, and more pernicious, however, is that the focus on whether gender expressions are status-like may actually reinforce gender stereotypes and encourage highly gender-stereotypical behavior in the workplace. To prove that a gender expression is status-like—and that its abandonment would have high compliance costs—employees must demonstrate that the attribute at issue is a core part of their gender identity. An attribute looks more central and essential the more it fits within a coherent gender package. As a result, in the quest for protection, gender-bending workers have an incentive to exaggerate their gender dysphoria by conforming those traits about which the worker feels less strongly to the gender of the traits for which the worker seeks protection. The result, somewhat oddly, is that workers may adopt a more extreme gender dysphoria than they actually feel, and manifest this dysphoria through more consistent and coherent expressions of the gender code associated with the opposite sex.

This pressure to overperform dysphoria to the point of adopting a stereotypical gender package is clear in the transsexual cases. Indeed, the very diagnosis of GID, which has been so important to transsexual victories, requires allegiance to a traditional gender script, including stories of childhood participation in stereotypically gender-inappropriate behavior,[59] evidence of "[a] strong and persistent cross-gender identification (not merely a desire for any perceived cultural advantages of being the other sex),"[60] and "the ability to inhabit and perform the new gender category 'successfully.' "[61] It pressures transsexuals to downplay or reject aspects of their gender that conform readily to their biological sex.[62] Transsexual workers are pushed to play the part of highly stylized men and women even if they would be more comfortable with more mixed or ambiguous gender packages.[63]

The pressure on nontranssexual workers is similar, though less obvious. A plaintiff seeking protection for gender-nonconforming conduct must convince a court that abandoning the trait at issue would be painful and difficult. One way to do so is to show that the challenged gender expression is a function of the plaintiff's core, stable personality rather than an expression of individual autonomy or personal taste. A plaintiff's gender-nonconforming conduct is likely to look more stable and immutable to the extent that it is part of a broad, consistent, and stereotypical pattern of gender nonconformity.

To see why this is so, consider again Darlene Jespersen's challenge to Harrah's makeup requirement for female bartenders. To win protection, Jespersen would need to convince the court that compliance with the rule would be psychically, if not physically, painful for her. This was, in fact, precisely the argument that transgender advocates made on her behalf in their amici brief. The National Center for Lesbian Rights and the Transgender Law Center argued that requiring Jespersen to wear makeup was "contrary to [her] innate identity and sense of self" and was "a serious, invasive, and demeaning experience . . . as debilitating to an individual as being subjected to sexual or gender-based harassment."[64] The court was unconvinced, instead treating Jespersen's desire to leave her face free of makeup as simply a matter of personal preference.[65]

Part of the reason for the court's skepticism may have been that Jespersen did not object to any of the other feminine grooming requirements imposed on her by Harrah's. If Jespersen had objected to all feminine grooming requirements and had sought to present herself consistently according to Harrah's masculine grooming code, the court might have viewed her opposition to makeup with a bit more respect. Certainly, she would then have looked more like the plaintiffs in *Smith* and *Yunits* who were granted gender nonconformity protection.

Indeed, the pressure on plaintiffs to prove their gender expressions are immutable not only encourages a particular kind of gender performance, it actually entrenches a particular understanding of what it means to be gender female or gender male. Reliance by courts on the medical definition of GID to understand how transsexuals experience their gender offers the clearest example. Transsexuals must experience and express a strong commitment to the gender norms typically associated with the other sex. There remains, however, a great deal that is unknown about transsexualism,[66] and it is certainly possible that this medical narrative may be erroneous or, at least, too narrow.[67] Nonetheless, once courts rely on a particular medicalized conception of transsexualism, that conception becomes entrenched in law and in society more generally.[68] Those who do not experience transsexualism in the prescribed ways will either be (newly) pathologized or discredited. Either way, they are likely to be excluded from the current antidiscrimination framework.[69] Those who seek to avoid such exclusion must articulate, if not actually experience, their gender in the ways courts say that they do.[70]

Courts' reliance on a medical narrative about transsexualism, however, reifies not only transsexualism but also gender more generally.[71] When medical experts testify that a plaintiff suffers from GID, the experts are saying something not only about transsexualism but also about femininity and masculinity more generally.[72] Consider, for example, the court's effort in *Doe v. Yunits*—the case involving the middle school boy who came to school in girls' clothing—to translate the medical evidence about transsexualism into "non-medical terminology."[73] According to the court, a diagnosis of GID means "Doe has the soul of a female in the body of a male."[74] Having the soul of a female meant that Doe needed to wear stereotypically female clothing,[75] and that coming to school in boys' clothing would "endanger her psychiatric health."[76] While this latter contention was made by Doe and did not need to be proven in the context of a motion to dismiss, the court did note approvingly, "[T]here is evidence in the court file to support this allegation."[77]

Similarly, in *Schroer v. Billington*[78]—a case involving a job candidate whose offer from the Library of Congress was rescinded after he told his employer he planned to have a sex change—the plaintiff presented testimony from two experts, a medical doctor and a licensed social worker who provided Schroer with therapy during her transition. The medical doctor testified that "gender identity can be viewed as the sex of the brain, which, once established, cannot be changed."[79] Transsexuals, he explained, "experience incongruence between their sex assigned at birth and their gender identity."[80] The therapist spoke more specifically about her diagnosis of Schroer as transsexual. She testified that Schroer "has a female gender identity and is a woman,"[81] explaining that she had reached this conclusion by "continually assess[ing] [Schroer's] female feelings and expression" and "evaluat[ing] Ms. Schroer's life story."[82] She had found evidence of Schroer's womanhood in her "level of crossdressing, her internal feelings about being female, [and] her inherent need to present as female."[83] In other words, in order to conclude that Schroer was transsexual, the therapist needed to conclude that Schroer was a woman trapped in a man's body. Schroer was a woman, the therapist decided, because she did and thought what women do and think.

Nevertheless, even if the current medical establishment is correct about how most transsexuals experience their gender, it may still be mistaken in equating transsexuals' experience of gender with that of nontranssexuals. It may be, for example, that male-to-female transsexuals are not in fact experiencing their gender in the same ways that nontranssexual women experience their gender.[84] It is possible, for example, that transsexuals may have particularly strong gender associations that make cross-gender manifestations particularly painful.[85] Transsexuals may experience gender more acutely than nontranssexuals. Nontranssexuals may not have as strong gender commitments.[86]

Alternatively, even if transsexuals and nontranssexuals experience their core gender identity in similar ways, outward manifestations may be intensely more important for transsexuals than they are for nontranssexuals. Transsexuals may find such behaviors critically important to their gender identity because they simply cannot be recognized as their true gender unless their outward manifestations of gender are clear, strong, and uniform. Nontranssexuals may have much less difficulty having their gender recognized, even if they send a range of more mixed and ambivalent signals through their clothes, hair, makeup, jewelry, and so on. For both reasons, cross-gender manifestations may be trivial for nontranssexuals while being truly painful for transsexuals.

If, however, courts believe that women have female souls and that such souls require women to wear stereotypically feminine clothing, then the pain of women like Jespersen, who seek to challenge some but not all feminine gender conventions, will always be invisible. For Jespersen, wearing makeup should be pleasing and certainly could not be painful. Similarly, the alleged pain or discomfort caused to women in nontraditional jobs may be too easily believed by courts, making them far too willing to accept employers' claims of a lack of interest defense in cases where women are excluded from nontraditional jobs. In her seminal article about the lack of interest defense, Professor Vicki Schultz described the importance for blue-collar employers of describing jobs as physically "dirty."[87] Particularly for conservative courts, Schultz explained, acceptance of the lack of interest defense often followed "merely as a matter of 'common sense' " from courts' acceptance of such a job description.[88] To the extent that femininity continues to be associated with concerns about dress, beauty, and appearance, women's exclusion from "dirty" jobs will continue to look, at least plausibly, like a matter of choice.

Perhaps even more troubling, however, is that judicial conceptions of gender may in fact become real and come to affect how people view themselves, what they aspire to, and what they ultimately accomplish. Those who identify as gender female may, for example, come to believe that they really are and that they must be most comfortable in skirts and makeup. Hence, they may shy away from jobs that require masculine attire and dirty physical labor. Those who identify as gender male may come to believe that they really are and that they must be aggressive and competitive. Hence they may shy away from jobs requiring nurturing and caregiving. Professor Richard Ford has identified a similar danger in the race context, explaining: "The harm of misrecognition is that members of the misrecognized group may internalize the deprecating stereotypes of others. Such individuals, then, may not always appropriately determine what is fundamental to their identity, or better put, what should be fundamental to their identity."[89] Legal scripts do have the power to shape the actual lives of women and men.[90] The irony of the recent sex discrimination victories of gender-nonconforming workers is that the prohibition against sex stereotyping is being applied in such a way as to give even progressive courts an incentive to adopt highly essentialized and traditional conceptions of masculinity and femininity.

CONCLUSION

Certainly there is something different and more compelling about discrimination based on one's status or immutable traits than that based upon one's conduct or traits that are easily changed. When Congress limited Title VII's protection to particular enumerated types of status, it reflected a broader social consensus that only when the causes of discrimination are beyond one's control do they (potentially) warrant state protection. Otherwise, individuals are expected to engage in self-help and to comply with an employer's workplace demands. As the cases referred to above show, courts have increasingly come to accept conceptions of gender status that incorporate a rich array of culturally contingent and constructed traits and attributes. As a result, concerns about status-based harms have led to an expansion of Title VII's sex discrimination protection in ways that would have been unthinkable at the time of the act's passage. Yet the benefits of this expansion in terms of protection for individual plaintiffs must be weighed against the potential dangers to women and men generally of increasingly entrenched, encompassing, and stereotypical gender categories.

CHAPTER FIVE

Perfectionism

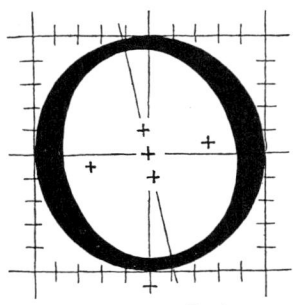N its face, Title VII of the Civil Rights Act of 1964 is a classic piece of liberal legislation—it is rights based and value neutral toward competing conceptions of the good. It requires that women have access to the work world on the same terms as men. It is agnostic, however, as to what women do with this right. Title VII requires that women can be doctors, not that they must be. The values discussed in the prior chapters are all consistent with the act's liberal goals. They seek to ensure access and opportunity—to break down barriers not to impel particular types of workplace participation. But a more controversial set of values is also at work in contemporary sex discrimination jurisprudence—values reflecting judges' own perfectionist beliefs about better and worse ways of life. Recognizing this perfectionism provides

a more complete picture of recent sex discrimination juris-prudence and helps explain in particular why courts resist so solidly employers' imposition of hypersexualized gender performance demands on female workers, ensuring instead that most of the work world remains, at least formally, a desexualized zone.

Perfectionism is a theory of the good life and of the kinds of activities that are and are not compatible with it. While rarely stated explicitly, judges' own perfectionist beliefs are doing important work in shaping and defining the structure of contemporary sex discrimination law and, in turn, the kinds of opportunities that are available to women and men in the workplace. Indeed, there are pockets of contemporary sex discrimination law—those cases raising privacy and sexual-titillation issues in particular—that are difficult to understand without recognizing the judicial values that often lie just be-low the surface of the formal opinions. The values reflect a distinct prioritization of intellectual agency over sexual objec-tification as well as a sense of the vulnerability of the former to the latter. This chapter seeks not only to articulate these values more fully but also to present a rich array of social sci-ence evidence suggesting that judges may be correct in their intuitive sense of the incompatibility of sex and intellect in the workplace.

PERFECTIONISM IN THEORY

Perfectionism, as legal philosopher Andrew Koppelman has defined it, "is the view that some ways of life are intrinsically better than others, and that the state may appropriately act to promote these better ways of life."[1] Perfectionist theories divide into those arguing that certain activities and traits are inherently valuable—valuable in light of human nature—and those arguing that certain activities and traits are intrinsically valuable—valuable regardless of human nature.[2]

Philosophers Thomas Hurka, George Sher, and Martha Nussbaum all offer inherent perfectionist theories. Hurka, for example, starts from the premise that a good human life is one that develops "human nature" to a "high degree."[3] He equates human nature "with the properties essential to humans and conditioned on their being living things"[4] and identifies physical perfection, theoretical rationality, and practical rationality as the goals of a good human life.[5] Sher, too, contends that human flourishing comes from the development of fundamental human capacities. He determines which capacities are fundamental by asking which characteristics are nearly universal and nearly inescapable for all persons. He then sets out to discover the telos, or end, toward which these capacities aim.[6] Like the other two theorists, Nussbaum focuses in her view of perfectionism on essential forms of human functioning and their requisite capacities.[7] However, instead of arguing that the good life requires that individuals develop and exercise these capacities to their fullest, she contends that a good human life requires merely that an individual possess them, regardless of whether they are actually utilized.[8]

Joseph Raz, in contrast to the other theorists, offers an intrinsic perfectionism that derives not from a theory of human nature or essence but from a belief in the intrinsic value of autonomy. Human flourishing for Raz requires that individuals possess the capacities and conditions for an autonomous life because autonomy is good in itself. In fact, Raz's perfectionism requires not only that individuals live autonomously but also that they direct their lives toward valuable ends. About what precisely constitutes valuable autonomy, however, Raz is vague.[9]

Despite their different points of origin, these contemporary perfectionist theorists share a commitment to the importance of intellectual and rational development for a meaningful human life. For Nussbaum such development must be only to the degree necessary to allow one to form and act upon one's own life plans and projects, while for Hurka, Raz, and Sher such development must be to some higher, if not the highest possible, degree.[10] Nonetheless, for all, human flourishing requires attention to and development of individuals' intellectual capacities.

Several theorists also stress the importance of certain kinds of sexual and intimate expression. Nussbaum argues that human flourishing requires that individuals be able to make "personal and self-defining choices" such as those regarding sexual expression without undue interference.[11] Raz and Sher both stress the importance of particularly valuable kinds of intimate personal relationships. For Sher such relationships are caring and nonmanipulative,[12] while for Raz such relationships are nonmonetized, requiring individuals to treat themselves, others, and their relationships as incommensurable and noncommodifiable.[13] Margaret Jane Radin, who offers a more narrowly circumscribed perfectionist theory than the other theorists, also emphasizes the importance for human flourishing of noncommodified conceptions of sexuality. "To see the rhetoric of the market—the rhetoric of fungibility, alienability, and cost-benefit analysis—as the sole rhetoric of human affairs is to foster an inferior conception of human flourishing," Radin argues.[14] To understand sexuality, as well as certain other aspects of ourselves, she continues, "as monetizable or as completely detachable from the person . . . is to do violence to our deepest understanding of what it is to be human."[15]

PERFECTIONISM APPLIED

Although contemporary American courts rarely refer openly to perfectionist political theories in order to ground their decisions, perfectionist commitments to intellectual and rational development and valued sexual expression do play a critical role in their decisions about when to permit explicit sex-based workplace discrimination. Title VII's bona fide occupational qualification (BFOQ) exception permits employers to engage in sex-based hiring if doing so is necessary to preserve the essence of the business. Perfectionist values, along with more explicit commitments to neutrality and antisubordination, help determine when courts permit sex-based discrimination and when they instead redefine jobs and demand sex-blind hiring.

Consider, for example, courts' responses to sex-based hiring in cases in which employers claim that discriminatory hiring is necessary in order to protect the personal privacy of customers and coworkers. As discussed in chapter 3, on antisubordination, courts are generally quite permissive of sex discrimination in privacy cases. One explanation may be that such cases sometimes, but not always, involve a parity of sex-based exclusion that minimizes the antisubordination impact of the exclusion. Women may be excluded from jobs as bathroom attendants in men's bathrooms because men are similarly excluded from jobs as bathroom attendants in women's bathrooms. Yet, antisubordination-oriented concerns do not seem to tell the whole story in these cases. Courts' permissiveness toward sex-based hiring in cases raising privacy concerns simply does not map closely enough onto instances in which the sex-based hiring has a reciprocal counterpart to explain everything.

A kind of customer-focused perfectionism that ties human flourishing to control over one's body and sexuality seems also to be at work in privacy-based BFOQ cases. Indeed, courts seem to permit discrimination in these cases so willingly precisely because of their belief that human dignity and flourishing is tied to one's ability to shield one's body and sexuality from unwanted and forced exposure.

In *Local 567, American Federation of State, County, & Municipal Employees v. Michigan Council 25*,[16] for example, the district court held that the need to provide personal hygiene care for patients could justify sex-based hiring of workers at state mental-health-care institutions.[17] In reaching its conclusion, the court explained: "We cannot conceive of a more basic subject of privacy than the naked body. The desire to shield one's unclothed figure from view of strangers, and particularly strangers of the opposite sex, is impelled by elementary self-respect and personal dignity."[18]

The Ninth Circuit expressed similar sentiments in *Michenfelder v. Sumner*.[19] In that case, the plaintiff, a prisoner in a maximum-security facility, sued Nevada state prison officials, alleging that their policy of conducting strip searches and otherwise exposing unclothed male inmates to view by female guards and visitors violated the Fourth and Eighth Amendments.[20] Although the court found no constitutional violation in the case because female officers at the prison were not routinely present for strip searches of male prisoners and because visitors were not in fact able to view such searches, it noted that prisoners "retain a limited right to bodily privacy" and that such preferences were directly linked to individuals' self-respect and personal dignity.[21]

Several courts have explained their decision to permit sex-based hiring in privacy cases by simply quoting approvingly from a well-known employment discrimination treatise: "Giving respect to deep-seated feelings of personal privacy involving one's own genital area is quite a different matter from catering to the desire of some male airline passengers to have . . . an attractive stewardess."[22] For these courts, customer preferences to shield their bodies and sexuality from exposure are simply different from and more valuable than other types of customer preferences, in particular those for commodified sexuality.

The perfectionist ideal underlying and driving courts' permissiveness toward discrimination in such cases is focused on the value and importance of protecting personal and sexual autonomy, particularly from forced exposure in the market. This view helps explain why privacy is treated as a negative rather than a positive right and, relatedly, why privacy preferences are respected even when they seem illogical. Privacy can be thought of as a negative right to the extent that it is protected only when one expresses a desire for it. Privacy can be thought of as a positive right, however, to the extent that it is protected regardless of whether one has expressed an actual desire for it. Our society generally treats privacy as a negative rather than a positive right: an individual's choice to seek personal privacy from individuals of the opposite sex is often protected, but such personal privacy is not required. For example, while individual women can choose to see only female gynecologists and obstetricians on privacy grounds, society does not require that women shield their naked bodies from male doctors and nurses. What matters is respecting individual privacy preferences, not ensuring individual privacy per se.

This focus on respecting privacy preferences—rather than on ensuring personal privacy—helps to explain why courts respect privacy preferences even when they appear to be illogical. For instance, courts respect women's preferences to be cared for only by female obstetrics and gynecology nurses and thus permit hospitals to discriminate on the basis of sex in hiring such nurses, even when the same women are having their babies delivered by male doctors.[23] Similarly, courts respect elderly women's preferences to be cared for only by female nurses, even when the same women are simultaneously being treated by male doctors.[24] Courts tolerate this seeming illogic because what is important is not protecting privacy per se, but protecting privacy preferences, which courts deem to be deeply intertwined with individuals' sense of self.

The flip side of privacy-based BFOQ cases are those involving sexual titillation. While in privacy cases employers discriminate to satisfy customers' desires to shield their bodies and sexuality from exposure, in sexual-titillation cases employers discriminate to satisfy customers' desires to purchase sexuality. Antisubordination concerns can also help explain courts' unwillingness to permit sexuality to become an explicit hiring requirement for mainstream jobs. Yet such concerns, again, do not tell the whole story. Although not as explicit as in the privacy cases, similar perfectionist ideals about the nature of valuable, as opposed to debased, sexuality, and the importance of rational development also seem to be at work. While it was courts' permissiveness toward discrimination in the privacy cases that revealed their perfectionism, it is their impermissiveness toward discrimination in the sexual-titillation cases that is so revealing.

When deciding sexual-titillation cases, courts effectively do two things: (1) they rigidly divide the work world between sex and nonsex businesses (they do not permit sex to become a "plus" or addition in traditionally nonsex businesses), and (2) they police the boundary between these two worlds to ensure that the nonsex world may grow but may not shrink. Courts do not go so far as to prohibit all sex jobs, but they do rigidly sequester and control them. Businesses may sell sexual titillation (and discriminate in hiring in order to do so) only if that is essentially all they are selling.[25] In other words, businesses explicitly selling sexual titillation must position themselves within the traditionally marginalized and stigmatized sex industry. Businesses may not bring explicit sexual titillation into the mainstream by combining it with the sale of other goods and services. Courts simply redefine the businesses so as to not involve the sale of sexual titillation and to not require sex-based discrimination. The businesses must either become sex businesses, and accept the resulting social marginalization, or become nonsex businesses, and get rid of their explicit sexual-titillation dimension.[26]

Moreover, courts scrupulously police this divide to be sure that the realm of nonsex jobs may expand but may not shrink. Although employers are generally permitted to change their business mission, impose new requirements and uniforms on employees, and fire those unwilling to comply, courts are simply unwilling to permit employers to redefine nonsex jobs as jobs requiring sexual titillation.

Consider, for example, the case of *Guardian Capital v. N.Y. State Division of Human Rights*,[27] discussed previously in the chapter on antisubordination. In the case, the New York Supreme Court would not let the Ramada Inn redefine its waitstaff positions to make female sexuality an explicit job requirement.[28] The court based its holding on its conclusion that the employer had not shown that sales at the Cabaret increased after the change to the all-female, gaze-object-plus-food format. Since this was the Cabaret's ostensible purpose for the change, the court concluded the change was not permissible. The court offered no explanation for why the Cabaret could not simply seek to restructure itself from a nonsex to a plus-sex establishment, even if its hope of increasing sales revenues was mistaken. Nor does this opinion shed any light on why, several years later, a federal district court in Texas ruled that Southwest Airlines was not permitted to sell sex along with air travel despite its ability to show that the new business strategy boosted its sales substantially.[29] Moreover, Justice Reynolds, writing in concurrence in *Guardian Capital*, noted that it was difficult to reconcile the court's ruling that the Cabaret could not explicitly sell female sexuality along with food with its prior decision upholding the right of the Playboy Clubs to do just that.[30] Reynolds attributed the seeming inconsistency in the decisions to the great difference in "wealth and influence" between the Playboy Clubs and the Cabaret. A better explanation for the difference might be that the Playboy Clubs were, in a sense, grandfathered into the sex side of the work world divide. The first Playboy Club opened in 1960 in Chicago, several years before sex discrimination became illegal.[31] Playboy Clubs, therefore, arose, and became known for their sale of both food and sexual titillation before Title VII raised a question about such hiring. Because the clubs already existed and their social meaning had already been defined, it was easier for courts to find that sexual titillation was a necessary part of their existence. The court in *Guardian Capital*, however, played a safekeeping role and was unwilling to let the Cabaret switch from being a nonsex to a sex-based business.

Consider, too, *EEOC v. Sage Realty*,[32] in which the district court of New York would not permit an office building to sexualize its lobby attendant. At issue in the case was the building's attempt to require its female lobby attendant to wear a Bicentennial uniform that was open on the sides and sexually revealing. The district court ruled that by requiring the plaintiff, Hasselman, to wear the sexually revealing Bicentennial uniform, Sage had engaged in illegal sex discrimination.[33] The court based its ruling on its finding that the Bicentennial uniform caused Hasselman to be subjected to sexual harassment.[34] The court's ruling, however, is far more interesting for what it implicitly holds than for what it explicitly says.

A growing body of case law and EEOC Guidances indicate that employers are liable for sexual harassment of their employees by nonemployees as well as by supervisors and co-workers.[35] What is less clear, and has not been squarely addressed by the courts, is whether standards for nonemployee sexual harassment vary depending upon the nature of the business. That is, courts have not answered the question of whether the standard for evaluating whether customer behavior constitutes sexual harassment is the same regardless of whether the leers and jeers are aimed at a librarian at the public library, an ice cream scooper at Baskin Robbins, or a stripper at a local strip club. Several commentators have argued that the same standards should not apply.[36] Indeed, sexual comments, propositions, and physical appraisals that would be totally inappropriate when aimed at a public librarian do seem less offensive and less worthy of legal redress when aimed at a performing stripper. It seems plausible to think sexual comments that might otherwise be actionable might not be actionable when aimed at employees who are explicitly selling sexual titillation—either alone or with other goods and services. In such contexts, the comments seem less unwelcome and less likely to alter the employees' work environment.

To the extent that the employer in *Sage Realty* was attempting to define the job of "lobby hostess" as involving the explicit sale of sexual titillation along with various lobby and elevator services, it is not at all clear that the sexual comments and gestures the plaintiff received would actually constitute sexual harassment. The court, of course, avoided this question because it did not take seriously the possibility that the lobby hostess position could be one in which sexual titillation and elevator services were (legitimately) combined into a single position. The court found sexual harassment in this case by applying the same standards applicable for nonsexualized jobs to the job at issue here.[37]

But the court did even more than this. The court not only found that Sage was liable for failing to stop the harassment of Hasselman, it actually ruled that Sage could not place Hasselman in a sexually revealing uniform.[38] It is unlikely that if a strip club were held liable for failing to prevent the sexual harassment of its strippers by customers, it would be ordered to have its strippers wear clothes. This was, in effect, the court's ruling in *Sage Realty*. Hasselman's employer was not only liable for failing to prevent the harassment, it was also liable for putting Hasselman in a sexually revealing outfit in the first place. The court, policing the boundary between sexualized and nonsexualized jobs, simply would not permit Sage to change a nonsexualized lobby attendant position into an explicitly sexualized lobby hostess position.

In *Priest v. Rotary*,[39] the plaintiff was hired to work as a cocktail waitress at a hotel lounge. When she refused to wear clothing that was sufficiently sexually revealing, however, she was reassigned to work in the hotel coffee shop in which the waitresses received significantly lower tips. In the course of her employment at the coffee shop, the plaintiff was subjected to repeated sexual touching by the supervisor who had originally hired her. Again, the court held not only that the supervisor had engaged in illegal sexual harassment of the plaintiff but also that the supervisor had acted illegally by requiring her to sell sexual titillation along with drinks as part of the job of cocktail waitress. The court explained that "Title VII is ... violated when an employer requires a female employee to wear sexually suggestive attire as a condition of employment."[40]

The EEOC issued a similar ruling in a case in which the plaintiff was required explicitly to add sexual-gaze object to her job requirements as a receptionist.[41] The plaintiff was hired for the position of traffic director assistance. Her job involved acting as a receptionist, typist, and clerk. The plaintiff's supervisor made repeated sexual requests and sexual comments to her. He then asked her to act as a hostess for four days for visiting businessmen in addition to performing her regular job duties. As a hostess, the plaintiff was required to wear a uniform of a halter-bra top and a skirt with a slit in the front running up to her thighs. When the plaintiff wore the costume she was subjected to sexual comments from male visitors to the office. In ruling on the plaintiff's sex discrimination action, the EEOC concluded that the "supervisor's sexual advances constituted sexual harassment."[42] But the EEOC also ruled that the supervisor acted illegally when he made sexuality or sexual titillation an explicit requirement of the plaintiff's job.[43] As in the cases above, the EEOC would simply not allow the employer to explicitly sexualize this form of employment or this employee.

As these cases reveal, courts permit sexiness requirements for a small set of traditionally sex-focused jobs, but they are vigilant in excluding explicit sexiness requirements from the rest of the workforce. This distrust of sexuality in the workplace, either as an explicit job requirement or as an implicit requirement for promotion or rewards, is also reflected in the

EEOC Policy Guidance on Employer Liability under Title VII for Sexual Favoritism.[44] In the Guidance, the EEOC advises that the widespread sexualization of women in a workplace (in the form of widespread sexual liaisons between supervisors and female employees), even if the sexualization is consensual, could establish a sexual harassment cause of action for other women and men in the workplace. According to the EEOC, such (consensual) sexualizing of women in the workplace is harmful in two primary ways. First, "in these circumstances, a message is implicitly conveyed that the managers view women as 'sexual playthings,' thereby creating an atmosphere that is demeaning to women."[45] Second, "managers who engage in widespread sexual favoritism may also communicate a message that the way for women to get ahead in the workplace is by engaging in sexual conduct, or that sexual solicitations are a prerequisite to their fair treatment."[46] In other words, even the consensual sexualizing of women in the workplace should be avoided and is potentially actionable because such sexualizing is harmful to women's ability to compete and participate in the work world as rational intellectual agents. The sexualization potentially dominates for women themselves, and for others, the way women are perceived, treated, and valued in the workplace.

Although inexplicit, the language and structure of these cases suggest that a worker-focused perfectionism—one focused on the harms that sexual-titillation requirements cause to women—may be at work. Indeed, courts' neat division of the work world into sex and nonsex jobs, and their unwillingness to allow employers to sexualize mainstream jobs, seems to reflect a desire to protect women's ability to develop as intellectual and rational actors by carving out a space for them in the work world where they cannot be formally and explicitly sexualized. Courts' rulings seem to reflect both a belief in the importance for human flourishing of one's self-development and social treatment as an intellectual, rational actor, and also a belief in the fragility, for women in particular, of this valued self-conception.

This perfectionist commitment to preserving and protecting women's intellectual development may reflect a set of pragmatic—rather than inherent or intrinsic—beliefs: namely, the work world is an important arena for encouraging adults' intellectual growth. Yet an explicit focus on sexuality in the work world may crowd out women's intellectual development in two distinct ways. First, the explicit sexualization and sexual valuation of women may obstruct men's attention to their intellectual and rational selves. Protecting the work world as a nonsexualized realm may be necessary in order for women to be perceived of and treated by men as rational intellectual beings. Second, to the extent that women themselves focus on their sexuality and sexual value, they too may overlook and deemphasize their development as intellectual and rational individuals. Maintaining the work world as a nonsexualized realm, free of the seductive temptation of self-sexualization, may, therefore, be critical to women's intellectual and rational development.

Women may choose to sexualize themselves in the work world, but they must do so wholly and explicitly. They must do so under conditions in which there is no confusion that what is being sought and provided is the woman's sexual self, rather than her cognitive self. Courts help ensure that women who do not choose to become dominantly sex objects in the work world will not have their cognitive selves overwhelmed and undermined by their sexualized selves by desexualizing their explicit job requirements. The problem, for example, with a job that requires a woman to work as a chemistry professor from nine to five and then perform a striptease for the administrative staff at five o'clock every afternoon is not that we cannot conceive of it or make its requirements clear to all prospective candidates. The problem is in the substance of the job and its effect on the jobholder. By explicitly combining the roles of cognitive and sexual actor, a job of this sort may cause women to underperform in their cognitive tasks. By eliminating the sexual aspects of the job, courts help encourage women's cognitive development.

Certainly, the work world has not been completely divided—sex and nonsex jobs are not perfectly separated. The Hooters restaurant chain, for example, hires only young, sexy women as food servers, requires them to wear revealing outfits, and explicitly combines sex and nonsex job requirements in the position of food server. Hooters has managed to maintain this policy by settling sex discrimination lawsuits and avoiding judicial judgment.[47] Nonetheless, under the worker-focused perfectionism I describe, Hooters probably is less dangerous to women than was the sexualized version of Southwest that was held by a court to be illegal. Hooters' primary product is its sexualized environment—offering a particular soft-core-porn sexual fantasy involving the "All-American Cheerleader / Surfer-Girl-Next-Door."[48] Cognitively, the choice to be a Hooters Girl looks a lot like the choice to be a stripper. In contrast, Southwest's dominant product was always air travel, but it used sexual titillation to boost its sales at the margin. More important, flight attendants at Southwest had a clear set of cognitive, nonsexual responsibilities. They had to master and carry out a range of safety procedures in addition to serving as eye candy. Therefore, Southwest's sexualized flight attendant positions seemingly pose a greater danger of role confusion than do the Hooters Girl positions.

Interestingly, the short-lived Hooters Air managed to avoid some of the problems of the old Southwest Airlines. Like the old Southwest, Hooters Air marketed itself as an airline explicitly selling heterosexual male sexual titillation along with air travel. Rather than sexualizing flight attendants as Southwest did, however, Hooters maintained the flight attendant position as a desexualized one, but placed two explicitly sexualized Hooters Girls on each flight.[49] By disaggregating the sexualized and nonsexualized jobs, Hooters Air avoided the dangers of role confusion that are the primary focus of worker-focused perfectionism. While courts have yet to rule on the legality of Hooters restaurants' sale of sexual titillation, they have taken aim at a wide range of businesses that have similarly, and even more brazenly, sought to challenge the sex/nonsex divide by demanding that women perform the role of eye candy along with their other standard role requirements.

EMPIRICAL SUPPORT

Although not relied on or even mentioned by courts deciding sex discrimination cases, empirical research actually supports both disaggregation contentions underlying the worker-focused perfectionism that seems to be at work in the sexual-titillation cases. First, studies suggest that the sexualization or hyperfeminization of women in the workplace alters the way they are treated by others so that their intellectual and professional attributes are less likely to be recognized and encouraged. Psychologists Brad Bushman and Angelica Bonnaci, for example, conducted a study in which subjects watched sexually explicit and neutral television programs. They found that after viewing sexual images, people of both sexes had impaired memory for the substance of whatever came next.[50] What this study finds with respect to television may also hold with respect to in-person contacts. It may be that the more explicitly sexualized women are, the more distracted men are and the less they listen to the substance of what women say. Other studies show that the simple feminization of women in the work world, even without their explicit sexualization, leads to perceptions of their diminished professional competency. Sandra Forsythe and her colleagues, for example, found that simply dressing female managerial job candidates in feminine clothing caused them to be perceived as less competent for managerial positions.[51] Similarly, Peter Glick and his colleagues found that study participants gave lower competence ratings to a female manager dressed in a sexy manner as opposed to a neutral manner.[52] One can reasonably assume that perceptions of diminished capability also affect the way others treat and interact with these feminized women.

Importantly, it is not only men who perceive scantily clad women to be less competent and intelligent. Studies have found that female observers often perceive such women the same way.[53] In one such study, Regan Gurung and colleagues showed female college students pictures of female Olympic athletes dressed either in their athletic clothes or in provocative attire. The researchers found that female participants rated these female athletes as less intelligent, less strong, and less capable when they appeared in provocative clothing.[54]

In addition, the fragility of women's intellectual development may be due not only to external forces but to internal ones as well. It may be that women too take themselves less seriously as intellectual and rational agents when they are focusing on their physical and sexual appearance.[55] That is, in any given sphere, the more women focus on their bodies and appearance, the less attention they have left to focus on intellectual challenges. Intellectual development, at least for women, may therefore be best accomplished by carving out a sphere in which they cannot be explicitly and overtly sexualized.[56]

This has been one argument made by supporters of single-sex high schools and colleges. Although research regarding the results of single-sex education has been mixed,[57] advocates of single-sex schools often argue that girls would perform better academically in such schools because they would be freed from the pressures to self-sexualize that are prevalent in coed classrooms.[58] Advocates have often relied on anecdotes or intuition to support their contentions that girls are likely to be sexualized in coed schools and that such sexualization leads to diminished academic performance.[59]

Recent work in psychology has shown that the dangers of sexualization are real. Sexualization of girls and women does seem to impair their intellectual focus and performance. In a 1997 article, psychologists Barbara Fredrickson and Tomi-

Ann Roberts outline what they call "objectification theory" to describe and explain the experiential effects on girls and women of their pervasive social sexualization.[60] The authors rely on extensive research showing the frequency with which women's bodies are the objects of men's sexualized gazes in interpersonal encounters and the frequency with which women are depicted as sexualized bodies in the visual media. "The sexual objectification of the female body," they conclude, "has clearly permeated our cultural milieu; it is likely to affect most girls and women to some degree, no matter who their actual social contacts may be."[61]

The authors further argue that the pervasive social sexualization of girls and women causes them to internalize the observer's perspective and, "at some level, [to] treat themselves as objects to be looked at and evaluated."[62] This internalization of the sexualized gaze leads, not surprisingly, to a preoccupation among girls and women with their own physical appearance. One consequence of this self-objectification, the authors contend, is that it impedes women's ability to reach peak motivational states. According to the authors, a person reaches peak motivational states when that person is "fully absorbed in challenging mental or physical activity."[63] Women's self-objectification and "habitual body monitoring" divides their attention, making them unable to focus fully on intellectual or physical tasks.[64]

In a 1998 article, Fredrickson, Roberts, and their colleagues sought to test empirically the impact that women's self-objectification had on their ability to perform intellectually demanding tasks.[65] The researchers tested this effect by having male and female students take a challenging math test while wearing either a swimsuit or a sweater. The swimsuit was meant to trigger, at least for women, the same body consciousness caused by their social sexual objectification.

The study was conducted on eighty-two undergraduate students at the University of Michigan, forty-two women and forty men. Participants were told they were taking part in a study concerning "emotions and consumer behavior." After first being asked to evaluate a fragrance to bolster the researchers' cover story, participants were left alone in a room and told over headphones to try on either a swimsuit or a sweater. Female participants were randomly assigned to try on either a one-piece swimsuit or a V-neck sweater. Male participants were randomly assigned to try on either swim trunks or a crew-neck sweater. While wearing either the swimsuit or the sweater, participants completed questionnaires asking how they felt about themselves both generally and at that moment. Participants were then asked, again via headphones, to complete a math test, which they were told was unrelated to the study.[66]

Fredrickson and her colleagues found that individuals in the swimsuit were more focused on their bodies and described themselves more in terms of their bodies than did individuals wearing the sweaters. According to the researchers, wearing the swimsuit caused an increase in self-objectification—an increase in the feeling that "I am my body"—for both women and men as compared to the women and men wearing the sweater.[67] Yet, this self-objectification differed in both its nature and effect for the female and male students.

Wearing the swimsuit prompted women to feel an increase in shame about their bodies, but did not raise such feelings of shame in men.[68] More important, wearing a swimsuit actually impaired women's, but not men's, intellectual performance. Controlling for students' past performance on standardized math tests, the researchers found that women wearing the swimsuits performed significantly worse on the math test than did women wearing the sweaters. Men's performance on the math test was not affected by what they were wearing.[69] The researchers concluded that women's self-objectification "does indeed draw on women's attentional resources and disrupt[s] their mental performance."[70]

Subsequent research suggests that the negative effects of self-objectification may not, in fact, be sex specific. Michelle Hebl and her colleagues hypothesized that the Fredrickson study found a sex-based performance impact because the study did not induce a parallel state of self-objectification for men and women.[71] Hebl and her colleagues replicated the Fredrickson study, but instead of asking male participants to wear either a sweater or swim trunks as Fredrickson had, they asked male participants to wear either a sweater or a Speedo bathing suit, which they believed would place men in comparably objectifying conditions to those experienced by their female counterparts.[72] The researchers found that men in the Speedo, just like women in the swimsuit, did indeed perform more poorly on the math test than their sweater-clad counterparts.[73] Together, these studies suggest that courts may indeed be right in viewing the explicit sexualization of the workplace as potentially dangerous to other arguably more valuable forms of individual development.

In another extension of the original Fredrickson study, researchers examined whether the negative effects of self-objectification held across different types of tasks and, importantly, whether the effects would hold for tasks, unlike math, that were not considered stereotypically male.[74] The idea was to see whether objectification undermined concentration and performance even on tasks that did not pose any kind of stereotype threat to women's sense of competence and confidence. In this 2006 study, Diane Quinn and her colleagues tested whether women wearing bathing suits were slower to respond to a basic Stroop color-naming task than were women wearing sweaters. The Stroop task asked participants to name the color of the ink in which words appeared. Consistent with prior studies, the researchers found that the women in the swimsuit took longer to respond to all types of Stroop words.[75]

Indeed, the effects of clothing on cognitive performance may be quite sweeping. Clothing, it seems, can enhance as well as detract from performance. Just as sexualized clothing may distract the agent and impair cognitive performance, professional clothing may actually encourage concentration and enhance performance. A study by Hajo Adam and Adam Galinsky, for example, found that subjects had improved attention and performance on a Stroop color-naming task when they wore a lab coat as compared to when they did not wear a lab coat.[76] Similarly, subjects showed greater sustained attention on a visual search task when wearing a lab coat described as a doctor's coat as compared to when wearing a lab coat described as a painter's coat.[77]

One potential problem with using a theory about the harms that sexualization causes to women's intellectual achievement in order to explain courts' unwillingness to recognize plus-sex jobs is that the jobs that are most likely to become plus-sex jobs are those that are least likely to demand intellectual achievement. It may, for example, seem implausible to contend that courts are not permitting businesses to require food servers to also act as gaze objects in order to preserve and protect food servers' ability to focus exclusively on mastering the intellectual challenges of their jobs. I think, however, this criticism underestimates both the intellectualism, or at least the genuine craftsmanship, present in many nonprofessional jobs, and the dangers that sexualizing the workplace poses to all women—not only those in positions closest to the borderline between sex and nonsex jobs. Low-wage and low-skill jobs often entail a distinct and legitimate craft aspect.[78] Women's ability to focus on the genuine craft component of their jobs may be undermined by sexualization in much the same way as is their ability to focus on more traditionally intellectual challenges. As recent studies suggest, sexualized clothing demands for women workers may impair their ability to focus on and pay sustained attention to a task of any sort. It is not just the performance of higher math that is at stake but also women's ability to pay careful attention—sustained attention—to the kind of rules and directions that must necessarily be followed for success in virtually all jobs.

Moreover, although the danger of allowing jobs to be explicitly sexualized is most immediate for women holding those jobs closest to the borderline between the sex and nonsex worlds, the dangers to women of broad sexualization are more widespread. It is possible, for example, that if employers were permitted to make sex appeal an explicit requirement for jobs such as waitress and flight attendant, employers could also make sex appeal an explicit requirement for hiring lawyers or professors. The fact that such jobs do not exist is probably more a function of the state of current antidiscrimination law than of their social inconceivability. In addition, to the extent that an increasing number of jobs available to women in the workplace require the explicit sale of their sexuality, this fact alone may cause women to focus heightened attention on their sexual valuation at the expense of their intellectual development.

CONCLUSION

As both this chapter and the last suggest, a close and deep examination of contemporary antidiscrimination law reveals that more controversial values are at work than is generally thought. Indeed, it is difficult to fully understand or make sense of courts' reactions to sex-based hiring in cases that involve personal privacy or sexual titillation without recognizing an unspoken judicial prioritization of intellectual development and a distrust of commodified sexuality. While the last chapter raised serious concerns about the judicial conceptions of gender as status that seemed to motivate recent expansions in protection for gender nonconformists, this chapter has largely defended the prioritization and protection of intellectual development that seems implicitly to underlie judicial constraint on women's sexualization in the workplace. The goal in both, however, has been to uncover the values at work so that they can be subjected to broader social analysis, review, and debate.

CHAPTER SIX

Expressive Freedom
A Short Discussion of a Value
That Is Not There

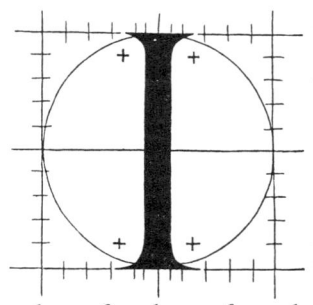 N the previous chapters, I sought to identify the work being done by several traditional and nontraditional antidiscrimination values in courts' recent decisions protecting gender nonconformists in the workplace. In this chapter, I consider another value—freedom of gender expression—which some scholars argue is also driving the recent case law. I show that despite judicial rhetoric to the contrary, courts are not in fact committed to protecting freedom of gender expression through antidiscrimination law, nor should they be.

Workplace fit demands—requirements that employees possess and present the "right" corporate image—have become a focus of contemporary antidiscrimination scholarship. Scholars argue that such demands are gendered because they require employees to embrace traditional conceptions of masculinity and femininity and that such demands are racial because they embody white middle-class norms of dress, speech, appearance, and behavior.[1] Increasingly scholars and activists argue in favor of a broad liberty-based protection for all workplace expressions of gender and racial identity.[2] With respect to gender expressions, for example, Dylan Vade urges legal and political changes to make society "more inclusive and protective of the gender galaxy in order to ensure that every person's self-identified gender is respected, [and] that every person can express their gender freely."[3] Franklin Romeo encourages courts to recognize "that all people have the inherent right to determine their own gender identity and expression."[4]

Some scholars have gone further, asserting that such protection is already required by existing antidiscrimination law. They argue that the prohibition on sex stereotyping as first announced by the Supreme Court in *Price Waterhouse v. Hopkins* and then restated by the Sixth Circuit in *Smith v. City of Salem* encompasses a right to free gender expression. As one scholar argues, *Smith* guarantees to all individuals the right "to control their own gender expression."[5] Another contends that *Smith* "preserve[s] liberty of self-identity in our 21st Century world."[6] Yet despite suggestive judicial rhetoric to the contrary, such an interpretation of the law's scope or underlying values is certainly wrong as a matter of legal reality.

THE CASE LAW

Courts' regular denial of protection to workers challenging sex-based grooming codes belies the claim that courts are committed in any serious or systematic way to freedom of gender expression in the workplace or that the prohibition on sex stereotyping demands such freedom. Indeed, after *Price Waterhouse*, as before, courts routinely permit sex-based grooming requirements that prescribe how employees may express their gender at work. For example, courts uphold workplace grooming codes requiring that male, but not female, workers keep their hair short.[7] Similarly, courts uphold grooming requirements prohibiting male, but not female, employees from wearing earrings, and, quite famously in *Jespersen v. Harrah's Operating Co.*, requirements that female, but not male, employees wear makeup.[8] Indeed, courts reaffirm such requirements even in cases in which they rely on sex-stereotyping rhetoric to check other kinds of conformity demands. In *Nichols v. Azteca Restaurant Enterprises, Inc.*, for example, the Ninth Circuit used the sex-stereotyping rhetoric of *Price Waterhouse* to hold that discrimination against a male worker because of his perceived effeminacy was a form of sex discrimination.[9] Nonetheless, the court emphasized that its "decision does not imply that there is any violation of Title VII occasioned by reasonable regulations that require male and female employees to conform to different dress and grooming standards."[10]

Although *Price Waterhouse* and *Smith* have not in fact signaled a new judicial commitment to free unfettered gender expression in the workplace, there is a narrower expressive rights principle that focuses on protecting expressions of group, rather than individual, identity that has been a goal of some feminist scholarship as well. I consider next whether this narrower principle has gained any traction in the case law.

Rather than protecting all personal and idiosyncratic expressions of gender identity, the narrower principle would protect only those expressions that are culturally group associated in some way. It would, for example, protect female workers who choose to wear traditionally feminine attire to work, such as skirts or frilly blouses, from being forced to dress in more masculine attire—at least without proof from their employer that feminine attire directly impaired job performance. More significantly, the principle would call for a reconceptualization of traditionally male jobs so as to protect and accommodate traditionally feminine attributes like empathy and relationship building. A law firm accustomed to hiring only highly aggressive and competitive litigators would, for example, be forced to consider whether individuals who were cooperative problem solvers might in fact be equally effective. Rather than protecting gender nonconformists, this narrow conception of expressive freedom would in effect protect job nonconformists—those who seem because of group identity to perform their job duties in a way different from that envisioned by the employer.

Feminists have championed protection of this sort for decades, both as a way to elevate the feminine and as a way to improve the status of women.[11] Professors Kathryn Abrams and Laura Kessler, for example, have sought greater protection for a culturally feminine caregiving norm. Both have argued that employers should be obligated to restructure jobs and workplaces so as to accommodate women's caregiving work.[12] Professor Mary Anne Case has argued for the protection of feminine styles in the workplace, whether performed by female or male workers. "Discrimination against the feminine," she notes, "is likely to have a disparate impact on women" and, as a result, "should be permitted only if job-related and justified by business necessity."[13]

Despite Case's argument that feminine expressions by both women and men should be protected, one could argue that culturally associated traits merit protection only when performed by in-group members because outsider performance represents only an imitative and inauthentic version of the trait. Interpreted in this way, the narrow expressive rights principle is consistent with courts' refusal to protect men wishing to express traditionally feminine traits at work—such as earrings and long hair. It is likewise consistent with the Ninth Circuit's refusal to protect Darlene Jespersen's desire to express a traditionally male attribute at work—an unmade-up face.

The narrow principle is, however, wholly inconsistent with courts' traditional and continued deference to employer demands that women leave their cultural femininity at the workplace door. In the famous case of *EEOC v. Sears, Roebuck & Co.*, for example, the court did not question the employer's conventionally masculine worker demands despite their exclusionary effect.[14] Sears, the Equal Employment Opportunity Commission alleged, had engaged in a pattern or practice of excluding women from commission sales positions.[15] The EEOC presented evidence showing that women were significantly underrepresented in commission sales jobs. Sears defended by arguing that lack of interest by women, rather than discrimination, caused the underrepresentation. Commission sales jobs, according to Sears's Retail Testing Manual, required a " 'special breed of cat,' ": someone who "possesses a lot of drive and physical vigor, is socially dominant, and has an outgoing personality."[16] Sears looked for candidates who possessed "aggressiveness," "assertiveness," and "competitiveness" and had a "social or extraverted personality."[17] Women, Sears argued, were simply less interested in the positions than men. In concluding that women's lack of interest, rather than Sears's discrimination, was to blame, the court did not pause to consider whether Sears's masculine-oriented job description and hiring criteria may have affected women's interest in the positions. Nor did it require Sears to demonstrate that such masculine attributes were in fact necessary for successful job performance. Far from protecting culturally feminine traits and attributes, the court used them to justify women's exclusion.[18]

In *Wislocki-Goin v. Mears* the plaintiff, who worked at a juvenile detention center, sued for sex discrimination after she was fired for wearing her hair down and wearing excessive makeup to work in violation of her employer's unofficial dress code demanding the " 'Brooks Brothers look.' "[19] The Seventh Circuit affirmed the district court's judgment in favor of the employer and echoed the lower court's deferential acceptance of the employer's grooming demands. Rather than requiring the employer to show that the plaintiff's feminine style actually impeded her job performance, the court simply presumed the reasonableness of the employer's grooming requirements.[20]

Price Waterhouse did not weaken such deference. Indeed, in *Price Waterhouse* itself the Supreme Court saw no problem with the masculine job demands placed on prospective partners. As Mary Anne Case has noted, "[T]here is little indication . . . that the Court would have found it to be sex discrimination if a prospective accounting partner had instead been told to remove her makeup and jewelry and to go to assertiveness training class instead of charm school."[21] It was the demand of femininity by Price Waterhouse at the same time that it devalued it that was the problem, not its devaluation of femininity standing alone.

Employers' freedom to define jobs in ways more consistent with masculine than feminine work styles continued in *Chi v. Age Group, Ltd.*[22] The plaintiff, Theresa Chi, had worked long hours coordinating imports for her employer before taking maternity leave for the birth of her second child. At the end of her leave, Chi told her employer that she would like to return to work on a part-time basis and would no longer be able to work overtime. Asserting that full-time work with regular overtime was required, Chi's employer deemed her unqualified for her position and fired her. In granting summary judgment against Chi on her sex discrimination claim, the court concluded that she had not even made out a prima facie case of discrimination, because she could not show she was "qualified for her position."[23] As Laura Kessler noted in her discussion of the case, "the court did not consider the possibility that Age Group might work out a flexible schedule with Chi" so that she might be "qualified" if only her job were reconceptualized.[24] Rather than protecting culturally feminine caregiving norms, the court uncritically accepted the employer's male-normative workplace demands.

THE PROBLEMS

Courts' failure to endorse a principle of workplace gender freedom is not surprising. True gender freedom is both conceptually complex and practically costly. At its most expansive, it requires protection for all forms of gender expression—those that are stereotypical, atypical, and idiosyncratic, those that are persistent, and those that are transient. Gender becomes whatever people say it is. Yet as gender becomes solely a matter of self-identification, the distinction between gender and personal idiosyncrasy becomes one of mere nominalism, and all conduct becomes potentially entitled to protection.

Title VII, however, prohibits discrimination on the basis of sex and gender,[25] not discrimination based on a whole host of other traits and attributes.[26] This distinction, to be meaningful, requires a definition of gender more stable than simple self-declaration. External criteria for identifying gender expressions are necessary, and two seem most plausible. First, gender expressions might be defined and limited to those commonly associated with masculinity or femininity. Gender would, in other words, be defined by those expressions that are socially group identified. Alternatively, gender expressions might be limited to those that are deemed integral to one's gender identity as determined, not by self-proclamation, but by external judge or expert. Versions of both approaches have also been argued for in the race context.[27]

Yet, once gender is defined using external or objective criteria, there will be some forms of expression experienced by the actor as gender expressions that do not satisfy the category requirements. Protections will necessarily be limited to a prescribed set, and some forms of gender expression will be defined out of the box. In particular, idiosyncratic or impermanent gender expressions are unlikely to be recognized and protected. Herein lies the core tension: complete gender freedom is incompatible with any kind of stable and workable definition of gender, but Title VII requires such a definition.

To make this tension more vivid, consider the following hypothetical. Imagine that instead of objecting to a requirement that she wear makeup at work, Darlene Jespersen objected to a requirement that she smile at customers. She objected not on the grounds that smiling would violate her gender identity but on the grounds that smiling inauthentically at strangers would violate her self-image and sense of self. Jespersen's challenge to the smile-at-customers rule would clearly lose under Title VII. Title VII does not provide blanket protection for personal expression. Indeed, it does not provide protection even for those forms of personal expression that are consistent with technical job requirements. Title VII does not protect against job irrational treatment; it protects only against treatment based on certain protected characteristics.

Imagine next that Jespersen had objected to the smile-at-customers rule on the grounds that it violated her gender identity. Smiling at strangers, Jespersen might have argued, is a particularly feminine attribute signaling deference and servility. Doing so would conflict with her more masculine and assertive gender identity. Under a broad gender freedom principle, Jespersen's refusal to smile would now be protected under Title VII. So too, of course, would be any attribute that Jespersen labeled or identified as an expression of her gender.

Without some guidelines for what differentiates an expression of gender from an expression of personal taste, Title VII would be left without form, predictability, or limit. With guidelines regarding gender in place, however, plaintiffs, like my second hypothetical Jespersen, will likely find their idiosyncratic expressions of gender unprotected. It is impossible to structure protection in a way that both relies on the category of gender and simultaneously transcends any conventional understanding of it.

Moreover, gender freedom, in either its broad or narrow version, would also impose dramatic costs, and constraints, on both employers and society more generally. The most conventional justification for Title VII's prohibition on race and sex discrimination is that these are job-irrelevant hiring criteria.[28] Race and sex per se are not relevant to (though they certainly may be highly correlated with) whether one possesses the range of skills and attributes necessary for (almost all) jobs.[29] Such is not the case with gender. Many jobs are distinctly gendered. That is, they demand a set of traits and attributes that are typically recognized as masculine or feminine. Prohibiting employers from requiring conduct that is traditionally gendered would force employers to restructure jobs so as to fit employees' preferred gender expressions—such accommodations would be costly and, in some cases, impossible.

Consider, for example, three jobs with traditionally feminine role demands—flight attendant, elementary school teacher, and paralegal. Flight attendants are (or at any rate were, pre-9/11) expected by employers to be warm, friendly, helpful, and at least somewhat deferential to customers.[30] Elementary school teachers are expected to be sensitive to children's needs, nurturing, and empathetic.[31] They are also expected to be collegial and cooperative in their dealings with other teachers and administrators.[32] Paralegals are expected to be organized and analytical. They are also expected to be deferential toward and emotionally supportive of the lawyers with whom they work.[33]

These jobs differ significantly from those with traditionally masculine role demands, such as litigation associate, debt collector, and Marine. Litigation lawyers are "expected to be tough, aggressive, and intimidating toward their opponents."[34] Bill collectors are expected—indeed, encouraged—to be aggressive and intimidating toward debtors.[35] Marines are expected to be strong, aggressive, and emotionally detached.[36]

Certainly, some jobs seem gendered for no reason other than social convention. The role of secretary, for example, came to include both caretaking and sexual titillation only after the job became dominated by women.[37] Such expectations were not part of the job when it was performed predominantly by men. As women came to dominate the profession, its norms changed so as to essentially preclude further male occupation.[38]

Other jobs seem gendered for reasons more intrinsic to the job itself. Nurturing treatment, for example, probably is important to the healthy development of young children. A nurturing disposition may then be required of elementary school teachers for reasons independent of the fact that most elementary school teachers are female.[39] The same may hold true of the role demands of Marines. The core functions of a Marine may simply be performed better by one who is physically strong, aggressive, and unemotional. Men may dominate the Marines because they have these qualities to a higher degree than women, but the role demands themselves may be defined this way for reasons independent of men's past or present dominance.

Jobs may be gendered not only in terms of the attributes they seek but also, more simply, in terms of the clothes and appearance they require. Construction, like other forms of physical labor, for example, often requires not just a kind of masculine strength but also the adoption of masculine dress and grooming styles in order for the jobs to be performed safely. An employer who is unable to force a femininely gendered construction worker to tie her hair back and wear pants to work will be unable to safely assign the worker to a range of duties. An employer who is unable to force a femininely gendered bill collector to scowl and talk in an aggressive manner may have to pair the feminine worker with a more masculine coworker, in a good-cop/bad-cop kind of ploy, in order for the worker to be effective. An employer who cannot force a masculinely gendered elementary school worker to smile and coo at his charges may not be able to create the kind of warm and nurturing atmosphere in which children thrive. In all cases, the costs to employers, and society more generally, of true gender freedom for workers would be significant.

CONCLUSION

Courts have not, in short, been persuaded by scholars' arguments that Title VII, to be meaningful, must protect freedom of gender expression in the workplace. Instead, restraints on gender expression seem to be viewed as just another workplace constraint—to be added to the list of many other controls—that can legitimately be expected in the workplace.

While it is true that courts have expanded protection for some gender nonconformists, a commitment to gender freedom—for either individuals or groups—is not the motivation. Gender-nonconforming expressions are protected only when other antidiscrimination values are implicated. The values pushing the boundaries of sex discrimination coverage are the more traditional ones discussed in previous chapters, most notably a concern about group subordination and status harms, as well as a rather covert perfectionist distrust of sexuality. Free gender expression itself is not an antidiscrimination demand.

CHAPTER SEVEN

The Race Paradox

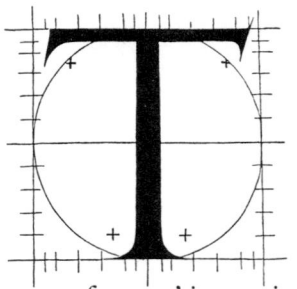HIS book's focus is on federal sex discrimination law and the rapid and quite remarkable changes in courts' interpretation of that law over the past two decades with respect to gender nonconformists. The prior chapters sought to make sense of courts' increasing willingness to interpret Title VII's prohibition on sex discrimination as prohibiting discrimination based on gender identity and gender performance as well. I seek to end the book with a brief comparative study that serves to highlight just how dramatic the changes taking place in sex discrimination jurisprudence have been by contrasting them with the virtual stagnation that has occurred in race discrimination jurisprudence over a similar period.

As the prior chapters made clear, it was the Supreme Court's pronouncement against sex stereotyping in *Price*

Waterhouse v. Hopkins that set the stage for Title VII's dramatically expanded protection of gender nonconformists.[1] What followed *Price Waterhouse* was widespread protection of male employees harassed because they were deemed too feminine, female employees harassed because they were deemed overly masculine, and growing protection of preoperative male-to-female transsexuals discriminated against for adopting feminine styles of dress and grooming. In the race context there has been no similar watershed moment and no similar expansion of coverage for expressions of racial identity. Courts uniformly and explicitly refuse to protect minority workers from demands that they conform to culturally white norms of dress, behavior, and appearance. Title VII's prohibition on race discrimination has remained narrow and constrained during a period in which its prohibition on sex discrimination has been interpreted in increasingly broad ways.

In a sense, this presents a paradox. Although Title VII prohibits employment discrimination on the basis of both race and sex, race was its primary target. The addition of sex was an afterthought, and, as I discussed earlier, one commonly thought of as an act of sabotage. Moreover, sex received weaker protection than race did under Title VII, just as it does under the Equal Protection Clause.[2] Why, then, are courts currently interpreting Title VII to provide workers with more expansive protection under its sex discrimination prohibition than under its race discrimination prohibition?

In order to make sense of this paradox, this chapter mines not only the values and beliefs motivating antidiscrimination law but also the values and beliefs that underlie our thinking about race and gender as social identities. Contemporary race and sex discrimination coverage looks so different not because of a divergence of legal principles but because of important differences in the ways in which workplace rules burden women and minorities and because of very different underlying assumptions about how individuals experience their race and gender.

Race scholars, like sex scholars, have focused considerable attention in recent years on the racial implications of workplace "fit" requirements. They contend that while racial minorities are rarely excluded anymore from jobs because of their race per se, their inclusion in the work world often comes at a cost. The cost is assimilation to corporate culture demands that require workers to downplay their race and to act, even if not be, white. Antidiscrimination law, they argue, should protect workers from workplace conformity demands that burden minority workers' expressions of racial or cultural identity. Professor Barbara Flagg, for example, argues that employers regularly engage in what she calls "transparently white decisionmaking," whereby employers make "unconscious use of criteria of decision that are more strongly associated with whites than with nonwhites."[3] The result is workplace demands that mimic the norms and styles of their predominantly white middle-class employees, even while being formally race neutral. Flagg argues that antidiscrimination law should protect racial minorities from demands that they adopt "behaviors and characteristics associated with whites" and abandon traits and attributes with which they are racially identified.[4] Professor Juan Perea makes a similar argument with respect to culturally associated traits and Title VII's prohibition on national origin discrimination.[5] Perea contends that most of the discrimination faced by ethnic minorities results from their possession of certain traits, not from the fact of their national origin or place of birth.[6] As a result, he argues, Title VII should protect against discrimination based on "physical and cultural characteristics that make a social group distinctive either in group members' eyes or in the view of outsiders."[7] He includes within this category "religion, shared history, traditions, values, and symbols."[8]

The belief that racial expressions should be protected in the workplace has not been uniformly shared by race scholars. Professor Richard Thompson Ford has been the most vocal skeptic. He has objected to protecting employees from conformity demands with which they can choose to comply, arguing that antidiscrimination law need not privilege workers' subjective preferences for self-presentation over employers' subjective preferences regarding workplace control.[9] Moreover, he worries that protecting workers' expressions of racial identity will essentialize these groups based on traits and attributes that may be both contested and harmful.[10] Nonetheless, the push for greater protection of minority workers from workplace conformity demands has been one of the most significant developments of recent race discrimination scholarship and has paralleled in important respects the movement taking place in sex discrimination jurisprudence to protect gender nonconformists. What is not obvious is why this push has been so much less successful.

NEUTRALITY

Certainly neutrality is as strong a value in race discrimination jurisprudence as in sex discrimination cases. In the aftermath of Title VII's passage, demands for neutral treatment of the races led to dramatic changes in the professional opportunities available to African Americans in this country, and to seismic shifts in the racial composition of the work world.[11] Yet while arguments in favor of neutrality have been used with some success by feminist scholars as a way to expand protection for gender nonconformists, such arguments have been used primarily as a shield by employers in race cases seeking to defend racially loaded conformity demands. To see why this is so, consider the different ways in which gender and racial conformity demands generally operate in the workplace. Workers who seek to express their gender in ways that flout convention generally seek to mimic the gender expressions typically associated with individuals of the opposite sex. For such individuals, arguments about antidiscrimination law's demand for sex-based neutrality are helpful, even if not altogether convincing for reasons I have already articulated. Neutrality arguments seek to narrow the safe harbor that courts have built for sex-based sex and grooming codes with the goal of giving women and men access to gender conventions on both sides of the divide.

In race cases, by contrast, workers who seek to express their race in ways that flout workplace convention generally seek to act in ways that are not permitted of anyone. Against these individuals, arguments about neutrality have become a shield used by employers to protect themselves from claims that workplace dress, behavior, or grooming codes are in fact discriminatory. In *Rogers v. American Airlines, Inc.*, for example, the court rejected the plaintiff's challenge to a no-corn-rows rule by emphasizing the neutral application of the rule.[12] As the *Rogers* court explained: "[A]n even-handed policy that prohibits to both sexes a style more often adopted by members of one sex does not constitute prohibited sex discrimination."[13] Similarly, in *Garcia v. Spun Steak Co.* the court rejected a challenge by bilingual Hispanic workers to their employer's English-only rule, again stressing the rule's formal neutrality.[14] The *Spun Steak* court noted as well that there was no suggestion in that case that the employer's formally neutral English-only rule had been adopted with discriminatory intent.[15] As a result, the plaintiffs in both *Rogers* and *Spun Steak* were left only with their disparate impact claims.

ANTISUBORDINATION

Antisubordination concerns, too, are as central to courts' race discrimination jurisprudence as they are to its sex discrimination jurisprudence. Indeed, *Griggs v. Duke Power Co.*, which established the disparate impact framework, was a race discrimination case.[16] Yet, in both *Rogers* and *Spun Steak*, the plaintiffs' disparate impact claims failed because the courts viewed compliance as a matter of choice and the traits at issue as mutable. In *Rogers*, the court focused on the mechanical ease with which black women could change their hairstyle and thereby avoid any adverse impact. According to the court, because "[a]n all-braided hair style is an 'easily changed characteristic,' " disadvantageous treatment based on the trait did not constitute an adverse impact for disparate impact purposes.[17] The *Spun Steak* court stated the disparate impact framework's limits even more clearly, explaining that "Title VII is not meant to protect against rules that merely inconvenience some employees, even if the inconvenience falls regularly on a protected class."[18] According to the court, it was just such mere inconvenience that was at issue in *Spun Steak*. As the court explained: "The fact that an employee may have to catch himself or herself from occasionally slipping into Spanish does not impose a burden significant enough to amount to the denial of equal opportunity."[19]

More interesting, perhaps, is why the particular antisubordination-oriented disparate treatment frameworks—those focusing on unequal burdens and double binds—that have provided such critical protection for workplace expressions of gender identity have not resulted in similar protection for workplace expressions of racial identity. Context is again critical.

Scholars have raised unequal-burden-type arguments in race cases. Many workplace demands, they argue, impose unequal burdens on minority workers because the demands are coded culturally white. As a result, minority workers must do extra work to comply with them.[20] Yet this is precisely the kind of unequal burden that courts did not care about in the sex context. It is not surprising, then, that they do not care about it in the race context either. Courts deciding racial discrimination cases, like those deciding sex discrimination cases, have refused to adopt a per se unequal burdens test for conformity demands that disproportionately burden members of one group in terms of the time, money, and energy costs of compliance as long as the demands match conventional professional norms. This is precisely the problem, according to many race discrimination scholars.[21] Nonetheless, it is also what renders the compliance costs for white and minority workers both invisible and immaterial to courts.

In the sex context, courts did care about conformity demands that distinguished between the sexes in ways not justified by conventional gender norms—regardless of whether the burdens imposed were equal or unequal—because such differentiation alone was deemed stigmatic to women. In the race context, conformity demands never distinguish between the races in this way. Conformity demands are always (at least formally) uniform.

Nonetheless, courts do seem to be as concerned about stigma in race cases as in sex cases, and they recognize that even formally neutral demands may be stigmatic. Conformity demands may stigmatize racial or ethnic minorities in two distinct ways. First, they may stigmatize group members by attacking and denigrating traits that are associated with group identity. The assimilationist nature of such trait requirements reinforces the privilege of the dominant culture and the outsider status of those whose cultural expressions differ from it. Second, trait requirements may stigmatize outsider group members by sending a broader social message about the group's perceived inferiority. Even if a particular hiring requirement does not degrade and devalue a group-identified trait, it may still send a social message of racial segregation or hierarchy. This second form of stigma is what Professor Charles Lawrence argues should drive courts' analysis of facially neutral laws under the Equal Protection Clause. Lawrence maintains that laws that have a racialized social meaning should be subject to heightened scrutiny even if they are racially neutral and not the product of intentional race discrimination. As easy examples of laws with racially stigmatizing cultural meanings, Lawrence points to the school segregation challenge in *Brown v. Board of Education* and the attempt by local government to construct a wall between white and black communities challenged in the case of *City of Memphis v. Green.*[22]

Social meanings do seem to matter to courts in race cases, though the concern is rarely articulated as such. In *Rogers*, for example, in the very same paragraph where the court explains that American Airlines could prohibit Rogers from wearing cornrows, the court says that a policy prohibiting employees from wearing an "Afro/bush" hairstyle might offend Title VII.[23] The court explains this difference in legal result as stemming from the mutability of the former trait and the immutability of the latter, but this explanation is unconvincing. In fact, both cornrows and Afros are highly mutable. In order to comply with the no-cornrows policy, Rogers could have undone her cornrows, cut them off, or covered them with a hairpiece. An employee with an Afro facing a no-Afro/bush hair policy could likewise straighten her hair, cut it off, or cover it with a scarf. Compliance in both cases is certainly physically possible, and it is not clear that complying with the no-Afro/bush hair policy is any more physically costly than complying with the no-cornrows policy. The *Rogers* court's great discomfort with a no-Afro policy seems more likely to stem from a sense that such a policy sends a strong and direct message of white physical, and cultural, superiority.

Consider also the hypothetical discussed in dicta by the Fifth Circuit in the case of *Garcia v. Gloor*, which involved a challenge to an English-only workplace rule.[24] The court explained that just as the English-only policy at issue in *Gloor* was permissible, "[i]n similar fashion an employer might, without business necessity, adopt a rule forbidding smoking on the job. The [Civil Rights] Act would not condemn that rule merely because it is shown that most of the employees of one race smoke, most of the employees of another do not and it is more likely that a member of the race more addicted to tobacco would be disciplined."[25] The court explained this similarity of result by asserting that the traits affected by both conformity demands—speaking only English for bilingual employees and not smoking, respectively—are mutable. In fact, the requirement that someone addicted to smoking refrain from doing so is not one that can be easily and painlessly met. As in *Rogers,* a concern about something other than mutability seems to be driving the courts' intuition that a rule prohibiting smoking is not problematic. The court's intuition that a no-smoking requirement should be permitted seems to have far more to do with judgments about the social meaning of the trait requirement than with concerns over trait mutability. In practice, however, concerns about stigma have simply not resulted in much actual protection in the race context because courts so rarely view formally neutral workplace conformity demands as racially stigmatic.

The double-bind framework also plays out in importantly different ways in the race and sex contexts. Racial conformity demands do not place workers in the kind of narrow double bind at issue in *Price Waterhouse*—where conformity demands conflict directly with professional demands. This difference is due to the different ways in which assimilation demands constrain female and minority workers.

Gender conformity demands require female workers to play to a distinctly feminine code. Women are expected to look and act like women; men are required to look and act like men; and these are not the same. Racially loaded conformity demands, in contrast, require minority workers to play to a unitary code—one that is applied to all workers regardless of race. The effect of this formal neutrality is that minority workers never face the kind of direct conflict between cultural conformity demands and professional demands that female workers sometimes do.

Consider, for example, a black man facing the same hurdle as Ann Hopkins. He is an associate at a large accounting firm being considered for partnership. He is evaluated, as Hopkins was, based in part on his compliance with cultural conventions as well as with more role-specific demands. In accord with cultural conventions, he is expected to speak standard, grammatically correct English, wear relatively expensive but understated clothes, and keep his hair and beard short and clean-cut. In accord with professional role expectations, he is expected to project strength, authority, and competence. The cultural conformity demands, rather than conflicting with role demands, as they did for Hopkins, work in concert with them. Indeed, satisfying cultural assimilation demands actually increases the likelihood that the minority candidate will also be viewed as satisfying role demands.

Certainly, one could conceive of a double-bind scenario in the race context that parallels the one faced by Ann Hopkins in the sex context. Imagine a world, perhaps in the not too distant past, in which cultural conformity demands for blacks and whites, just as for women and men, were explicitly different. Blacks were expected to be deferential, reverential, and subservient to whites. Whites, at least white men, were expected to be confident and assertive. Consider again the black applicant for partnership. In order to satisfy the role demands of a successful accountant, the candidate must project strength, authority, and competence. Now, however, the applicant's cultural conformity demands directly conflict with his professional role demands. If the black man satisfies his role demands, he fails his cultural conformity demands and is likely to be viewed as uppity and arrogant—much as Ann Hopkins was viewed as a "bitchy woman."[26] If he satisfies the cultural conformity demands, he almost certainly fails his role demands. Double-binding assimilation demands of this sort would constitute actionable race discrimination.[27] In practice, however, assimilationist demands do not double-bind racial minorities in this way.

A focus on the market consequences of such conformity demands may also help reveal the race-sex difference in the application of a narrow double-bind prohibition. While traditionally gendered assimilation demands tend to help women in low-level jobs, they tend to hurt women in high-level jobs.[28] Women in high-level jobs receive market rewards by resisting traditionally female assimilation demands. The demands double-bind them. In contrast, assimilation demands always and only help minority workers to satisfy professional role demands. There is no professional or market penalty for minority workers for abiding by such demands and no market reward for minorities who resist assimilationist demands.

In the sex context, I argued that a broad double-bind principle—one requiring only that professional demands are in tension with, rather than in direct conflict with, cultural conformity demands—was also at work. Such a broad principle

might seem to hold more promise for checking racial conformity demands. One could argue that just as sexualized conformity demands double-bind female workers by distracting
their attention from the nonsexualized aspects of their jobs, so
too do culturally white conformity demands double-bind racial minorities by diminishing the attention they have left to
expend on other aspects of their jobs.

Indeed, the fact that courts have not used Title VII to
protect minority workers from racially loaded conformity
demands may mean that courts are simply unwilling to adopt
as broad a double-bind principle in the race context as they do
in the sex context. The difference in coverage may, in other
words, be due to doctrinal differences in the two contexts.
Alternatively, however, it may be that the only kinds of double
binds that courts care about are structural, not personal. For
example, courts may care about the double bind created by
sexualization demands because such demands undermine all
female workers both by taking their attention away from
nonsexualized skill development and by diminishing how
seriously they are taken by others. The double bind does not
depend on the specific subjectivity of any particular female
worker. However, the double bind imposed on racial minorities by normatively white conformity demands is different.
The extent to which a minority worker is distracted and disadvantaged by having to conform to culturally white norms
depends on the subjectivity of the particular employee and
especially on the degree to which he or she is already comfortable, or identified, with white norms. For a minority
worker who is fully acculturated to white middle-class norms,
such conformity demands would not impose a double bind

even in the broad sense. Rather than rejecting the broad double-bind antidiscrimination principle in race cases, then, courts may simply not be seeing conformity demands that double-bind in the structural manner they care about.

HARMS

While courts' narrow and particular antisubordination concerns may not have a good parallel in the race context, their concerns about status harms do. Indeed, they help to explain one of the few types of conformity demands that courts readily treat as racially discriminatory. These are demands that black men with pseudofolliculitis barbae (PFB), a skin condition that makes shaving painful, comply with no-beard requirements.[29]

The medical diagnosis of PFB as a disease makes it look a lot like GID: a condition for which the individual is blameless and over which he lacks easy control. Indeed, critical to the success of plaintiffs in such cases has been their ability to convince a court of the physical pain and hardship associated with shaving because of this racially correlated condition.[30] In *Richardson v. Quik Trip Corp.*, for example, the plaintiff was fired for refusing to shave his beard in violation of the company's grooming code.[31] The plaintiff sued, alleging that enforcement of the policy against black men like him who suffered from PFB constituted race discrimination. The court agreed, declaring that for PFB sufferers like the plaintiff, shaving was "insufferable."[32] Similarly, in *University of Maryland at Baltimore v. Boyd*, the plaintiff, a black man with PFB, claimed that, as applied to him, a no-beard requirement for university police officers was racially discriminatory.[33] In upholding his claim, the Maryland Court of Special Appeals emphasized the pain associated with shaving for PFB sufferers and the particular severity of the plaintiff's own case.[34]

When PFB makes it extremely painful for black men to shave, their cost of compliance with a no-beard policy is very high, and courts tend to grant protection from this conformity requirement. In contrast, when compliance costs are low, nonconformity looks less like a matter of racial status and more like a matter of personal choice. As a result, in low-compliance-cost cases courts refuse to use antidiscrimination law to protect workers from no-beard requirements.[35] Consider, for example, the Eighth Circuit's ruling in *Bradley v. Pizzaco of Nebraska*, a case brought by the EEOC on behalf of an African American man who suffered from PFB.[36] Langston Bradley, a deliveryman for Domino's Pizza, was fired for failing to comply with the company's no-beard policy.[37] The EEOC sought an injunction requiring Domino's to recognize an exception to its no-beard policy for PFB sufferers.[38] Although the court ultimately ruled that Domino's was required to recognize such an exception,[39] it denied Bradley protection because it found that he suffered from only a mild case of PFB.[40] Although the no-beard requirement constituted impermissible race discrimination as applied to those PFB sufferers for whom shaving was really painful, as applied to Bradley, for whom compliance costs were low, it was a legitimate workplace conformity demand.[41]

Yet, such status-based protection from racially loaded conformity demands is rare. Unlike the PFB cases, the vast majority of racial conformity cases involve demands whose satisfaction is perceived by courts to be well within the control of minority workers. Indeed, it is the employee's ready control over the traits at issue that courts point to when denying antidiscrimination protection. For example, in *Rogers*, the case involving a challenge to an airline's no-cornrows requirement for customer service personnel, the court emphasized that the plaintiff could easily comply physically with the no-cornrows rule by covering her hair or wearing it in a bun.[42] Similarly, in *Garcia v. Spun Steak Co.*, the case involving a challenge to an employer's English-only rule, the court noted that the bilingual plaintiffs could simply choose to speak English in order to comply.[43] In these cases, because the traits at issue have not been medicalized as they have in GID and PFB cases, courts discount and ignore both the physical and the psychic harm that would result from their abandonment. In addition, because the contested traits are discrete and clearly defined, unlike in the effeminate men cases, courts view compliance as easily attainable. Minority workers' nonconformity with racially dominant workplace norms is therefore seen as a matter of choice rather than as a reflection of status, and is left unprotected.

Though perhaps counterintuitive, it is likely that courts' refusal to treat virtually any expressions of racial identity as status-like is, at least in part, a legacy of the civil rights movement. As civil rights activists struggled to define and promote a conception of racial justice and equality, two competing positions fought for prominence within the movement: integrationism and nationalism.[44] Integrationists responded to the country's racist legacy of essentializing blacks as different and inferior to whites by denying the significance of race altogether. They equated racial justice with racial transcendence, whereby individuals would interact and compete with each other in a race- and color-blind world.[45] Black nationalists, in contrast, argued that race did matter. They maintained that blacks and whites had distinct communities, histories, and traditions that should be recognized and preserved.[46] Rather than racial transcendence, they sought the distribution and equalization of power across races.[47] Integrationism, they contended, would lead not to some idyllic color-blind society but instead to assimilation to white norms and the abandonment of black culture.[48]

To integrationists, black nationalism smacked of the same kind of essentialism as white supremacy.[49] They believed that both ideologies needed to be suppressed and surpassed in the interests of racial justice. As Professor Gary Peller has argued, this equation of black nationalism with white supremacy, and the subsequent marginalization of both, was the compromise required to incorporate civil rights into the mainstream. He explains: "Along with the suppression of white racism that was the widely celebrated aim of civil rights reform, the dominant conception of racial justice was framed to require that black nationalists be equated with white supremacists, and that race consciousness on the part of either whites or blacks be marginalized as beyond the good sense of enlightened American culture."[50] Integrationism won mainstream support, and color blindness became the dominant social and legal conception of racial equality.[51] It is this commitment to racial transcendence, and the corresponding aversion to racial essentialism, that helps ensure that courts virtually never regard expressions of racial identity by minority workers as a necessary or inherent component of their racial status as such.

In the race context, as in the sex context, scholars have also sought to expand the scope of Title VII's protection by making freedom-of-expression-type arguments. Such arguments, however, have focused on the importance of free expression for the purpose of protecting group, rather than individual, identity. In the race context, as in the sex context, such arguments have been wholly unsuccessful. In *Rogers v. American Airlines, Inc.*, for example, the plaintiff's core argument for protection from her employer's no-cornrows rule was that cornrows were an integral part of her identity as a black woman.[52] "The completely braided hair style," she asserted, "has been and continues to be part of the cultural and historical essence of Black American women."[53] The argument was wholly unavailing. Mincing no words, the court explained that "an all-braided hair style ... even if socioculturally associated with a particular race or nationality, is not an impermissible basis for distinctions in the application of employment practices by an employer."[54] Expressions of racial identity as such were not entitled to antidiscrimination protection.[55]

The employees in *Garcia v. Spun Steak Co.* in challenging their employer's English-only rule as a form of national origin discrimination also emphasized their right to express their group identity.[56] The English-only rule, they argued, should be invalidated because "it denies them the ability to express their cultural heritage on the job."[57] The court rejected the plaintiffs' claim for protection of their group culture in no uncertain terms. "Title VII," the court explained, "does not protect the ability of workers to express their cultural heritage at the workplace."[58] Title VII, courts have made clear, is not in the business of preserving racial and ethnic group identities in the face of mainstream cultural assimilation demands. Preservation of group culture is not the purpose of Title VII.

CONCLUSION

The paradox of contemporary antidiscrimination law is that at a time when the scope of Title VII's sex discrimination protection is expanding dramatically to protect individual expressions of gender identity in the workplace, no similar expansion has occurred in race discrimination case law. The difference appears to have more to do with culture and context than with law. Sex is treated as rich and complex in ways that race is not. Individuals are viewed as having not only a sex but also a gender. While the two are no longer seen as invariably aligned, both are viewed as meaningful. Both are treated as biologically—or physiologically—based and as having some recognizable external manifestations. Race, in contrast, is viewed as a mere technical difference of skin tone unassociated with meaningful differences in behavior or self-presentation. In short, race is empty, while sex is loaded.

These differences explain why similar legal values lead to such different results. Because some gendered behaviors seem "natural" and immutable, they receive protection from workplace conformity demands. Because no racial expressions are viewed the same way, they do not. Moreover, because gender conformity demands are sex specific they do impact the workplace success of women and men differently. Again, the same is not true for race. Racially loaded conformity demands are unitary and do not impose different obligations or impediments on different racial groups. As a result, the former trigger antisubordination-oriented protections that the latter do not.

What this comparative analysis makes clear is that a real understanding of antidiscrimination law requires recognizing not only the values underlying the law itself but also the values and beliefs that inhere in our thinking about race and sex as identities. It is not just antidiscrimination values that push and modulate the law's coverage, it is our core conception of how individuals experience their race and sex.

Conclusion

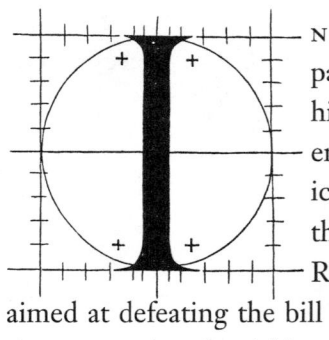N the fifty years since Title VII's passage, the scope of the law's prohibition on sex discrimination in employment has expanded dramatically. When viewed most cynically, the inclusion of sex in the Civil Rights Act was merely a strategy aimed at defeating the bill and undercutting antidiscrimination protection for African Americans. When viewed more optimistically, the inclusion of sex in the act was an attempt to end the categorical exclusion women faced from many jobs and industries. Title VII's passage, with sex included, belied its cynical beginnings, and, over time, the act's coverage has far exceeded the aspirations of its sponsors. Not only did Title VII's prohibition on sex discrimination end women's categorical exclusion from the work world, it has also been interpreted increasingly expansively so as to protect the ways

in which both men and women express their gender, as opposed to their biological sex. In this book, I have sought to show the trajectory of this expansion and to uncover the values and beliefs that are driving it. I have also sought to raise a note of caution by highlighting the unintended and potentially reactionary consequences of the expansion-at-all-costs strategy that has dominated sex discrimination litigation since the act's passage.

At the core of American antidiscrimination law is a commitment to neutrality—a belief that like must be treated alike. Title VII's demand for neutral treatment with regard to hiring requirements and job criteria was critical to its early success in breaking down formal barriers and gaining women access and opportunity. Yet a commitment to neutrality has not explained much of the recent expansion of Title VII's sex discrimination coverage. In fact courts have never demanded that women and men be treated alike with respect to all workplace demands. Instead, because courts both before and after the passage of Title VII have viewed women and men as importantly different, physically, emotionally, and socially, they have always permitted gender-differentiated treatment in the work world in those areas that most directly implicate widely shared gender conventions. In other words, gender norms have always served as a check on neutrality demands in sex discrimination litigation. Recent expansions in sex discrimination coverage have been the result neither of courts' heightened commitment to principles of neutrality nor of courts' weakened commitment to conventional gender norms. Expansion has resulted instead from competing value commitments.

For example, concerns about group-based antisubordination, rather than individual neutrality, have been responsible for important expansions. The expansion has not, however, been generated through the disparate impact framework—the act's explicit mechanism for addressing group-based disadvantage. Instead, antisubordination concerns have infiltrated and informed courts' application of the disparate treatment framework. Indeed, it is such concerns that help determine when courts are willing to challenge the gender norms and assumptions left largely untouched by the neutrality principle. Courts have whittled away at and weakened those particular gender norms they have deemed most dangerous to group-based equality—such as those requiring women to be demure, complacent, or sexy. Rather than mounting a full-frontal attack on gender norms, courts have focused on more precise targets—undermining and dismantling those norms that do the most damage to the group. They have done this, moreover, through disparate treatment cases in which the concerns of the group have largely been implicit rather than overt.

Yet, as this book has shown, the most significant and dramatic expansions in sex discrimination protection and coverage have not resulted from a heightened commitment to either of Title VII's core antidiscrimination values—neutrality or antisubordination. Instead, it has resulted from a set of values, commitments, and beliefs that are significantly more controversial. In particular, recent protection for transsexuals as well as those deemed inappropriately masculine or feminine in their demeanor has flowed most directly from a reinforced and newly medicalized commitment to binary gender categories.

Gender nonconformists have increasingly won protection under Title VII by convincing courts that their nonconformity is not a matter of personal choice or taste but a product of necessity—a core aspect of their being, demanded not by their physical sex but by their psychological gender.

The result has been expanding protection for some individual nonconformists but with costs to women and men more generally that have been largely overlooked. I have sought in this book to shine a light on these costs. Courts' increasing tendency to view gender as something fixed and binary and to condition antidiscrimination protection for gender nonconformists on their fit within an established gender category—regardless of their biological sex—actually encourages gender nonconformists to adopt more highly dysphoric gender packages than they might otherwise. In the quest for protection for nonconforming traits and attributes, such workers are actually required to enact more conventional gender performances, albeit performances traditionally associated with the opposite sex. Whether pressure on gender nonconformists to overperform their dysphoria is any worse than pressure to overperform their sex-based gender code is a question about which I am agnostic. It is important to recognize, however, that such pressure results in neither more authentic gender expressions in the workplace nor more gender fluidity and flexibility.

More troubling, however, is the increased medicalization of gender in sex discrimination cases, which is narrowing and ossifying gender categories and codes for all workers—not only for transsexuals seeking protection for sex-atypical gender expressions. As courts increasingly treat an individual's femininity or masculinity as fixed, stable, and legally meaningful, they are also potentially redrawing the social boundaries that limit and define workers' lives. No longer does sex define the aspirations and future possibilities of girls and boys in the ways it once did. The danger, at present, however, is that gender will come to circumscribe life choices and possibilities in the ways sex once did. Victory for some nonconformists may come at the expense of greater rigidity of gender roles and expectations for all workers. The result will be not only a loss of human potential but also a loss of dynamism both within and outside the work world. To the extent that antidiscrimination protection depends upon satisfying recognized gender categories, neither workers nor employers will have an incentive to experiment with or protect a wider range of gender possibilities that might lead to more personally fulfilling lives for individuals and more creative and adaptable environments in the workplace.

As I mentioned at the outset, my goal in this book is not to argue against recent expansions of sex discrimination coverage. The expansions have gained important protection for individuals and groups that have been widely and needlessly degraded and excluded. My goal instead has been to explore the often inexplicit values and beliefs that have been driving this expansion and to raise a note of caution about unintended and largely unrecognized consequences.

Notes

1. See, e.g., Price Waterhouse v. Hopkins, 490 U.S. 228 (1989); Hopkins v. Price Waterhouse, 920 F.2d 967 (1990).

2. See, e.g., Nichols v. Azteca Restaurant Enterprises, Inc., 256 F.3d 864 (2001).

3. See, e.g., Barnes v. Cincinnati, 401 F.3d 729 (6th Cir. 2005).

4. See, e.g., Jespersen v. Harrah's Operating Co., 444 F.3d 1104 (9th Cir. 2006).

5. See, e.g., Albermarle Paper Co. v. Moody, 422 U.S. 405, 409 (1975) (employer had operated a racially segregated plant reserving high-pay and high-skill jobs for whites); Griggs v. Duke Power Co., 401 U.S. 424, 426–28 (1971) (employer had refused to hire blacks for any but its lowest-paying jobs).

6. Diane L. Bridge, for example, describes a Westinghouse manual from the early 1900s which provided that "the lowest paid male job was not [to] [*sic*] be paid a wage below that of the highest paid female job, *regardless of the job content and value to the firm.*" "The Glass Ceiling and Sexual Stereotyping: Historical and Legal Perspectives of Women in the Workplace," 4 *Virginia Journal of Social Policy & the Law* 581, 599 (1997) (alterations in original) (quoting Ray Marshall & Beth Paulin, "Employment and Earnings of Women: Historical Perspectives," in Karen S. Koziara et al., eds., *Working Women: Past, Present, Future*

(Washington, DC: Bureau of National Affairs, 1987), 1, 12. In the same article, Bridge also quotes the International Ladies' Garment Workers' Union contract from 1913, which limited women to the less skilled jobs and provided that "the highest paid female could not earn more than the lowest paid male."

7. See Erickson v. Bartell Drug Co., 141 F. Supp. 2d 1266, 1269 (W.D. Wash. 2001) ("What is clear from the law itself, its legislative history, and Congress' subsequent actions, is that the goal of Title VII was to end years of discrimination in employment and to place all men and women, regardless of race, color, religion, or national origin, on equal footing in how they were treated in the workforce.").

CHAPTER 1. THE CASE LAW

1. Hopkins v. Price Waterhouse, 618 F. Supp. 1109, 1112 (1985).

2. Hopkins v. Price Waterhouse, 825 F.2d 458, 462 (D.C. Cir., 1987).

3. *Hopkins*, 618 F. Supp. at 1113.

4. *Hopkins*, 618 F. Supp. at 1116.

5. *Hopkins*, 618 F. Supp. at 1117.

6. *Hopkins*, 618 F. Supp. at 1117.

7. *Hopkins*, 618 F. Supp. at 1117.

8. Of the eighty-eight candidates nominated to the partnership in 1982, forty-seven were invited to join, twenty-one were rejected, and the remaining twenty were placed on hold. Hopkins v. Price Waterhouse, 825 F.2d at 462.

9. *Hopkins*, 618 F. Supp. at 1117.

10. *Hopkins*, 618 F. Supp. at 1118.

11. *Hopkins*, 618 F. Supp. at 1119–20.

12. *Hopkins*, 618 F. Supp. at 1120.

13. Hopkins v. Price Waterhouse, 825 F.2d 458, 468 (D.C. Cir. 1987).

14. *Hopkins*, 825 F.2d at 473.

15. See 42 U.S.C. § 2000e-2(m); 42 U.S.C. § 2000e-5(g)(2)(B).

16. *Price Waterhouse*, 490 U.S. 228, 251 (citations omitted) (1989).

17. See Hopkins v. Price Waterhouse, 920 F.2d 967 (D.C. Cir. 1997).

18. Doe v. City of Belleville, 119 F.3d 563 (7th Cir. 1997).

19. *City of Belleville*, 119 F. 3d at 568.

20. *City of Belleville*, 119 F.3d at 580.

21. *City of Belleville*, 119 F.3d at 581.

22. *City of Belleville*, 119 F.3d at 577.

23. Oncale v. Sundowner Offshore Servs., Inc., 523 U.S. 75 (1998).

24. *Oncale*, 523 U.S. at 80.

25. *Oncale*, 523 U.S. at 80–81.

26. See Bibby v. Philadelphia Coca Cola Bottling Co., 260 F.3d 257, 263 n.5 (3d Cir. 2001) (opining that "there is nothing in *Oncale* . . . that would call into question" the holding in *Belleville* that harassment based on a failure to live up to gender stereotypes is sex discrimination).

27. See, e.g., Nichols v. Azteca Restaurant Enterprises, Inc., 256 F.3d 864, 874–75 (9th Cir. 2001) (holding that the rule from *Price Waterhouse* prohibiting sex stereotyping also barred the discrimination in this case where the plaintiff was harassed based on a belief that he did not act as a man should act); Bibby v. Philadelphia Coca Cola Bottling Co., 260 F.3d 257, 262–63 (3d Cir. 2001) ("A plaintiff may be able to prove that same-sex harassment was discrimination because of sex by presenting evidence that the harasser's conduct was motivated by a belief that the victim did not conform to the stereotypes of his or her gender."); Simonton v. Runyon, 232 F.3d 33, 38 (2d Cir. 2000) ("The Court in *Price Waterhouse* implied that a suit alleging harassment or disparate treatment based upon nonconformity with sexual stereotypes is cognizable under Title VII as discrimination because of sex."); Higgins v. New Balance Athletic Shoe, Inc., 194 F.3d 252, 261 n.4 (1st Cir. 1999) ("Just as a woman can ground an action on a claim that men discriminated against her because she did not meet stereotyped expectations of femininity, a man can ground a claim on evidence that other men discriminated against him because he did not meet stereotyped expectations of masculinity." (citation omitted)). Female workers harassed for their perceived masculinity have also received protection. See, e.g., Heller v. Edgewater Country Club, 195 F. Supp. 2d 1212, 1224, 1229 (D. Or. 2002) (denying the employer's motion for summary judgment because the plaintiff had presented evidence such that a jury could find she had been harassed because she was deemed inappropriately masculine in her traits and appearance).

28. Ulane v. Eastern Airlines, Inc., 742 F.2d 1081, 1085 (7th Cir. 1984). See also Sommers v. Budget Marketing, Inc., 667 F.2d 748 (8th

Cir. 1982) (holding that Title VII does not prohibit discrimination against transsexuals); Holloway v. Arthur Andersen, 566 F.2d 659 (9th Cir. 1977) (refusing to extend Title VII protection to transsexuals because discrimination against transsexuals is discrimination because of "gender" rather than "sex").

29. Smith v. City of Salem, 378 F.3d 566 (6th Cir. 2004). In *Smith*, and in all cases involving transsexual plaintiffs, I refer to the plaintiff by the same gendered pronoun that the court used.

30. The district court had concluded that Smith's claim of discrimination was in fact based on his transsexuality rather than his failure to conform to sex stereotypes and hence was not actionable under Title VII. Smith v. City of Salem, 2003 WL 25720984 at *3 (N.D. Ohio, 2003).

31. *Smith*, 378 F.3d at 574.

32. Barnes v. City of Cincinnati, 401 F.3d 729 (6th Cir. 2005).

33. *Barnes*, 401 F.3d at 734.

34. *Barnes*, 401 F.3d at 737–38. The Ninth Circuit has endorsed similar protection for transsexuals. See Kastle v. Maricopa County Community College District, 325 Fed. Appx. 492, 493–94 (9th Cir. 2009) (explaining that "after *Hopkins* and *Schwenk*, it is unlawful to discrimination against a transgender (or any other) person because he or she does not behave in accordance with an employer's expectations for men or women," but, nonetheless, holding that employer's ban on transsexual plaintiff's use of women's restroom for safety reasons did not constitute sex discrimination); Schwenk v. Hartford, 204 F.3d 1187, 1202 (9th Cir. 2000) (holding that the Gender Motivated Violence Act parallels Title VII in prohibiting victimization of a transsexual because he is "a man who 'failed to act like' one").

Several district courts have also asserted similar protection for transsexual workers. See Glenn v. Brumby, 724 F. Supp. 2d 1284, 1299, 1305 (N.D. Ga. 2010) (finding that plaintiff had shown a violation of the Equal Protection Clause based on sex stereotyping and noting that "this Court concurs with the majority of courts that have addressed this issue, finding that discrimination against a transgendered individual because of their failure to conform to gender stereotypes constitutes discrimination on the basis of sex"); Schroer v. Billington, 577 F. Supp. 2d 293, 305–6 (finding discrimination against transitioning male-to-female transsexual, explaining: "Ultimately, I do not think it matters for purposes of Title VII liability whether the library withdrew its offer of employment because it perceived Schroer to be an insufficiently masculine man, an insufficiently feminine woman, or an inherently gender-nonconforming transsexual. . . . While I would therefore conclude that Schroer is entitled to judgment based on a *Price Waterhouse*-type claim for sex stereotyping, I also conclude that she is entitled to judgment based on the language of the statute itself."); Lopez v. River Oaks Imaging Diagnostic Group, Inc., 542 F. Supp. 2d 653, 660 (S.D. Tex. 2008) (denying defendant's motion for summary judgment and explaining that "Title VII is violated when an employer discriminates against any employee, transsexual or not, because he or she has failed to act or appear sufficiently masculine or feminine enough for an employer"); Trevino v. Center for Health Care Services, Civil Action No. SA-08-CV-0140 NN, 2008 WL 4449939 (W.D. Tex., Sept. 29, 2008) (holding that plaintiff could state a claim for sex discrimination because she alleged discrimination based on gender and not discrimination based on transsexualism; Creed v. Family Express Corp., No. 3:06-CV-465RM, 2007 WL 2265630 (N.D. Ind., Aug. 3, 2007) (noting that "Ms. Creed's allegation she was terminated after refusing to present herself in a masculine way permits the inference she was terminated as a result of [her employer's] stereotypical perceptions, rather than simply her gender dysphoria"); Mitchell v. Axcan Scandipharm, Inc., No. Civ. A 05-234, 2006 WL 456173 *1 (W.D. Pa., Feb. 17, 2006) (explaining that "having included facts showing that his failure to conform to sex stereotypes of how a man should look and behave was the catalyst behind defendant's actions, plaintiff has sufficiently pleaded claims of gender discrimination"); Myers v. Cuyahoga County, Ohio, 182 F. Appx. 510 (6th Cir. 2006) (explaining that "Title VI protects transsexual persons from discrimination for failing to act in accordance and/ or identify with their perceived sex or gender," but ruling against plaintiff, a postoperative transsexual, on her sex discrimination claim because there was no evidence that plaintiff was treated differently because of her gender nonconformity).

35. Jespersen v. Harrah's Operating Company, 444 F.3d 1104 (9th Cir. 2006).

36. *Jespersen*, 444 F.3d at 1107. Female bartenders were also required to have their hair "teased, curled, or styled every day." Male

bartenders were required to keep their hair short and their fingernails trimmed, and to wear no facial makeup.

37. Jespersen v. Harrah's Operating Company, 392 F.3d 1076, 1077 (9th Cir. 2004) (panel decision).

38. *Jespersen*, 392 F.3d at 1083.

39. *Jespersen*, 444 F.3d at 1106.

40. *Jespersen*, 444 F.3d at 1112.

41. *Jespersen*, 444 F.3d at 1116.

42. *Jespersen*, 444 F.3d at 1112.

CHAPTER 2. NEUTRALITY

1. See, e.g., R. Richard Banks, "Class and Culture: The Indeterminacy of Nondiscrimination," 5 *Stanford Journal of Civil Rights & Civil Liberties* 1, 17–18 (2009) (explaining that the nondiscrimination mandate is premised on the "simple sense of neutrality" that "directs one to treat likes alike"); George Rutherglen, "Disparate Impact, Discrimination, and the Essentially Contested Concept of Equality," 74 *Fordham Law Review* 2313, 2325 (2006) (noting that "[b]road agreement across the political spectrum supports the concept of discrimination as colorblindness"); Kendall Thomas, "The Political Economy of Recognition: Affirmative Action Discourse and Constitutional Equality in Germany and the U.S.A.," 5 *Columbia Journal of European Law* 329, 341 (1999) (describing the antidiscrimination principle as informed by the injunction that "likes must be treated alike"); Martha Albertson Fineman, "Feminist Legal Theory," 12 *American University Journal of Gender Social Policy & Law* 13, 16 (2005) (explaining that Title VII's "primary commitment" was "to equality and gender neutrality").

Legal scholars often refer to this demand for neutrality as an "anticlassification" requirement. See Bradley A. Areheart, "The Anticlassification Turn in Employment Discrimination Law," 63 *Alabama Law Review* 955, 961 (2012) ("anticlassification principles prohibit practices that classify people on the basis of a forbidden category"). Jack M. Balkin & Reva B. Siegel, "The American Civil Rights Tradition: Anticlassification of Antisubordination?" 59 *University of Miami Law Review* 9, 10 (2003) (explaining that the anticlassification principle "holds that the government may not classify people either overtly or surreptitiously on the basis of a forbidden category").

2. See Deborah L. Rhode, *Justice and Gender: Sex Discrimination and the Law* (Cambridge, MA: Harvard University Press, 1989), 57 (explaining that "although Smith had been a sponsor of the Equal Rights Amendment, he had opposed civil rights legislation in general and the Equal Pay Act in particular."). See also Diane L. Bridge, "The Glass Ceiling and Sexual Stereotyping: Historical and Legal Perspectives of Women in the Workplace," 4 *Virginia Journal of Social Policy & Law* 581, 610 (1997); Robert Stevens Miller Jr., "Sex Discrimination and Title VII of the Civil Rights Act of 1964," 51 *Minnesota Law Review* 877 (1966–67); Francis J. Vaas, "Title VII: Legislative History," 7 *Boston College Industrial & Commercial Law Review* 441 (1965–66).

Some scholars have suggested that Smith's motives may have been more complex, and that he might have been acting in genuine support of women's rights. See, e.g., Robert C. Bird, "More Than a Congressional Joke: A Fresh Look at the Legislative History of Sex Discrimination of the 1964 Civil Rights Act," 3 *William & Mary Journal of Women & Law* 137, 150–53, 156–58 (1997); Carl M. Brauer, "Women Activists, Southern Conservatives, and the Prohibition of Sex Discrimination in Title VII of the 1964 Civil Rights Act," 49 *Journal of Southern History* 37, 41–50 (1983).

3. 110 Cong. Rec. 2577–84 (1964) *reprinted in* U.S. Equal Employment Commission, *Legislative History of Titles VII and XI of Civil Rights Act of 1964* (Washington: For sale by the Supt. Of Docs., U.S. Govt. Print. Off., 1968), 3213–14.

4. U.S. Equal Employment Commission, *Legislative History of Titles VII and XI of Civil Rights Act of 1964*, 3215.

5. U.S. Equal Employment Commission, *Legislative History of Titles VII and XI of Civil Rights Act of 1964*, 3222.

6. U.S. Equal Employment Commission, *Legislative History of Titles VII and XI of Civil Rights Act of 1964*, 3222.

7. U.S. Equal Employment Commission, *Legislative History of Titles VII and XI of Civil Rights Act of 1964*, 3221.

8. U.S. Equal Employment Commission, *Legislative History of Titles VII and XI of Civil Rights Act of 1964*, 3221.

9. U.S. Equal Employment Commission, *Legislative History of Titles VII and XI of Civil Rights Act of 1964*, 3225.

10. See Miller, "Sex Discrimination and Title VII," 877.

11. Miller, "Sex Discrimination and Title VII," 882–83. The lack of legislative history was remedied to an extent when Congress amended Title VII several years later with the Equal Opportunity Act of 1972. The 1972 act was the product of extensive debate and did produce a legislative history making clear Congress's intent for Title VII to be a powerful tool against sex discrimination. The act enabled the EEOC to bring direct enforcement actions and extended Title VII's coverage to public employers. See Cary Franklin, "Inventing the 'Traditional Concept' of Sex Discrimination," 125 *Harvard Law Review* 1307, 1346–47 (2012).

12. Miller, "Sex Discrimination and Title VII," 882 n.29.

13. Phillips v. Martin Marietta Corp., 400 U.S. 542, 544 (1971).

14. Bowe v. Colgate-Palmolive Co., 416 F.2d 711 (1969).

15. *Bowe*, 416 F.2d at 719 ("Colgate may, if it so desires, retain its 35-pound weight-lifting limit as a general guideline for all of its employees, male and female. . . . Each employee who is able to so demonstrate must be permitted to bid on and fill any position to which his or her seniority may entitle him or her.").

16. Rosenfeld v. Southern Pacific Co., 293 F. Supp. 1219, 1225 (C.D. Ca. 1968).

17. See William J. Carrington, Kristin McCue, & Brooks Pierce, "Using Establishment Size to Measure the Impact of Title VII and Affirmative Action," 35 *Journal of Human Resources* 503, 504 (2000) (showing that federal laws helped to increase women's labor market participation in the 1960s and 1970s).

18. See 1980 Statistical Abstract of the United States, at 394 (table 653).

19. See Laura T. Kessler, "The Attachment Gap: Employment Discrimination Law, Women's Cultural Caregiving, and the Limits of Economic and Liberal Legal Theory," 34 *University of Michigan Journal of Law Reform* 371, 374 (2001).

20. Women and men's voices differ not only in pitch but also in a number of other aspects stemming from hormonal differences between them. See Jean Abitbol, Patrick Abitbol, & Beatrice Abitbol, "Sex Hormones and the Female Voice," 13, no. 3 *Journal of Voice* 424, 431 (1999) (explaining that "Voice is a secondary sexual 'characteristic' and is influenced by sexual hormones. . . . The hormonal impact acts not only on

the genital tract, but also on the essential elements [of the vocal physiology], which are the mucosa, the muscles, the bony tissues, the laryngeal instrument, and the cerebral cortex."). Indeed, producing plausible female voices remains a significant problem for male-to-female transsexuals. See Kerstin Neumann et al., "Cricothyroidopexy in Male-to-Female Transsexuals—Modification of Thyroplasty Type IV," *International Journal of Transgenderism* 6, no. 4 (2002): 3 ¶ 1, http://www.symposion.com/ijt/ijtvoo6noo3_03htm (explaining that "the secondary sex characteristic of the larynx with its vocal function remains a major obstacle to male-to-female transsexuals 'passing' as female"); Susan D. Clark, "To Sound Like a Woman," GENDYS Conference, Fifth International Gender Dysphoria Conference, Manchester, England, 1998 (available at http://www.gender.org.uk/conf.1998/clark.htm) (providing therapeutic techniques to assist male-to-female transsexuals in developing female voices).

21. Geduldig v. Aiello, 417 U.S. 484 (1974).

22. General Electric Co. v. Gilbert, 429 U.S. 125 (1976).

23. *Geduldig,* 417 U.S. at 486–87.

24. *Geduldig,* 417 U.S. at 496–97, n.20.

25. *Gilbert,* 429 U.S. at 138–40.

26. *Gilbert,* 429 U.S. at 136–40.

27. *Gilbert,* 429 U.S. at 127–29, 136–40, 138–39, 139.

28. The Pregnancy Discrimination Act was added to Title VII in 1978 and amended its definitions portion. It provides in relevant part: "The terms 'because of sex' or 'on the basis of sex' include, but are not limited to, because of or on the basis of pregnancy, childbirth, or related medical conditions; and women affected by pregnancy, childbirth, or related medical conditions shall be treated the same for all employment-related purposes, including receipt of benefits under fringe benefit programs as other persons not so affected but similar in their ability or inability to work." 42 U.S.C. § 2000e(k) (1998); see also Newport News Shipbuilding & Dry Dock Co. v. EEOC, 462 U.S. 669, 684 (1983) ("The [PDA] makes clear that it is discriminatory to treat pregnancy-related conditions less favorably than other medical conditions.").

29. *Compare* Ensley-Gaines v. Runyon, 100 F.3d 1220, 1226 (6th Cir. 1996) (holding that in order to determine whether there is a PDA violation, the treatment of pregnant women should be compared with the treatment of nonpregnant individuals who are similar in terms of

their ability or inability to work regardless of the place of their injury), *with* Urbano v. Continental Airlines, Inc., 138 F.3d 204, 208 (5th Cir. 1998) (holding that the treatment of pregnant women must be compared with that of similarly abled nonpregnant workers who were injured off the job), *and* Spivey v. Beverly Enterprises, Inc., 196 F.3d 1309, 1313 (11th Cir. 1999) (holding that the PDA required that pregnant women be treated the same as other similarly abled workers who suffered nonoccupational disabilities). The Supreme Court addressed this question in Young v. United Parcel Service, 135 S. Ct. 1338 (2015) but provided little clarity as to which companion group was appropriate. Instead, the Court held that an employer could treat pregnant workers worse than other categories of workers similar in their inability to work as long as the employer had "a legitimate nondiscriminatory" reason for doing so. See generally Jamie L. Clanton, "Toward Eradicating Pregnancy Discrimination at Work: Interpreting the PDA to 'Mean What It Says,' " 86 *Iowa Law Review*, 703 (2001) (analyzing the disagreement among courts over who is similarly situated under the PDA).

30. See, e.g., Derungs v. Wal-Mart Stores, Inc., 374 F.3d 428, 439 (6th Cir. 2004) ("No judicial body thus far has been willing to take the expansive interpretive leap to include rules concerning breast-feeding within the scope of sex discrimination."); Wallace v. Pyro Mining Co., 951 F.2d 351 (6th Cir. 1991) (PDA did not give employee right to breastfeed at work, because doing so was not a medical necessity); Barrash v. Bowen, 846 F.2d 927, 931 (4th Cir. 1988) (plaintiff could not establish disparate impact claim based on denial of breastfeeding leave, because the PDA applied only to incapacitating illnesses). Recently, the Fifth Circuit held that lactation is a related medical condition of pregnancy for purposes of the PDA and that discrimination against a woman because she is lactating or expressing breast milk violates Title VII and the PDA. Importantly, however, the plaintiff in the case did not seek any accommodation to breastfeed and was allegedly fired simply for raising the issue of breastfeeding at work with her employer. See EEOC v. Houston Funding II, 2013 WL 2360114 (5th Cir., May 30, 2013). The Patient Protection and Affordable Care Act, H.R. 3590, which President Obama signed into law on March 23, 2010, does provide some limited protection to breastfeeding mothers. The act amended the Fair Labor Standards Act of 1938 (29 U.S. Code 207) to require an employer to provide reasonable break time for a nonexempt employee to express breast milk for one year after a child's birth.

31. The plaintiff in *Oiler* was not in fact transsexual but was described by the court as a "male crossdresser." See *Oiler,* 2002 WL 31098541, at *5.

32. James v. Ranch Mart Hardware, 881 F. Supp. 478, 481 (D. Kan. 1995).

33. Duncan Kennedy has written an essay that discusses "sexy dressing" in relation to patriarchal dominance. The essay explores, for example, attitudes toward sexy dressing in the workplace in which the sexy dresser, by deviating from established norms, invites disciplinary abuse, such as sexual harassment. Duncan Kennedy, "Sexual Abuse, Sexy Dressing, and the Eroticization of Domination," in *Sexy Dressing Etc.: Essays on the Power and Politics of Cultural Identity* (Cambridge, MA: Harvard University Press, 1993), 170–71, 182.

34. In *Oiler v. Winn-Dixie Louisiana, Inc.,* for example, the district court saw a man dressing as a woman not only as dissimilar from a woman dressing as a woman but also as disordered. 2002 WL 31098541, at *5.

35. I suspect there is significantly less social consensus regarding what constitutes sexy dressing for men than there is about what constitutes sexy dressing for women.

36. Craft v. Metromedia, Inc., 766 F.2d 1205 (8th Cir. 1985).

37. *Craft,* 766 F.2d at 1208, 1209, 1221.

38. Craft v. Metromedia, Inc., 572 F. Supp. 868, 877 (W.D. Mo. 1983).

39. *Craft,* 766 F.2d at 1215 (citations omitted).

40. Craft and supporting Amici Curiae argued both that the television station enforced appearance standards more strictly on female than male on-air personnel and that the socially gendered appearance standards themselves were discriminatory. *Craft,* 766 F.2d at 1212–14. Craft presented evidence showing that "only females were subject to daily scrutiny of their appearance or were ever required to change clothes at the station before going on the air and that no male was ever directed to take time from his journalistic duties to select clothing, with the help of a consultant from Macy's and to test that clothing on camera for the approval of another consultant." Ibid., 1213. In addition, Craft, but seemingly no one else at the station, was eventually required to use a clothing calendar. Ibid., 1209, 1213. According to the court of appeals: "The 'clothing calendar' was a calendar given to Craft showing in detail for each day the blazer, blouse, and skirt (or occasionally slacks) she was to wear. A note in one corner indicated that the appropriate accessory would be either a single strand of pearls or a single gold chain." Ibid., 1209 n.2.

41. Laurie A. Rudman & Peter Glick, "Prescriptive Gender Stereo-types and Backlash Toward Agentic Women," 57 *Journal of Social Issues*, 743, 747 (2001). The study involved as participants 172 undergraduates at Rutgers University (105 women and 67 men). Ibid., 749.

42. Rudman & Glick, "Prescriptive Gender Stereotypes," 757.

43. See Dore Butler & Florence L. Geis, "Nonverbal Affect Responses to Male and Female Leaders: Implications for Leadership Evaluations," 58 *Journal Personality & Social Psychology* 48, 54–57 (1990). The study involved 168 student participants (84 women and 84 men). Ibid., 49. Participants took part in small discussion groups composed of one male and one female participant and one male and one female confederate who were trained by the researchers to perform the role of group leader in a standardized manner. The study used two leader scripts, A and B, in all discussions. In half the sessions the male leader used script A and the female leader used script B, and in the other sessions it was reversed. Coders sat in an adjacent room behind one-way mirrors and tallied each participant's nonverbal affect expressions. Coders tallied nonverbal cues of pleasure such as smiling or nodding in agreement and coded nonverbal cues of displeasure such as a furrowed brow, tightening of the mouth, and nods of disagreement. In addition to controlling what the female and male leaders actually said, the researchers monitored the male and female leaders to make sure that they did not differ in eye contact, gaze direction, body posture, or amount of body movement. Ibid., 50–51; see also Alice H. Eagly et al., "Gender and the Evaluation of Leaders: A Meta-Analysis," 111 *Psychological Bulletin* 3, 16 (1992) (finding that women managers with a direct task-oriented leadership style are evaluated more negatively than men with similar management styles).

44. Butler & Geis, "Nonverbal Affect Responses to Male and Female Leaders," 54.

45. Victoria L. Brescoll & Eric Luis Uhlmann, "Can an Angry Woman Get Ahead? Status Conferral, Gender, and Expression of Emotion in the Workplace," 19 *Psychological Science* 268, 273 (2008).

46. Price Waterhouse v. Hopkins, 490 U.S. 228 (1989).

47. Mary Anne Case, "Disaggregating Gender from Sex and Sexual Orientation: The Effeminate Man in the Law and Feminist Jurisprudence," 105 *Yale Law Journal* 7 (1995).

48. See, e.g., Case, "Disaggregating Gender from Sex and Sexual Orientation," 1, 7 (explaining that under *Price Waterhouse,* "if their employer tolerates feminine behavior or attire in women but not in [men], the employer is subjecting them to disparate treatment in violation of Title VII."); Colleen C. Keaney, "Expanding the Protectional Scope of Title VII 'Because of Sex' to Include Discrimination Based on Sexuality and Sexual Orientation," 51 *St. Louis University Law Journal* 581, 594 (2007) ("Smith upturns rigid sex categories and allows both sexes to participate in the full range of gender expressions"); Ilona M. Turner, "Sex Stereotyping Per Se: Transgender Employees and Title VII," 95 *California Law Review* 561, 590 (2007) (interpreting Smith to mean that "discrimination against a person for acting 'like' the other sex—no matter what the reason—is sex discrimination.").

49. *Price Waterhouse,* 490 U.S. at 228, 235.

50. See Valorie K. Vojdik, "Gender Outlaws: Challenging Masculinity in Traditionally Male Institutions," 17 *Berkeley Women's Law Journal* 68, 70–71 (2002); see also Brief Amici Curiae of the Center for Military Readiness et al., United States v. Virginia, 518 U.S. 515 (1995) (Nos. 94-1941, 94-2107), 1995 WL 744997, at *14 (describing the Department of Justice's arguments to the district court that a buzz haircut simply did not fit into the range of traits and attributes deemed socially acceptable for women). This, of course, is why other employers discriminate against women with buzz cuts.

51. See Vojdik, "Gender Outlaws," 70–71 (noting the Citadel's argument that equal treatment "meant the same treatment afforded male cadets").

52. Imposing a formally neutral hair requirement on Faulkner in this case would probably seem discriminatory even if the requirement were not so clearly being used by the Citadel as simply a pretext for her exclusion. See Vojdik, "Gender Outlaws," 70–71 (describing the desperation with which the Citadel tried to exclude Faulkner).

53. Vojdik, "Gender Outlaws," 71.

54. Brief Amici Curiae of the Center for Military Readiness et al., United States v. Virginia, 518 U.S. 515 (1995) (Nos. 94-1941, 94-2107), at *14 (source of quotation omitted from original). One could likewise imagine an employer that refused to hire anyone with hair longer than one-quarter inch in length. The employer would argue that its policy

was neutral as between women and men, while women challenging the policy would argue for nondiscrimination required something other than formal neutrality.

55. Vojdik, "Gender Outlaws," 71.

56. This is, of course, the insight of the disparate impact doctrine of Title VII.

57. See Case, "Disaggregating Gender from Sex and Sexual Orientation," 4 (arguing that "masculine women" and "effeminate men . . . should already unequivocally be protected under existing law from discrimination on the basis of gender-role-transgressive behavior"); see also Taylor Flynn, "Transforming the Debate: Why We Need to Include Transgender Rights in the Struggles for Sex and Sexual Orientation Equality," 101 *Columbia Law Review* 392, 399 (2002) (arguing that women's freedom to exhibit certain gender-specific traits in the workplace is necessarily tied to men's freedom to do the same).

58. This is a possibility that Case herself clearly recognizes. See Case, "Disaggregating Gender from Sex and Sexual Orientation," 8 (acknowledging "the risks in insisting that employers impose the same grooming standards on men and women: Haunted by the specter of a man in a dress, employers may choose to impose a unisex, conventionally masculine grooming code on all employees"). Another alternative would be for employers to increase their preemployment screening measures so as to exclude applicants with a propensity to gender bend. In this way, employers could maintain more expansive clothing and grooming options for their employees while ensuring that the individuals they hire will not in fact engage in gender bending behavior. Under this approach, individuals with a desire to gender bend will not be formally prevented from doing so, but they simply will not be hired.

CHAPTER 3. ANTISUBORDINATION

1. Bradley A. Areheart, "The Anticlassification Turn in Employment Discrimination Law," 63 *Alabama Law Review* 955, 964 (2012) ("Title VII—though seemingly designed to combat irrational discrimination and a statute that holds out the hope of moving beyond the consideration of, for example, race—has also sought to effect the redistribution of resources through policies such as affirmative action, reasonable accommodation (in certain instances), and the disparate impact

doctrine."); Jack M. Balkin & Reva B. Siegel, "The American Civil Rights Tradition: Anticlassification or Antisubordination?" *58 University of Miami Law Review*, 9, 33 (2003) ("To claim that the struggle for equality in this country has not been about subordinated groups seeking to dismantle the social structures that have kept them down makes a travesty of American history. The moral insistence that the low be raised up—that the forces of subordination be named, accused, disestablished, and dissolved—is our story, our civil rights tradition."); Samuel R. Bagenstos, "Rational Discrimination: Accommodation, and the Politics of (Disability) Civil Rights," 89 *Virginia Law Review* 825, 838 (2003) (describing the goal of antidiscrimination law as "reducing subordination and social inequality").

2. Griggs v. Duke Power Co., 401 U.S. 424, 430 (1971). Congress codified the disparate impact framework in the Civil Rights Act of 1991, § 703(k)(1)(A), 32 U.S.C.A. § 2000e-2(k)(1)(A).

3. *Griggs*, 401 U.S. at 432 (quoting Griggs v. Duke Power Co., 420 F.2d 1225, 1232 (4th Cir. 1971)).

4. *Griggs*, 401 U.S. at 430.

5. *Griggs*, 401 U.S. at 432 (explaining that "good intent or absence of discriminatory intent does not redeem employment procedures or testing mechanisms that operated as 'built-in headwinds' for minority groups and are unrelated to measuring job capability.").

6. Laffey v. Northwest Airlines, 366 F. Supp. 763, 790 (D.D.C. 1973).

7. Gerdom v. Continental Airlines, 692 F.2d 602, 603, 610 (9th Cir. 1982) ("Continental's policy of requiring an exclusively female category of flight attendants, and no other employees, to adhere to the weight restrictions at issue here constitutes discriminatory treatment on the basis of sex.").

8. Frank v. United Airlines, Inc., 216 F.3d 845, 854 (9th Cir. 2000) (en banc).

9. *Frank*, 216 F.3d at 855 (noting that "even if United's weight rules constituted an appearance standard, they would still be invalid" because they impose unequal burdens on women and men); *Gerdom*, 692 F.2d at 605–6 (concluding that the female-only weight requirement imposed a significantly greater burden on women than men); *Laffey*, 366 F. Supp. at 774 (emphasizing that the contact lenses female flight attendants were

required to wear were more expensive than the eyeglasses male flight attendants were permitted to wear).

10. See Jespersen v. Harrah's Operating Co., 392 F.3d 1076, 1081 (9th Cir. 2004) (majority decision) (applying the unequal burdens test by comparing the complete set of appearance requirements for women to the complete set of requirements for men); Jespersen v. Harrah's Operating Co., 444 F.3d 1104, 1110 (9th Cir. 2006) (en banc) (explaining that Jespersen could not demonstrate that the makeup requirement imposed an unequal burden on women, because she "did not submit any documentation or any evidence of the relative cost and time required to comply with the grooming requirements by men and women").

11. See, e.g., Willingham v. Macon Telegraph Publishing Co., 507 F.2d 1084, 1086, 1092 (5th Cir. 1975) (upholding a male-only short-hair requirement); Knott v. Missouri Pacific Railroad Co., 527 F.2d 1249, 1249 (8th Cir. 1975) (same); Baker v. California Land Title Co., 507 F.2d 895, 896 (9th Cir. 1974) (same); Fagan v. National Cash Register Co., 481 F.2d 1115, 1116 (D.C. Cir. 1973) (same).

12. See, e.g., Thomas v. Firestone Tire & Rubber Co., 392 F. Supp. 373, 374 (N.D. Tex. 1975) (upholding an employer's no-beard policy against a sex discrimination challenge); Rafford v. Randle Eastern Ambulance Service, Inc., 348 F. Supp. 316, 317 (S.D. Fla. 1972) (same).

13. Craft v. Metromedia, Inc., 766 F.2d 1205, 1207 (8th Cir. 1985).

14. *Craft*, 766 F.2d at 1212–13.

15. *Craft*, 766 F.2d at 1214.

16. The court noted that "evidence showed a particular concern with appearance in television; the district court stated that reasonable appearance requirements were 'obviously critical' to KMBC's economic well-being." *Craft*, 766 F.2d at 1215.

17. *Craft*, 766 F.2d at 1215–16.

18. *Jespersen*, 444 F.3d at 1111 ("Having failed to create a record establishing that the 'Personal Best' policies are more burdensome for women than for men, Jespersen did not present any triable issue of fact.").

19. *Jespersen*, 444 F.3d at 1117.

20. *Jespersen*, 444 F.3d at 1110 (quoting *Knott*, 527 F.2d at 1252).

21. For example, in *Fagan v. National Cash Register*, the court upheld a short-hair requirement for male employees by explaining: "Perhaps

no facet of business life is more important than a company's place in public estimation. That the image created by its employees dealing with the public when on company assignment affects its relations is so well known that we may take judicial notice of an employer's proper desire to achieve favorable acceptance. Good grooming regulations reflect a company's policy in our highly competitive business environment." 481 F.2d at 1124–25.

22. See Diaz v. Pan American World Airways, Inc., 442 F.2d 385, 388 (5th Cir. 1971) (holding that "a pleasant environment, enhanced by the obvious cosmetic effect that female stewardesses provide" is "tangential to the essence of the business involved").

23. Carroll v. Talman Federal Savings & Loan Association of Chicago, 604 F.2d 1028 (7th Cir. 1979).

24. O'Donnell v. Burlington Coat Factory Warehouse, 656 F. Supp. 263 (S.D. Ohio 198).

25. See *Frank*, 216 F.3d at 855 (citing *Carroll* as an example of a case applying the unequal burdens test); see also Dianne Avery & Marion Crain, "Branded: Corporate Image, Sexual Stereotyping, and the New Face of Capitalism," 14 *Duke Journal of Gender Law & Policy* 13, 53 (2007) (referring to the " 'unequal burdens' test as articulated in *Carroll*"); Hilary J. Bouchard, "*Jespersen v. Harrah's Operating Co.:* Employer Appearance Standards and the Promotion of Gender Stereotypes," 58 *Maine Law Review* 204, 209 (2006) (citing *Carroll* as a case decided using the unequal burdens test); Michael Selmi, "The Many Faces of Darlene Jespersen," 14 *Duke Journal of Gender Law & Policy* 467, 470–71 n.10 (2007) (same); Allison T. Steinle, "Appearance and Grooming Standards as Sex Discrimination in the Workplace," 56 *Catholic University Law Review* 261, 279 n.137 (2006) (citing *O'Donnell* as a case decided using the unequal burdens case); Deborah Zalesne, "Lessons from Equal Opportunity Harasser Doctrine: Challenging Sex-Specific Appearance and Dress Codes," 14 *Duke Journal of Gender Law & Policy* 535, 540 n.28 (2007) (citing *Carroll* and *O'Donnell* as cases involving conformity requirements struck down under the unequal burdens test).

26. *Carroll*, 604 F.2d at 1029.

27. *Carroll*, 604 F.2d at 1029.

28. *O'Donnell*, 656 F. Supp. at 264.

29. 604 F.2d at 1032–33.

30. 656 F. Supp. at 266.

31. See *Carroll*, 604 F.2d at 1030 (explaining that "the written dress code for female employees even discriminates with respect to their compensation, for defendant treats the cost of the two-piece uniform which it furnishes as income to women employees, withholding income tax on that amount from their wages").

32. See *O'Donnell*, 656 F. Supp. at 266 (stating that "unlike the case at bar, the female employees in [*Carroll v.*] *Talman* incurred the initial cost of their uniforms as well as subsequent cleaning and maintenance expenses").

33. *Carroll*, 604 F.2d at 1033.

34. *O'Donnell*, 656 F. Supp. at 266.

35. Price Waterhouse v. Hopkins, 490 U.S. 228, 251 (1989).

36. See, e.g., Tavora v. N.Y. Mercantile Exchange, 101 F.3d 907, 908 (2d Cir. 1996) (explaining that grooming codes requiring that men but not women have short hair have been held not to violate Title VII, because they "have only a *de minimis* effect"); *Willingham*, 507 F.2d at 1091 (holding that an employer's short-hair requirement only for male workers did not violate Title VII, and explaining that a grooming code imposing sex-specific hair-length requirements "is related more closely to the employer's choice of how to run his business than to equality of employment opportunity"); Pecenka v. Fareway Stores, 672 N.W.2d 800, 804 (Iowa 2003) (upholding an employer's no-earring rule for men and explaining that "Title VII . . . [was] not meant to prohibit employers from instituting personal grooming codes which have a *de minimis* effect on employment").

37. *Price Waterhouse*, 490 U.S. at 235 (quoting Hopkins v. Price Waterhouse, 618 F. Supp. 1109, 1117 (D.D.C. 1985)).

38. *Jespersen*, 444 F.3d at 1112.

39. See Avery & Crain, "Branded," 92.

40. See Avery & Crain, "Branded," 95 (noting that "of all full-time bartenders in 2004, 95,000 were men and 102,000 were women").

41. Avery & Crain, "Branded," 97 (describing the "sexing up" of bartenders); see also Linda A. Detman, "Women Behind Bars: The Feminization of Bartending," chap. 12 in *Job Queues, Gender Queues: Explaining Women's Inroads into Male Occupations*, ed. Barbara F. Reskin and Patricia A. Roos (Philadelphia: Temple University Press, 1990), 252 (describing the growth of "sex specific demand for female bartenders").

42. See Peter Glick et al., "Evaluations of Sexy Women in Low- and High-Status Jobs," 29 *Psychology of Women Quarterly* 389 (2005).

43. According to the study: "For the neutral condition, the woman wore little makeup, black slacks, a turtleneck, a business jacket, and flat shoes. In the sexy condition, the same woman wore more makeup and her hair was tousled. She wore a tight, knee-length skirt, a low-cut shirt with a cardigan over it, and high-heeled shoes." Glick et al., "Evaluations of Sexy Women," 391.

44. Glick and his coauthors found that "participants rated the receptionist as equally competent whether she was dressed in a sexy or a neutral manner. In contrast, participants rated the manager as less competent when she dressed in a sexy manner than when she dressed in a conservative manner." Glick et al., "Evaluations of Sexy Women," 393.

45. *Price Waterhouse*, 490 U.S. at 233.

46. EEOC v. Sage Realty, 507 F. Supp. 599, 604 (S.D. N.Y. 1981).

47. *Sage Realty*, 507 F. Supp. at 609–10 ("In requiring Hasselman to wear the revealing Bicentennial uniform in the lobby of 711 Third Avenue, defendants made her acquiescence in sexual harassment by the public, and perhaps by building tenants, a prerequisite of her employment as a lobby attendant.").

48. According to the court, Sage was not justified in putting Hasselman in a sexually revealing uniform, because sexual titillation was not a BFOQ [bona fide occupational qualification] of the position. The court explained: "While it may well be a [BFOQ] for Sage to require female lobby attendants in its buildings to wear certain uniforms designed to present a unique image, in accordance with its philosophy of urban design, it is beyond dispute that the wearing of sexually revealing garments does not constitute a [BFOQ]." *Sage Realty*, 507 F. Supp. at 611.

49. See also Priest v. Rotary, 634 F. Supp. 571, 581 (N.D. Cal. 1981) ("Title VII is . . . violated when an employer requires a female employee to wear sexually suggestive attire as a condition of employment."); E.E.O.C. Decision No. 81-17, 1981 WL 40388, at *2–3, 27 Fair Empl. Prac. Cas. (BNA) 1791 (1981) (striking down an employer's requirement that a receptionist wear a special sexually revealing costume consisting of "a halter-bra top and a mi[n]i-skirt with a slit in front running up to her thighs" in order to entertain visiting VIPs).

50. Gerdom v. Continental Airlines, 692 F.2d 602, 603 (9th Cir. 1982).

51. *Gerdom*, 692 F.2d at 604.

52. *Frank*, 216 F.3d at 848. United began hiring male flight attendants after *Diaz v. Pan American World Airways, Inc.*, in which the Fifth Circuit held that sex was not a BFOQ for the position of flight attendant. 442 F.2d at 388.

53. *Laffey*, 366 F. Supp. at 773–75. Although these cases are regularly cited as exemplars of the unequal burdens test, I believe the cases are better understood as reflecting a broad double-bind prohibition.

54. Wilson v. Southwest Airlines, 517 F. Supp. 292, 302 (N.D. Tex. 1981) (explaining, with respect to flight attendants and ticket agents, that "mechanical, non-sex-linked duties dominate both these occupations").

55. *Wilson*, 517 F. Supp. at 304.

56. Guardian Capital v. N.Y. State Division of Human Rights, 360 N.Y.S.2d 937 (N.Y. App. Div. 1974).

57. *Guardian Capital*, 360 N.Y.S.2d at 938.

58. *Guardian Capital*, 360 N.Y.S.2d at 938.

59. See Barbara Fredrickson et al., "That Swimsuit Becomes You: Sex Differences in Self-Objectification, Restrained Eating, and Math Performance," 75 *Journal of Personality & Social Psychology* 269 (1998) (finding that women wearing a swimsuit while taking a challenging math test performed worse than those wearing a sweater while taking the test).

60. See Brad J. Bushman & Angelica M. Bonacci, "Violence and Sex Impair Memory for Television Ads," 87 *Journal of Applied Psychology* 557, 561 (2002) (finding that after viewing sexual images on television, people of both sexes had impaired memory for the substance of whatever came next); Sandra Forsyth et al., "Influence of Applicant's Dress on Interviewer's Selection Decisions," 70 *Journal of Applied Psychology* 374, 378 (1985) (finding that dressing female managerial job candidates in feminine clothing caused them to be perceived as less competent for managerial positions); Glick et al., "Evaluations of Sexy Women," 389 (finding that sexy dressing diminished perceptions of the competence of female manager).

61. See, e.g., *Craft*, 766 F.2d at 1214 n.11 (noting that some focus on appearance for new anchors was unavoidable "since television is a visual

medium"); *Jespersen*, 444 F.3d at 1111–12 (noting that bartenders' appearance was important because Harrah's was part of the "entertainment industry").

62. See Dothard v. Rawlinson, 433 U.S. 321, 333 (1977) (stating that sex discrimination " 'is valid only when the *essence* of the business operation would be undermined' " if the business eliminated its discriminatory policy) (quoting *Diaz*, 442 F.2d at 388); see also International Union, United Auto., Aerospace and Agr. Implement Workers of America, UAW v. Johnson Controls, Inc., 499 U.S. 187, 206 (1991) (holding that sex discrimination is permissible under the BFOQ exception only if those aspects of a job that allegedly require discrimination fall within the " 'essence' of the particular business"); Healey v. Southwood Psychiatric Hospital, 78 F.3d 128, 132 (3d Cir. 1996) (same); Fesel v. Masonic Home of Delaware, Inc., 447 F. Supp. 1346, 1350 (D. Del. 1978) (same).

63. See Kimberly A. Yuracko, "Private Nurses and Playboy Bunnies: Explaining Permissible Sex Discrimination," 92 *California Law Review* 147 (2004).

64. See, e.g., *Healey*, 78 F.3d at 133 (permitting sex to be a BFOQ for psychiatric hospital staff treating emotionally disturbed and sexually abused children and adolescents because "child patients often [had to be] accompanied to the bathroom, and sometimes . . . bathed"); Jones v. Hinds General Hospital, 666 F. Supp. 933, 935 (S.D. Miss. 1987) ("The job duties of male and female nurse assistants and male orderlies often require that such employee view or touch the private parts of their patients"); *Fesel*, 447 F. Supp. at 1352 ("The Home has the responsibility of providing twenty-four hour supervision and care of its elderly guests. Fulfillment of that responsibility necessitates intimate personal care including dressing, bathing, toilet assistance, geriatric pad changes and catheter care. Each of these functions involves a personal touching.").

65. See Jennings v. N.Y. State Office of Mental Health, 786 F. Supp. 376, 381–82 (S.D. N.Y. 1992) (permitting sex to be a BFOQ for staffing of treatment assistants at a state-run psychiatric hospital because the positions sometimes necessitated that the treatment assistants view patients naked or partially undressed); Brooks v. ACF Industries, Inc., 537 F. Supp. 1122, 1125 (S.D. W. Va. 1982) (holding sex was a BFOQ for cleaning men's bathhouses at a railroad car plant because of the likelihood

that male workers would be viewed in various states of undress by the janitor cleaning the bathhouse).

66. Compare Norwood v. Dale Maintenance Systems, Inc., 590 F. Supp. 1410, 1418 (N.D. Ill. 1984) (holding that sex was a BFOQ for staffing attendants who cleaned single-sex restrooms in a large office building, not because of a concern that office workers might be seen naked by someone of the opposite sex, but because of a concern that office workers would feel "embarrassment" and "increased stress" from being expected to use washrooms in the presence of someone of the opposite sex), with EEOC v. Hi 40 Corporation, Inc., 953 F. Supp. 301, 303–4 (W.D. Mo. 1996) (holding that sex was not a BFOQ in the hiring of weight-loss counselors, even though the employer's predominantly female clientele was uncomfortable with male counselors taking their body-fat measurements either on bare skin or through clothing).

67. See Arthur Larson & Lex K. Larson, *Employment Discrimination*, § 15.10, at 4–27 (1992) (contending that the job of a prostitute is an "obvious" example of a BFOQ).

68. See *Wilson*, 517 F. Supp. at 301 (explaining that "in jobs where sex or vicarious sexual recreation is the primary service provided, e.g., a social escort or topless dancer, the job automatically calls for one sex exclusively"); Larson & Larson, *Employment Discrimination*, § 15.10, at 4–29 (1992) (contending that sex is a BFOQ for hiring in business where the "distinctive product inherently includes a component of female sexiness"); Larry Alexander, "What Makes Wrongful Discrimination Wrong? Biases, Preferences, Stereotypes, and Proxies," 141 *University of Pennsylvania Law Review*, 149, 205 (1992) (noting that hiring only females as strippers is permissible).

69. See, e.g., *Wilson*, 517 F. Supp. at 292 (prohibiting sex discrimination in hiring flight attendants and ticket agents); *Guardian Capital*, 360 N.Y.S.2d at 937 (prohibiting sex discrimination in hiring food servers). Hooters restaurants are perhaps the most obvious current example of a plus-sex business. The EEOC did initiate litigation against Hooters in the 1990s to challenge its sex-based hiring of Hooters Girls but settled the case after Hooters launched a public relations campaign mocking the EEOC's position. See Kenneth L. Schneyer, "Hooting: Public and Popular Discourse about Sex Discrimination," 31 *University of Michigan Journal of Law Reform* 551 (1998).

70. *Hi 40*, 953 F. Supp. at 301.

71. *Hi 40*, 953 F. Supp. at 304. See also Robino v. Iranon, 145 F.3d 1109, 1110–11 (9th Cir. 1998) (upholding women's prison's policy of hiring only female guards to six posts requiring guards "to observe the inmates in the showers and toilet areas," and concluding that the court did not need to reach the question of whether the privacy issues raised in this case were sufficient to justify the sex-based hiring in these positions, because of the policy's negligible impact on men's overall job opportunities in the prison).

72. Hardin v. Stynchcomb, 691 F.2d 1364 (11th Cir. 1982).

73. *Hardin*, 691 F.2d at 1369, 1371.

74. *Jones*, 666 F. Supp. at 933.

75. Norwood v. Dale Maintenance Systems, Inc., 590 F. Supp. 1410 (N.D. Ill. 1984).

76. Robbins v. White-Wilson Medical Clinic, Inc., 660 F.2d 1064 (5th Cir. Unit B, Nov. 1981), *vacated on other grounds*, 456 U.S. 969 (1982).

77. *Robbins*, 660 F.2d at 1065.

78. *Robbins*, 660 F.2d at 1068.

79. Chapman v. AI Transport et al., 229 F.3d 1012, 1034 (11th Cir. 2000) (en banc).

80. See *Chapman*, 229 F.3d at 1024 (holding that subjective employment criteria are legitimate as long as "the defendant articulates a clear and reasonably specific factual basis upon which it based its subjective opinion"); Byrnie v. Town of Cromwell, Board of Education, 243 F.3d 93, 105 (2d Cir. 2001) (noting that subjective hiring criteria are legitimate as long as the bases for the subjective criteria are clear, specific, and honest); *Robbins*, 660 F.2d at 1067 (noting that "the Supreme Court's requirement that 'the defendant's explanation of its legitimate reasons . . . be clear and reasonably specific' provides the plaintiff with some protection against the potential for discrimination inherent in a subjective selection process involving subjective job criteria"); Millbrook v. IBP, Inc., 280 F.3d 1169 (7th Cir. 2002) (rejecting plaintiff's challenge to defendant's use of subjective criteria, such as communication skills, in hiring decisions and noting that, as a general matter, there is nothing problematic about the use of subjective evaluation criteria for job applicants).

81. EEOC v. Joe's Stone Crab, Inc., 969 F. Supp. 727, 730 (S.D. Fla. 1997).

82. *Joe's Stone Crab*, 969 F. Supp. at 731–32.

83. *Joe's Stone Crab*, 969 F. Supp. at 741.

84. EEOC v. Joe's Stone Crab, Inc., 220 F.3d 1263 (11th Cir. 2000). The court of appeals explained: "The record extant and some of the district court's findings of fact can be read to support the alternate conclusion that Joe's management intentionally excluded women from food serving positions in order to provide its customers with an 'Old World,' fine-dining ambience." Ibid. at 1281.

85. *Joe's Stone Crab*, 969 F. Supp. at 732.

86. See Frederick Schauer, "Slippery Slopes," 99 *Harvard Law Review* 361, 381 (1985).

87. In *Johnson v. Transportation Agency, Santa Clara County, California, et al.*, the Supreme Court held that an employer "appropriately took into account as one factor the sex of Diane Joyce in determining that she should be promoted to the road dispatcher position. The decision to do so was made pursuant to an affirmative action plan that represents a moderate, flexible, case-by-case approach to effecting a gradual improvement in the representation of minorities and women in the Agency's work force. Such a plan is fully consistent with Title VII, for it embodies the contribution that voluntary employer action can make in eliminating the vestiges of discrimination in the workplace." 480 U.S. 616, 640–41 (1987). In its analysis, the court concluded: "The promotion of [the female employee applicant] satisfie[d] the first requirement enunciated in *Weber*, since it was undertaken to further an affirmative action plan designed to eliminate Agency work force imbalances in traditionally segregated job categories." Ibid. at 637 (citing United Steelworkers of America, AFL-CIO-CLC v. Weber et al., 443 U.S. 193 (1979)). See also Deborah Ballam, "Affirmative Action: Purveyor of Preferential Treatment or Guarantor of Equal Opportunity?" 18 *Berkeley Journal of Employment & Labor Law* 1, 15 (1997) (confirming that sex is a permissible "plus factor" that may be considered under affirmative action doctrine). Ballam further acknowledges the 1987 decision in *Johnson v. Transportation Agency* as the Court's official "sanction to voluntary affirmative action plans for women." Ibid. at 15 (citations omitted).

CHAPTER 4. STATUS

1. See Karen Engle, "The Persistence of Neutrality: The Failure of the Religious Accommodation Provision to Redeem Title VII," 76 *Texas Law Review* 317, 353 (1997). ("For the most part . . . a line between status and volitional conduct separates employer actions that are prohibited by Title VII from those that fall under the discretion of the employer, outside of Title VII's scope."); Camille Gear Rich, "Performing Racial and Ethnic Identity: Discrimination by Proxy and the Future of Title VII," 79 *New York University Law Review* 1134, 1200–1201 (2004) (describing the "involuntary/voluntary or 'status/conduct' distinction in Title VII cases"); Charity Williams, "Misperceptions Matter: Title VII of the Civil Rights Act of 1964 Protects Employees from Discrimination Based on Misperceived Religious Status," 2008 *Utah Law Review* 357, 360 (2008) ("Immutable traits are characteristics of status, whereas mutable traits are considered conduct, and only discrimination based on status is forbidden." (internal quotation marks and footnote omitted)). See also Garcia v. Gloor, 618 F.2d 264, 269 (5th Cir. 1980) (explaining that "the EEO Act does not prohibit all arbitrary employment practices. It does not forbid employers to hire only persons born under a certain sign of the zodiac or persons having long hair or short hair or no hair at all. It is directed only at specific impermissible bases of discrimination race, color, religion, sex, or national origin. . . . Save for religion, the discriminations on which the Act focuses its laser of prohibition are those that are either beyond the victim's power to alter . . . or that impose a burden on an employee on one of the prohibited bases." (internal citations omitted)); Frontiero v. Richardson, 411 U.S. 677, 686 (1973) ("Since sex, like race and national origin, is an immutable characteristic determined solely by the accident of birth, the imposition of special disabilities upon the members of a particular sex because of their sex would seem to violate 'the basic concept of our system that legal burdens should bear some relationship to individual responsibility' ").

2. Manfred Rehbinder, "Status, Contract, and the Welfare State," 23 *Stanford Law Review* 941, 954 (1971) ("The development from status to contract is more accurately a movement from 'ascriptive' status, fixed by birth and family rights, to status acquired on the basis of individual achievement." (internal quotation marks and footnote omitted)); Douglas Dribben, "Homosexuals and the Military: Strange Bedfellows," 57

University of Missouri-Kansas City Law Review 123, 126 (1988) ("The current suspect classes recognized by the Supreme Court are race and national origin, are defined by genetics and do not share any conduct or desire for a particular conduct peculiar to the class. It is because of the very nature of their trait—immutable, unchosen, and unrelated to any action on their part—that they have received suspect class status.").

3. Mathews v. Lucas, 427 U.S. 495, 505 (1976) ("The legal status of illegitimacy . . . is, like race or national origin, a characteristic determined by causes not within the control of the illegitimate individual"); Weber v. Aetna Casualty & Surety Company et al., 406 U.S. 164, 176 (1972) (suggesting heightened scrutiny is triggered by discrimination based on "status of birth"); see also Richard T. Ford, "Beyond 'Difference': A Reluctant Critique of Legal Identity Politics," in *Left Legalism/Left Critique*, ed. Wendy Brown & Janet Halley (Durham, N.C.: Duke University Press, 2002), 38 (arguing that civil rights law "properly focuses on ascriptive racial status, not on a metaphysics of ancestry or the unplumbed depth of subjective identity").

4. See American Psychiatric Association, *Diagnostic and Statistical Manual of Mental Disorders*, 4th ed. (Washington, DC: American Psychiatric Association, 2000), 581 (hereinafter *DSM-IV-TR*).

5. See J. Michael Bailey, *The Man Who Would Be Queen: The Psychology of Gender-Bending and Transsexualism* (Washington, DC: Joseph Henry Press, 2003), 169 (explaining that "femininity in boys and homosexuality in men are probably caused by incomplete masculinization of the brain during sexual differentiation"); Leslie M. Lothstein, "The Scientific Foundations of Gender Identity Disorders," in *Mental Disorders in the New Millennium*, ed. Thomas G. Plante (Westport, CT: Praeger, 2006), 227, 246 ("Newer findings . . . suggest that brain circuitry and specific brain nuclei may be responsible for organization and arousal, gender identity, sexual orientation, and love relationships.").

6. The *Diagnostic and Statistical Manual of Mental Disorders* defines GID as follows:

(A) A strong and persistent cross-gender identification (not merely a desire for any perceived cultural advantages of being the other sex). . . .

(B) Persistent discomfort with his or her sex or sense of inappropriateness in the gender role of that sex. . . .

(C) The disturbance is not concurrent with a physical intersex condition.

(D) The disturbance causes clinically significant distress or impairment in social, occupational, or other important areas of functioning.

DSM-IV-TR, 581; see also Franklin H. Romeo, "Beyond a Medical Model: Advocating for a New Conception of Gender Identity in the Law," 36 *Columbia Human Rights Law Review* 713, 731 (2005) (arguing that in order to get a medical diagnosis of GID and access to a sex-change operation, individuals are required to possess the conventional gender attributes of their psychological gender).

7. Indeed, it was courts' allegiance to an ascriptive notion of status that helps explain their previous unwillingness to protect transsexuals from discrimination. See, e.g., Holloway v. Arthur Andersen & Co., 566 F.2d 659, 664 (9th Cir. 1977) ("Holloway has not claimed to have [been] treated discriminatorily because she is male or female, but rather because she is a transsexual who chose to change her sex.").

8. Robinson v. California, 370 U.S. 660, 666–67 (1962) (explaining that "we deal with a statute which makes the 'status' of narcotic addiction a criminal offense" and holding that "a state law which imprisons a person thus afflicted as a criminal, even though he has never touched any narcotic drug within the State or been guilty of any irregular behavior there, inflicts a cruel and unusual punishment in violation of the Fourteenth Amendment.").

9. *Robinson*, 370 U.S. at 667.

10. Mark Kelman, "Interpretive Construction in the Substantive Criminal Law," 33 *Stanford Law Review* 591, 600 (1981) (noting that "the tensions of time-framing are evident in the status versus conduct distinction").

11. *Robinson*, 370 U.S. at 666.

12. Smith v. City of Salem, 378 F.3d 566 (6th Cir. 2004); Barnes v. City of Cincinnati, 401 F.3d 729 (6th Cir. 2005).

13. See Schwenk v. Hartford, 204 F.3d 1187, 1200 (9th Cir. 2000) (providing that Gender Motivated Violence Act protections apply to transsexuals); Schroer v. Billington, 424 F. Supp. 2d 203, 213 (D.D.C. 2006) (stating that refusal to hire someone based on his or her sexual identity was sex discrimination); Mitchell v. Axcan Scandipharm, Inc.,

No. Civ. A 05-234, 2006 WL 456173, at *2 (W.D. Pa., Feb. 17, 2006) (stating that terminating a transsexual employee for "his failure to conform to sex stereotypes of how a man should look and behave" is gender discrimination); Kastl v. Maricopa County Community College District, No. 02-1531-PHX-SRB, 2004 WL 2008954, at *2 (D. Ariz., June 3, 2004) ("Neither a woman with male genitalia nor a man with stereotypically female anatomy, such as breasts, may be deprived of a benefit or privilege of employment by reason of that nonconforming trait."); Tronetti v. TLC Healthnet Lakeshore Hospital, No. 03-CV-0375E(SC), 2003 WL 22757935, at *4 (W.D. N.Y., Sept. 26, 2003) ("Transsexuals are not gender-less, they are either male or female and are thus protected under Title VII to the extent that they are discriminated against on the basis of sex."); Doe v. United Consumer Financial Services, No. 1:01 CV 1112, 2001 WL 34350174, at *5 (N.D. Ohio, Nov. 9, 2001) ("Since Doe may have been fired, at least in part, because her appearance and behavior did not fit into her company's sex stereotypes, rather than solely because of her transgendered status, dismissal of Doe's Title VII claims is not warranted."). But see Ulane v. Eastern Airlines, Inc., 742 F.2d 1081, 1085 (7th Cir. 1984) (holding that Title VII does not provide "protection to transsexuals"); Sommers v. Budget Marketing, Inc., 667 F.2d 748, 750 (8th Cir. 1982) ("We hold that discrimination based on one's transsexualism does not fall within the protective purview of [Title VII]."); Holloway, 566 F.2d at 664 (holding that a claim of discrimination on the basis of being a transsexual was not actionable under Title VII); Etsitty v. Utah Transit Authority, No. 2:04CV616 DS, 2005 WL 1505610, at *3–5 (D. Utah, June 24, 2005) (holding that Title VII's ban on discrimination does not extend to transsexuals); Oiler v. Winn-Dixie Louisiana, Inc., No. Civ. A. 00-3114, 2002 WL 31098541, at *6 (E.D. La., Sept. 16, 2002) (holding that Title VII does not protect against discrimination based on "sexual identity disorders"); Underwood v. Archer Management Services, Inc., 857 F. Supp. 96, 98 (D.D.C. 1994) (stating that the definition of sex did not encompass transsexuality); Dobre v. National Railroad Passenger Corp., 850 F. Supp. 284, 286–87 (E.D. Pa. 1993) ("Congress did not intend Title VII to protect transsexuals from discrimination on the basis of their transsexualism."); Doe v. United States Postal Service, No. Civ. A. 84-3296, 1985 WL 9446, at *2 (D.D.C., June 12, 1985) (holding that plaintiff failed to state a claim when alleged discrimination was based on being a transsexual). Antidiscrimination protection for transsexual and transgender employees continues to vary widely. See Katie Koch & Richard Bales, "Transgender Employment Discrimination," 17 *UCLA Women's Law Journal* 243, 250–64 (2008).

14. Doe v. Yunits, No. 00-10060A, 2000 WL 33162199, at *1 (Mass. Super., Oct. 11, 2000).

15. *Doe v. Yunits,* 2000 WL 33163199, at *2.

16. *Doe v. Yunits,* 2000 WL 33163199, at *1.

17. *Doe v. Yunits,* 2000 WL 33163199, at *2.

18. *Doe v. Yunits,* 2000 WL 33163199, at *6. In addition to the sex discrimination claim, Doe brought state law claims alleging a denial of freedom of expression, disability discrimination, denial of liberty interest in appearance, denial of due process, and denial of the right to personal dress and appearance. Ibid. at *2.

19. Doe v. Yunits, No. 00-1060A, 2001 WL 36648072, at *6 (Mass. Supp., Feb. 26, 2001).

20. Harper v. Edgewood Board of Education, 655 F. Supp. 1353 (S.D. Ohio 1987).

21. *Doe v. Yunits,* 2000 WL 33163199, at *6 n.5.

22. *Doe v. Yunits,* 2000 WL 33163199, at *6 n.5.

23. Smith v. City of Salem, Ohio, 378 F.3d 566, 568 (6th Cir. 2004).

24. See Abigail W. Lloyd, "Defining the Human: Are Transgender People Strangers to the Law?" 20 *Berkeley Journal of Gender Law & Justice* 150, 179 (2005) ("Although the [*Smith*] court did not say so explicitly, this medical authority seemed to influence the court in seeing Smith's behavior as pursuant to trustworthy medical advice, and therefore less her fault or choice.").

25. Lie v. Sky Publishing Corp., No. 013117J., 2002 WL 31492397 (Mass. Super., Oct. 7, 2002).

26. *Lie,* 2002 WL 31492397, at *2.

27. *Lie,* 2002 WL 31492397, at *2.

28. Etsitty v. Utah Transit Authority, 502 F.3d 1215 (10th Cir. 2007).

29. *Etsitty,* 502 F.3d at 1218.

30. *Etsitty,* 502 F.3d at 1219.

31. *Etsitty,* 502 F.3d at 1219.

32. *Etsitty,* 502 F.3d at 1218.

33. *Etsitty,* 502 F.3d at 1224.

34. *Etsitty*, 502 F.3d at 1226.

35. *Etsitty*, 502 F.3d at 1224.

36. *Etsitty*, 502 F.3d at 1224.

37. See Kastl v. Maricopa County Community College District, No. CV-02-1531-PHX-SRB, 2006 WL 2460636, at *8 (D. Ariz., Aug. 22, 2006) (granting defendant's motion for summary judgment on female transsexual worker's claim of sex discrimination stemming from employer's requirement that she could not use the women's restroom until she had presented proof that she had completed a sex-change operation), *aff'd*, 325 Fed. Appx. 492, 493–94 (9th Cir. 2009); Johnson v. Fresh Mark, Inc., 98 Fed. Appx. 461 (6th Cir. 2004) (affirming without explanation district court's dismissal of female transsexual worker's Title VII sex discrimination claim based on employer's requirement that she use men's rather than women's restroom). But see Michaels v. Akal Security, Inc., No. 09-cv-01300-ZLW-CBS, 2010 WL 2573988, at *4 (D. Col. June 24, 2010) (agreeing with *Etsitty* that restrictions on a transsexual worker's bathroom usage does not itself establish sex discrimination, but holding that the plaintiff had sufficiently pled pretext to survive a motion to dismiss). Bathroom discrimination claims brought under state law sexual orientation discrimination statutes have been similarly unsuccessful. See Goins v. West Group, 635 N.W.2d 717 (Minn. 2001) (holding that employer's requirement that female transsexual use only unisex restroom rather than women's restroom did not constitute discrimination based on sexual orientation under the Minnesota Human Rights Act, which defined sexual orientation to include "having or being perceived as having a self-image or identity not traditionally associated with one's biological maleness or femaleness").

Certainly these are not the first cases in which courts have subordinated employees' antidiscrimination interests to the privacy interests of customers or coworkers. Courts regularly privilege such privacy interests in cases in which employers seek to engage in sex-based hiring of workers engaged in positions that involve the seeing or touching of unclothed customers or coworkers. See Kimberly A. Yuracko, "Private Nurses and Playboy Bunnies: Explaining Permissible Sex Discrimination," 92 *California Law Review* 147, 156–57 (2004).

38. Pecenka v. Fareway Stores, Inc., 672 N.W.2d 800 (Iowa 2003).

39. *Pecenka*, 672 N.W.2d at 805.

40. *Pecenka*, 672 N.W.2d at 805. The court also emphasized that the no earring for men rule did not reinforce women's or men's subordination in the workplace. The court noted, "Nor does [plaintiff] contend that the unwritten personal grooming code perpetuates a sexist or chauvinistic attitude in employment that significantly affects his employment opportunities." Ibid. See also Lockhart v. Louisiana-Pacific Corp., 795 P.2d 602, 603 (Or. Ct. App. 1990) (upholding no facial jewelry rule for male but not female employees, explaining that "only those distinctions between the sexes which are based on immutable, unalterable, or constitutionally protected personal characteristics are forbidden").

41. Austin v. Wal-Mart Stores, Inc., 20 F. Supp. 2d 1254, 1258 (N.D. Ind. 1998).

42. *Austin*, 20 F. Supp. 2d at 1256. Like the court in *Pecenka*, the *Austin* court also emphasized that the sex-specific grooming requirement at issue did not raise antisubordination-oriented concerns. As the court explained: "The objective of Title VII is to equalize employment opportunities. Consequently, discrimination based on either immutable sex characteristics or constitutionally protected activities such as marriage or child rearing violate Title VII because they present obstacles to the employment of one sex that cannot be overcome. . . ." Ibid.

43. Jespersen v. Harrah's Operating Co., 444 F.3d 1104, 1113 (9th Cir. 2006) (en banc).

44. *Jespersen*, 444 F.3d at 1112.

45. Nichols v. Azteca Restaurant Enterprises, Inc., 256 F.3d 864, 875 (9th Cir. 2001).

46. *Nichols*, 256 F.3d at 870.

47. *Nichols*, 256 F.3d at 870.

48. Doe v. City of Belleville, Ill., 119 F.3d 563 (7th Cir. 1996).

49. In addition to other incidents of physical and verbal harassment, H. Doe was regularly called "queer" and "fag," was asked, "Are you a boy or a girl?" and was referred to by his primary harasser as his "bitch." *Doe v. Belleville*, 119 F.3d at 566–67.

50. *Doe v. Belleville*, 119 F.3d at 567.

51. Indeed, H.'s brother J. was also harassed, albeit less severely, despite not wearing an earring. *Doe v. Belleville*, 119 F.3d at 566.

52. As the court explained: "H. Doe is not suing Belleville in order to challenge a workplace rule that forbade him from wearing an earring,"

he was suing because "his gender had something to do with the harassment heaped upon him." *Doe v. Belleville*, 119 F.3d at 582.

53. Devon Carbado, Mitu Gulati, and Gowri Ramachandran have offered a slightly different status-oriented reading of the effeminate men harassment cases, one focused on the status of homosexuality rather than gender. They contend that by using the sex stereotyping rhetoric of *Price Waterhouse* to protect effeminate men from harassment, courts, "quite possibly, . . . were engaging in subversive judging—namely, enacting a minor rebellion against the Constitutional refusal to provide any protection against sexual orientation discrimination." "The Jespersen Story: Makeup and Women at Work," in *Employment Discrimination Stories*, ed. Joel Wm. Friedman (New York: Foundation Press, 2006), 105, 137.

· 54. See Employment Non-Discrimination Act of 2007, H.R. 2015, 110th Cong. § 4(a) (2007) (the act also prohibited discrimination based on sexual orientation).

55. ENDA, H.R. 2015, 110th Cong. § 3(a)(6).

56. ENDA, H.R. 2015, 110th Cong. § 8(a)(4).

57. The Employment Non-Discrimination Act of 2007: Hearing on H.R. 2015 before the Subcomm. on Health, Emp., Lab. & Pensions, 110th Cong. 12–13 (2007) (statement of Rep. Barney Frank, Sponsor, Employment Non-Discrimination Act of 2007).

58. Bill Summary & Status, 110th Congress (2007–8), H.R. 3686, All Congressional Actions, The Library of Congress, http://thomas.loc.gov/cgi-bin/bdquery/z?d110:H.R.3686: (last visited Sept. 22, 2014) (noting the last major action of H.R. 3686 was its referral to House subcommittee on Oct. 17, 2007).

59. See Dean Spade, "Resisting Medicine, Re/Modeling Gender," 18 *Berkeley Women's Law Journal* 15, 24 (2003) ("Symptoms of GID in the Diagnostic and Statistical Manual (DSM-IV) describe at length the symptom of childhood participation in stereotypically gender inappropriate behavior." Boys with GID "particularly enjoy playing house, drawing pictures of beautiful girls and princesses, and watching television or videos of their favorite female characters. . . . They avoid rough-and-tumble play and competitive sports and have little interest in cars and trucks." Girls with GID do not want to wear dresses, "prefer boys' clothing and short hair," are interested in "contact sports, [and] rough-and-tumble play.").

60. *DSM-IV-TR*, 537.

61. Spade, "Resisting Medicine," 26. Spade is critical of the fact that "success" necessarily means adherence to established gender norms. For a female-to-male transsexual, tips for successful performance of masculinity "focus on an adherence to traditional aesthetics of masculinity, warning FTMs to avoid 'punky' hair cuts, black leather jackets and other trappings associated with butch lesbians. A preppy, clean-cut look is often suggested as the best aesthetic for passing. Again, this establishes the requirement that gender transgressive people be even more 'normal' than 'normal people' when it comes to gender presentation." Ibid. at 27.

62. Franklin Romeo, "Beyond a Medical Model: Advocating for a New Conception of Gender Identity," 36 Columbia Human Rights Law Review 713, 731 (2005). As Romero has explained: "The diagnostic criteria of GID do not challenge gender norms so much as they provide a mechanism for some people to substitute the gender norms of their lived gender for the norms of their birth sex. Moreover, the medical model holds transgender people to hyper-normative standards regarding their lived gender—thereby reifying the idea that 'real' men and women look and act a certain way. These hyper-normative standards do not reflect the experience of a great number of gender nonconforming people, and fail to recognize the complexity of experiences among gender transgressive people."

63. See Dylan Vade, "Expanding Gender and Expanding the Law: Toward a Social and Legal Conceptualization of Gender That Is More Inclusive of Transgender People," 11 *Michigan Journal of Gender & Law* 253, 297 (2005) ("In my experience, a person who was assigned male at birth and identifies as female has the best chance of having her self-identified gender confirmed by the courts if her medical experts testify that she is a feminine woman, a woman who played with dolls when she was young, a heterosexual woman, a woman with genital surgery, and so on. A gender non-conforming transgender person stands very little chance of having their self-identified gender recognized by the courts.").

64. Brief of Amici Curiae the National Center for Lesbian Rights and the Transgender Law Center in Support of Plaintiff-Appellant, Jespersen v. Harrah's Operating Co., Inc., 444 F.3d 1104 (9th. Cir. 2006) (No. 03-15045), 2005 WL 1501598, at *12–13. More generally, the groups argued: "Just as a person's core gender identity as male or female is

innate, a person's relative degree of masculinity or femininity is also deep-seated and generally impervious to manipulation or change. . . . Workplace rules affecting a person's core gender identity and outward expression of masculinity or femininity are not trivial, but rather touch on profound and fundamental aspects of the self. For an employer to require a person to adopt a gendered appearance that conflicts with the person's core identity is intrusive and humiliating and may seriously impair a person's well-being and ability to function." Ibid.

65. The court explained: "We respect Jespersen's resolve to be true to herself and to the image that she wishes to project to the world. We cannot agree, however, that her objection to the makeup requirement, without more, can give rise to a claim of sex stereotyping under Title VII. If we were to do so, we would come perilously close to holding that every grooming, apparel, or appearance requirement that an individual finds personally offensive, or in conflict with his or her own self-image, can create a triable issue of sex discrimination." *Jespersen*, 444 F.3d at 1112.

66. See "Gender Variance (Dysphoria)," version 2.0, *Gender Identity Research & Education Society*, 4, last revised Aug. 31, 2008, http://www.gires.org.uk/dysphoria.php (hereinafter "Gender Variance (Dysphoria)") ("The experience of extreme gender variance is increasingly understood in scientific and medical disciplines as having a biological origin. The current medical viewpoint . . . is that this condition . . . is strongly associated with unusual neurodevelopment of the brain at the fetal stage."); "Definition & Synopsis of the Etiology of Gender Variance," version 2.1, *Gender Identity Research & Education Society*, 3, last revised July 18, 2009, http://www.gires.org.uk/etiology.php (hereinafter "Etiology of Gender Variance") (hypothesizing that hormones significantly influence the "dimorphic development" of gender though noting that "the exact mechanism is incompletely understood"); Randi Ettner, "The Etiology of Transsexualism," in *Principles of Transgender Medicine and Surgery*, ed. Randi Ettner et al. (New York: Hawthorne Press, 2007), 1, 9 ("The sheer sweeping heterogeneity of the condition [transsexualism] itself impends a strictly biological explanation."); P.T. Cohen-Kettenis & L. J. G. Gooren, "Transsexualism: A Review of Etiology, Diagnosis and Treatment," 46 *Journal of Psychosomatic Research* 315, 318–19 (1999) (describing studies linking transsexualism to prenatal hormone

exposure or to sex differences in the hypothalamus); Frank P. M. Kruijver et al., "Male-to-Female Transsexuals Have Female Neuron Numbers in a Limbic Nucleus," 85 *Journal of Clinical Endocrinology & Metabolism* 2034, 2041 (2000) (presenting data "supporting the view that transsexualism may reflect a form of brain hermaphroditism such that this limbic nucleus *itself* is structurally sexually differentiated opposite to the transsexual's genetic and genital sex. It is conceivable that this dichotomy is just the tip of the iceberg and holds also true for many other sexually dimorphic brain areas.").

67. See, e.g., Vade, "Expanding Gender and Expanding the Law," 260 (explaining that "some male-to-female transgender people are butch lesbians. Some female-to-male transgender people like to cook and bake. And there are many transgender people who do not identify as either female or male, but as a third or other gender, such as trans or boy-girl, just to name a few."); Leslie Feinberg, *Transgender Warriors: Making History from Joan of Arc to Dennis Rodman* (Boston: Beacon Press, 1996), ix ("There are no pronouns in the English language as complex as I am, and I do not want to simplify myself in order to neatly fit one or the other."); Riki Anne Wilchins, *Read My Lips: Sexual Subversion and the End of Gender* (Ithaca, NY: Firebrand Books, 1997); Sandy Stone, "The Empire Strikes Back: A Posttranssexual Manifesto," in *Body Guards: The Cultural Politics of Gender Ambiguity*, ed. Julia Epstein & Kristina Straub (New York: Routledge, 1991), 292, 299 (encouraging transsexuals to speak openly about the complexities of their gender experiences); Susan Etta Keller, "Operations of Legal Rhetoric: Examining Transsexual and Judicial Identity," 34 *Harvard Civil Rights–Civil Liberties Law Review* 329, 332–33 (1999) (describing the varied ways in which transsexuals themselves understand transsexual identity).

68. For a general discussion of the effect of categorization in antidiscrimination law, see Laura Grenfell, "Embracing Law's Categories: Anti-Discrimination Laws and Transgenderism," 15 *Yale Journal of Law & Feminism* 51, 52 (2003) ("Through the process of categorization, legal narratives effectively strip the subject of agency by denying the subject the possibility of self-definition—for example, the agency to assert whether one is female, male, or neither. In this way, legal categories become constitutive of one's identity (e.g. not male equals female, not white equals black, not middle- (or upper-) class equals poor).").

69. See Andrew Gilden, "Toward a More Transformative Approach: The Limits of Transgender Formal Equality," 23 *Berkeley Journal of Gender Law & Justice* 83, 103 (2008) ("Much as an essentialized male/female binary renders unintelligible alternative gender identities, the articulation of an essentialized tertiary identity similarly marginalizes radical alternatives. If transsexuality only encompasses those trans people like Schroer who have been medically diagnosed as transsexuals and who conform to sex-stereotypes, then those trans people who most challenge normative sex/gender ideologies remain marginalized by trans jurisprudence.").

70. Dylan Vade makes this point quite concretely: "When courts only recognize as 'real' those transgender people who fit narrow gender stereotypes, have multiple medical interventions, and engage in heterosexual intercourse, then courts only grant custody, health benefits, and employment protections to transgender people who fit narrow gender stereotypes, have multiple medical interventions, and engage in heterosexual intercourse. Those clients of mine who do not fit the above requirements cannot make use of the legal protections. As a legal advocate for transgender people, this is a concern I face every day." Vade, "Expanding Gender and Expanding the Law," 256. For a more positive account of the role medical professionals play in improving the social and legal treatment of transsexuals, see Jennifer L. Levi, "A Prescription for Gender: How Medical Professionals Can Help Secure Equality for Transgender People," 4 *Georgetown Journal of Gender & the Law* 721, 735 (2003) (explaining that "medical experts can help to develop empathy in the greater community toward transgender litigants and, more specifically, help individual litigants to secure rights by chipping away at deeply held cultural prejudices that do not reflect medical realities.").

71. For a similar point, see Gilden, "Toward a More Transformative Approach," 96–97 ("In describing a 'biologically male' transsexual as performing feminine acts, it furthers the construction of particular acts as inherently feminine and normatively conflated with biological femaleness.").

72. See Levi, "A Prescription for Gender," 736 (describing the "classic description" of transsexuals as being "trapped in the 'wrong body'"); Vade, "Expanding Gender and Expanding the Law," 285 ("Transgender people often are defined as 'having a mismatch of gender

and sex.' "); Keller, "Operations of Legal Rhetoric," 353 (explaining that "the most common or notorious model for describing the transsexual condition, by academics writing about transsexuals, by transsexuals themselves, and by judges, is a vision of the transsexual as a woman/man trapped in a man/woman's body").

73. *Doe v. Yunits*, 2001 WL 664947, at *1.

74. *Doe v. Yunits*, 2001 WL 664947, at *1. Similarly, in ruling on a motion for preliminary injunction in the case, a different judge explained: "Plaintiff has been diagnosed with gender identity disorder, which means that, although plaintiff was born biologically male, she has a female gender identity." *Doe v. Yunits*, 2000 WL 33163199, at *1.

75. For Doe, female clothing involved "such items as skirts and dresses, wigs, high-heeled shoes, and padded bras with tight shirts." *Doe v. Yunits*, 2000 WL 33163199, at *1.

76. *Doe v. Yunits*, 2001 WL 664947, at *6.

77. *Doe v. Yunits*, 2001 WL 664947, at *6.

78. Schroer v. Billington, 577 F. Supp.2d 293 (D.D.C. 2008).

79. Expert Report of Walter O. Bockting, Ph.D., Schroer v. Billington (D.D.C. 2006) (No. 05CV01090), 2006 WL 4517046, at ¶ 32 (internal citation omitted).

80. Supplemental Report of Walter O. Bockting, Ph.D., Schroer v. Billington (D.D.C., Dec. 21, 2006) (No. 05CV01090), 2006 WL 4517047, at ¶ 5.

81. Expert Report of Martha L. Harris, LCSW, Schroer v. Billington (D.D.C. 2006) (No. 05CV01090), 2006 WL 4517048, at ¶ 22(a).

82. Expert Report of Martha L. Harris, LCSW, Schroer v. Billington (D.D.C. 2006) (No. 05CV01090), 2006 WL 4517048, at ¶ 26.

83. Expert Report of Martha L. Harris, LCSW, Schroer v. Billington (D.D.C. 2006) (No. 05CV01090), 2006 WL 4517048, at ¶ 28.

84. See Sherry F. Colb, *When Sex Counts: Making Babies and Making Law* (Lanham, MD: Rowman & Littlefield, 2007), 140 (describing a reaction she observed at a conference by female academics to a transsexual scholar presenting a paper where the female academics complained that the transsexual did not understand what made them "women" and mistook being a woman for wearing very stereotypically feminine clothing).

85. See Cohen-Kettenis & Gooren, "Transsexualism," 320 (noting that "not all children with GID will turn out to be transsexuals after

puberty" and explaining that it might be that "only very few extreme cases would become transsexuals, whereas the mild cases would become homo- or heterosexuals"); "Standards of Care for Gender Identity Disorders," version 6, *The Harry Benjamin International Gender Dysphoria Association*, 2, last revised February 2001, http://www.wpath.org/documents2/socv6.pdf ("A clinical threshold [for transsexualism] is passed when concerns, uncertainties, and questions about gender identity persist during a person's development, become so intense as to seem to be the most important aspect of a person's life, or prevent the establishment of a relatively unconflicted gender identity.").

86. There exist highly divergent views about how nontranssexuals experience their gender. Compare Romero, "Beyond a Medical Model," 738–39 (arguing that gender should be recognized as "a fundamental aspect of human life, which every person has the capacity and inherent right to control"); with Jennifer L. Levi, "Clothes Don't Make the Man (or Woman), but Gender Identity Might," 15 *Columbia Journal of Gender & Law* 90, 91 (2006) ("until courts understand the inelasticity of gender for most individuals alongside its social construction, sex discrimination claims will have limited utility").

87. Vicki Schultz, "Telling Stories about Women and Work: Judicial Interpretations of Sex Segregation in the Workplace in Title VII Cases Raising the Lack of Interest Argument," 103 *Harvard Law Review* 1749, 1800–1803 (1990).

88. Schultz, "Telling Stories about Women and Work," 1802.

89. See Ford, "Beyond 'Difference,'" 55 ("If misrecognition can lead people to fail to take advantage of opportunities even after 'objective obstacles to their advancement fall away,' then misrecognition might also lead those same people to push for rights to self-detrimental traits and adopt misconceived legal strategies in the name of safeguarding an identity that was shaped by the misrecognition of others.").

90. For a similar point about the dangers of entrenched categories in other contexts, see Richard T. Ford, "Race as Culture? Why Not?" 47 *UCLA Law Review* 1803, 1811 (1999–2000) ("The rights argument that protects culture as the authentic expression of the individual litigant must invite—in fact it must require—courts to determine which expressions are authentic and therefore deserving of protection. The result will often be to discredit anyone who does not fit the culture style

ascribed to her racial group."); K. Anthony Appiah, "Identity, Authenticity, Survival: Multicultural Societies and Social Reproduction," in *Multiculturalism: Examining the Politics of Recognition*, ed. Amy Gutmann (Princeton: Princeton University Press, 1994), 162–63 ("Demanding respect for people as blacks and as gays requires that there are some scripts that go with being an African-American or having same-sex desires. There will be proper ways of being black and gay, there will be expectations to be met, demands to be made."); Janet E. Halley, "Gay Rights and Identity Imitation: Issues in the Ethics of Representation," in *The Politics of Law: A Progressive Critique*, 3rd ed., ed. David Kairys (New York: Basic Books, 1998), 124 ("If advocacy constructs identity, if it generates a script that identity bearers must heed, and if that script restricts group members, then identity politics compels its beneficiaries. Identity politics suddenly is no longer mere or simple resistance: It begins to look like power. . . . Whenever activists invoke identity in ways that transform it, they may approach and even cross the dangerous line . . . between advocacy and coercion; they may interpellate subjects just as invidiously as Althusser's imagined cop in the street.").

CHAPTER 5. PERFECTIONISM

1. Andrew Koppelman, "The Fluidity of Neutrality," 66 *Review of Politics* 633, 634 (2004).

2. George Sher, *Beyond Neutrality: Perfectionism and Politics* (Cambridge: Cambridge University Press, 1997), 9. Vinit Haksar describes these views as weak and strong perfectionism, respectively. According to Haksar, weak perfectionism asserts that some forms of human life are superior to others because they "are more suited to human beings." In contrast, strong perfectionism says there are x's and y's such that "whatever human nature turns out to be . . . it would still be the case that x would be superior to y." Vinit Haksar, *Equality, Liberty and Perfectionism* (Oxford: Oxford University Press, 1979), 3–4.

3. Thomas Hurka, *Perfectionism* (New York: Oxford University Press, 1993), 3.

4. Hurka, *Perfectionism*, 17.

5. Hurka, *Perfectionism*, 37.

6. Sher, *Beyond Neutrality*, 202.

7. See Martha C. Nussbaum, "Human Capabilities, Female Human Beings," in *Women, Culture, and Development: A Study of Human Capabilities,* ed. Martha Nussbaum and Jonathan Glover (Oxford: Clarendon Press, 1995), 83–85; Martha C. Nussbaum, "Nature, Function, and Capability: Aristotle on Political Distribution," in *Oxford Studies in Ancient Philosophy* (Supplementary Volume), ed. Julia Annas and Robert H. Grimm (Oxford: Oxford University Press, 1988), 160–64.

8. Nussbaum, "Human Capabilities," 94–95.

9. Joseph Raz, *The Morality of Freedom* (Oxford: Clarendon Press, 1986), 6–7.

10. For Nussbaum, human flourishing requires that individuals have the cognitive and intellectual capacities necessary to be able to plan and direct a course for their lives. Nussbaum, "Nature, Function, and Capability," 160–61. For Hurka human flourishing requires the development and exercise of humans' capacities to form and act on sophisticated beliefs. Hurka, *Perfectionism,* 41. Likewise, for Raz autonomy requires that an individual possess the mental abilities necessary to form intentions, develop complex plans, and connect means with their probable ends. Raz, *Morality of Freedom,* 372–73. For Sher human flourishing requires the development of individuals' capacities for reason and knowledge to their highest degree. Sher, *Beyond Neutrality,* 203.

11. Nussbaum, "Human Capabilities," 83–85.

12. For Sher human flourishing requires social interaction aimed at mutual respect and recognition. Sher, *Beyond Neutrality,* 208. Sher contends that friendships or romantic relationships between people who care for and respect each other are far more successful at achieving mutual recognition than are "interpersonal relations that are (e.g.) manipulative, exploitative, coercive, or destructive." Ibid., 205–7.

13. Raz contends that certain valuable social forms, like intimate personal relations, can only exist if people recognize that the social relations are incommensurable with other kinds of market goods. Raz, *Morality of Freedom,* 347–53.

14. Margaret Jane Radin, "Market Inalienability," 100 *Harvard Law Review* 1849, 1885–86 (1987).

15. Radin, "Market Inalienability," 1905–6.

16. Local 567, American Federation of State, County, & Municipal Employees v. Michigan Council 25, 635 F. Supp. 1010 (E.D. Mich. 1986).

17. The court made clear, though, that whether sex-based hiring was actually permissible in that case depended on the state's ability to show that there were no reasonable alternatives by which the state could protect patients' privacy interests without engaging in sex-based hiring. *Local 567*, 635 F. Supp. at 1014.

18. *Local 567*, 635 F. Supp. at 1013 (quoting York v. Story, 324 F.2d 450, 455 (9th Cir. 1963)). The court went on to emphasize the connection between personal dignity and the preference for personal physical privacy: "Obviously most people would find it a greater intrusion of their dignity and privacy to have their naked bodies viewed (or any number of personal services performed) by a member of the opposite sex." Ibid. at 1013–14; see also Torres v. Wisconsin Department of Health & Social Services, 838 F.2d 944, 950–51 (7th Cir. 1988).

19. Michenfelder v. Sumner, 860 F.2d 328 (9th Cir. 1988).

20. *Michenfelder*, 860 F.2d at 329–34.

21. *Michenfelder*, 860 F.2d at 333–34. Contra Jordan v. Gardner, 986 F.2d 1521, 1531 (9th Cir. 1993) (*en banc*) (holding that a policy at a women's prison permitting random cross-gender clothed-body searches of female inmates constituted cruel and unusual punishment in violation of the Eighth Amendment).

22. Arthur Larson & Lex K. Larson, *Employment Discrimination*, § 14.30 (1987); see also Veleanu v. Beth Israel Medical Center, No. 98 CIV. 7455(VM), 2000 WL 1400965 (S.D. N.Y., Sept. 25, 2000) at *8 (citing Backus v. Baptist Medical Center, 510 F. Supp. 1191, 1194–95 (E.D. Ark. 1981) (quoting Arthur Larson & Lex K. Larson, *Employment Discrimination*, § 14.30 (3rd ed. 1980)), *vacated as moot*, 671 F.2d 1100 (8th Cir. 1981)).

23. In *EEOC v. Mercy Health Center*, the district court held that sex was a BFOQ for nurses in the labor and delivery area of the hospital and concluded that the hospital's refusal to hire male nurses to work in the labor and delivery area was permissible. In reaching this conclusion, the court relied in part on the complaints from women about male nurses made to the hospital's two main obstetrics and gynecology doctors, both of whom were male. EEOC v. Mercy Health Center, No. Civ. 80-1374-W, 1982 WL 3108, *3 (W.D. Okla., Feb. 2, 1982). Similarly, in *Backus v. Baptist Medical Center*, the district court upheld the hospital's policy of hiring only women as nurses in the obstetrics and gynecology department. In reaching this conclusion, the court relied in part on a doctor's

testimony that a majority of his patients would object to a male nurse. *Backus*, 510 F. Supp. at 1196.

24. See Fesel v. Masonic Home of Delaware, Inc., 447 F. Supp. 1346 (D.C. Del. 1978) (holding that sex was a BFOQ for nurses' aides serving predominantly female patients in a retirement home because at least some of the female residents objected to being cared for by a male nurses' aide, but also noting that the female patients consented to care by male doctors).

25. The district court in *Wilson* explained that in order for sex discrimination to be permissible, the sex-linked aspects of the job must predominate. Wilson v. Southwest Airlines, 517 F. Supp. 292, 301 (N.D. Tex. 1981). Some examples offered by the court in which "vicarious sexual recreation is the primary service provided" were a social escort, a topless dancer, and a Playboy Bunny. Ibid. The court made it clear, however, that only jobs within the narrow range of categories conventionally treated as exclusively sexual titillation based could include sexual titillation as a job requirement. Jobs outside that range, on the other hand, could never include sexual titillation as a job requirement. Jobs were either about sexual titillation or about something else.

26. To use again the analogy of bundled commodities: the more nonsexual goods or services sexual titillation is bundled with, the more likely courts are to conclude that sexual titillation is not, in fact, a necessary part of the commodity at all.

27. Guardian Capital v. N.Y. State Division of Human Rights, 360 N.Y.S.2d 937 (N.Y. App. Div. 1974).

28. *Guardian Capital*, 360 N.Y.S.2d at 939.

29. Wilson v. Southwest Airlines, 517 F. Supp. 292, 302 (N.D. Tex. 1981).

30. *Guardian Capital*, 360 N.Y.S.2d at 939 (citing Margarita St. Cross v. Playboy Club, Appeal No. 773, Case No. CSF 22618–70 (New York Human Rights Appeal Board, 1971) (quoted in Aromi v. Playboy Club, Inc., Case No. CS-32986-74 at 6 (1985)). In *St. Cross*, the New York State Human Rights Appeals Board had upheld the Playboy Clubs' policy of hiring only young, beautiful women as "Bunnies" in its clubs. *St. Cross*, CSF 22618–70 at 5. The court noted that the purposes of the Playboy Clubs were to serve their members and guests food and drink along with heterosexual male sexual titillation. *St. Cross*, CSF 22618–70

at 7. In *Guardian Capital,* Justice Reynolds noted: "Petitioner was attempting to emulate the Playboy Club atmosphere and it is difficult . . . to understand what the special duties of the 'Bunnies' were that the waitresses in the Cabaret don't have." *Guardian Capital,* 360 N.Y.S.2d at 940.

31. Playboy Clubs sold 2.5 million "membership keys" and eventually included forty properties. The last Playboy Club closed in 1986. See Ramona Paden, "FAQs about the House that Hef Built," *Examiner.com,* last visited Oct. 28, 2014, http://www.examiner.com/article/faqs-about-the-house-that-hef-built.

32. EEOC v. Sage Realty, 507 F. Supp. 599 (S.D. N.Y. 1981).

33. *Sage Realty,* 507 F. Supp. at 610–11.

34. *Sage Realty,* 507 F. Supp. at 609–10 (explaining that "in requiring Hasselman to wear the revealing Bicentennial uniform in the lobby of 711 Third Avenue, defendants made her acquiescence in sexual harassment by the public, and perhaps by building tenants, a prerequisite of her employment as a lobby attendant").

35. See, e.g., Folkerson v. Circus Circus Enterprises, Inc., 107 F.3d 754, 756 (9th Cir. 1997) (noting in dicta: "We now hold that an employer may be held liable for sexual harassment on the part of a private individual, such as the casino patron, where the employer either ratifies or acquiesces in the harassment by not taking immediate and/or corrective actions when it knew or should have known of the conduct."); Henson v. City of Dundee, 682 F.2d 897, 910 (11th Cir. 1982) (pointing out that sex harassment can be committed by a supervisor, a coworker, or "even strangers to the workplace"); Hernandez v. Miranda Velez, Civ. No. 92-2701 (JAF), 1994 WL 394855, at *7 (D.P.R. July 20, 1994) (finding employer liability for sexual harassment of a female manager by an official of one of employer's clients), *aff'd,* 132 F.3d 848 (1st Cir. 1998); Magnuson v. Peak Technical Services, Inc., 808 F. Supp. 500 (E.D. Va. 1992) (finding employer liability for sexual harassment of female automobile sales trainer when she visited with customer car dealerships); Powell v. Las Vegas Hilton Corp., 841 F. Supp. 1024 (D. Nev. 1992) (ruling that an employer could be held liable for nonemployee sexual harassment); Llewellyn v. Celanese Corp., 693 F. Supp. 369 (W.D. N.C. 1988) (finding employer liability for nonemployee sexual harassment of a female truck driver involving sexual propositions, sexual touching, and

exposure by male coworkers and one male customer); E.E.O.C. Decision No. 84-3, 1984 WL 23399, at *5, 34 Fair Empl. Prac. Cas. (BNA) 1887 (1984) (ruling on behalf of a waitress on her charge of sexual harassment against her employer based on customer harassment, and explaining that "it is the Commission's position that an employer is responsible under Title VII for the sexual harassment of an employee by a non-employee where the employer fails to take corrective measures within its control once it knows or has reason to know of the non-employee's conduct."); EEOC's Guidelines on Discrimination Because of Sex: Sexual Harassment, 29 C.F.R. § 1604.11(e) (1992) ("An employer may also be responsible for the acts of non-employees, with respect to sexual harassment of employees in the workplace, where the employer (or its agents or supervisory employees) knows or should have known of the conduct and fails to take immediate and appropriate corrective action.").

36. See, e.g., Kelly Ann Cahill, "Hooters: Should There Be an Assumption of Risk Defense to Some Hostile Work Environment Sexual Harassment Claims?" 48 *Vanderbilt Law Review* 1107, 1146–47 (1995); Robert J. Aalberts and Lorne H. Seidman, "Sexual Harassment of Employees by Non-employees: When Does the Employer Become Liable?" 21 *Pepperdine Law Review* 447, 466–67 (1994).

37. *Sage Realty*, 507 F. Supp. at 610–11.

38. According to the court, Sage was not justified in putting Hasselman in a sexually revealing uniform, because sexual titillation was not a bona fide occupational qualification of the position. The court explained: "While it may well be a bfoq for Sage to require female lobby attendants in its buildings to wear certain uniforms designed to present a unique image, in accordance with its philosophy of urban design, it is beyond dispute that the wearing of sexually revealing garments does not constitute a bfoq." *Sage Realty*, 507 F. Supp. at 611.

39. Priest v. Rotary, 634 F. Supp. 571 (N.D. Cal. 1981).

40. *Priest*, 634 F. Supp. at 581. The court continued: "Plaintiff Priest established a prima facie violation of Title VII by demonstrating that defendant Rotary removed her from her full-time, permanent employment as a cocktail lounge waitress because she refused to wear such sexually suggestive dress. Defendant Rotary failed to articulate any legitimate non-discriminatory reason for the imposition of the dress requirement on Ms. Priest." Ibid.

41. E.E.O.C. Decision No. 81-17, 1981 WL 40388, 27 Fair Empl. Prac. Cas. (BNA) 1791 (1981).

42. *E.E.O.C. Decision No. 81-17*, WL 40388 at *3.

43. According to the Commission, "the requirement that [plaintiff] wear revealing attire had the purpose and effect of unreasonably interfering with [plaintiff's] work performance and created an intimidating and offensive working environment." *E.E.O.C. Decision No. 81-17*, WL 40388 at *3.

44. See EEOC, Policy Guidance on Employer Liability under Title VII for Sexual Favoritism (Guidance), N-915.048 (Jan. 12, 1990).

45. Ibid.

46. Ibid.

47. For a description of Hooters' settlement of such cases see "Would-Be Hooters Guy Settles Discrimination Suit," at http://www.onpointnews.com/NEWS/Would-Be-Hooters-Guy-Settles-Discrimination-Suit.html (last visited Mar. 19, 2013).

48. See http://www.hooters.to/usvi/employment.php (last visited Oct. 28, 2014).

49. See Julie Busman, "Short-Shorts at 35,000 Feet," *New York Times*, Mar. 23, 2004, at TR 3.

50. See Brad J. Bushman & Angelica M. Bonacci, "Violence and Sex Impair Memory for Television Ads," 87 *Journal of Applied Psychology* 557 (2002). Bushman and Bonacci studied the effects that watching violent, sexually explicit, or neutral television shows had on individuals' ability to recall the substance of commercials embedded within the shows. Bushman and Bonacci found that memory recall was impaired for individuals watching either violent or sexually explicit shows and suggested that the impairment might be due to the fact that individuals focus more of their attention on violent and sexually explicit shows than they do on neutral shows, and this increased attention decreases the amount of attention they can direct to any other competing message. Bushman & Bonacci, "Violence and Sex," 561.

51. See Sandra Monk Forsythe et al., "Dress as an Influence on the Perceptions of Management Characteristics in Women," 13 *Home Economics Research Journal* 112 (1984); Sandra Forsyth et al., "Influence of Applicant's Dress on Interviewer's Selection Decisions," 70 *Journal of Applied Psychology* 374, 375 (1985). Forsythe and her colleagues had

seventy-seven personnel administrators (80 percent of whom were male) evaluate videotapes of four applicants for a managerial position. The applicants were dressed in outfits that differed in their degree of masculinity and femininity. Participants rated video applicants as being least forceful, self-reliant, dynamic, aggressive, and decisive when they wore the most distinctly feminine dress. Interestingly, though, participants viewed the female candidates as most strongly possessing these traits not when they wore the most masculine outfit but when they wore the second-most masculine outfit. Ibid. at 376. The researchers hypothesized that this occurred because the participants viewed the most masculine outfit as being inappropriate for women and it therefore resulted in lower managerial competency ratings. Ibid. at 377.

52. Peter Glick et al., "Evaluations of Sexy Women in Low- and High-Status Jobs," 29 *Psychology of Women Quarterly* 389 (2005). Glick and his coauthors found that "participants rated the receptionist as equally competent whether she was dressed in a sexy or a neutral manner. In contrast, participants rated the manager as less competent when she dressed in a sexy manner than when she dressed in a conservative manner." Ibid., 393.

53. Regan A. R. Gurung & Carly J. Chrouser, "Predicting Objectification: Do Provocative Clothing and Observer Characteristics Matter?" 57 *Sex Roles* 91 (2007).

54. Gurung & Chrouser, "Predicting Objectification," 95–96.

55. Barbara Fredrickson et al., "That Swimsuit Becomes You: Sex Differences in Self-Objectification, Restrained Eating, and Math Performance," 75 *Journal of Personality & Social Psychology* 269 (1998).

56. It is probably essential that courts carve out this sphere instead of leaving its creation to market forces. First, employers will likely have an incentive to sexualize jobs because male customers will be willing to pay a premium for sexualized services. Women may not have sufficient bargaining power to eliminate these jobs by driving up the hiring costs to such a degree that they are no longer profitable. Second, even if women had sufficient bargaining power to eliminate these jobs, they might choose not to. Women might believe that the pay premium attached to these jobs is sufficient to cover the value of their lost intellectual development, or they may believe that for them sexual and intellectual development are indeed compatible. It is therefore unlikely that the

market itself would carve out this kind of sex-free zone without judicial interference. Courts, though, are properly guided by social concerns other than profit maximization, and courts may be in a better position than even women themselves to weigh the social costs of women's lost intellectual development.

57. See Alexander W. Astin, *Four Critical Years: Effects of College on Beliefs, Attitudes and Knowledge* (San Francisco: Jossey Bass, 1977), 232–33 (arguing that single-sex colleges are likely to lead to higher academic and professional aspirations but not necessarily to higher academic achievement); Valerie E. Lee & H. M. Marks, "Sustained Effects of the Single-Sex Secondary School: Experience on Attitudes, Behaviors and Value in College," 82 *Journal of Educational Psychology*, 578 (1990) (study of students in seventy-five Catholic high schools finding that single-sex schools result in advantages to girls in terms of attitudes and behavior toward academics); Cornelius H. Riordan, *Girls and Boys in School: Together or Separate?* (New York: Teachers College Press, 1990), 95, table 5.2 (finding that girls in single-sex schools outscore girls in coed schools on general academic ability tests, with the most notable differences on science tests); Ed Cairns, "The Relationship Between Adolescent Perceived Self-Competence and Attendance at Single-Sex Secondary School," 60 *British Journal of Educational Psychology*, 207, 210 (1990) (concluding, based on a study of 2,890 sixteen-year-olds in their last year of compulsory education in Northern Ireland, that "being a pupil at a single-sex school may contribute to an increased sense of cognitive competence and a more inner-oriented locus of control"); Valerie E. Lee & Anthony S. Bryk, "Effects of Single-Sex Secondary Schools on Student Achievement and Attitudes," 78 *Journal of Educational Psychology*, 381 (1986) (showing that single-sex schools perform better than coed schools in terms of student academic achievement, faculty-student interaction, intellectual self-esteem, and all aspects of a student's experience except for social life). *But see*, American Association of University Women (AAUW), *Separated by Sex: A Critical Look at Single-Sex Education for Girls*, ed. Susan Morse (Washington, DC: AAUW, 1998), 22 (asserting that studies on single-sex classes have not shown improved achievement among girls); Herbert W. Marsh, "Effects of Attending Single-Sex and Coeducational High Schools on Achievement, Attitudes, Behaviors, and Sex Differences," 81 *Journal of Educational Psychology*, 70 (1989) (noting

that some of the seeming benefits of single-sex schools may be attributed to the fact that these private schools are likely to be more competitive than public schools).

58. See AAUW, *Separated by Sex*, 34 n.219 (noting that studies show that "girls in single-sex schools may draw greater confidence from academic competence, whereas girls in mixed-sex contexts draw more esteem from physical appearance"); Kristin S. Caplice, "The Case for Public Single-Sex Education," 18 *Harvard Journal of Law & Public Policy* 227, 242 (1994–95) (arguing that single-sex schools have advantages for girls because the single-sex environment frees girls to focus on their academic achievement rather than on their sexual attractiveness).

59. See Liz Vivanco, "New Charter School Is for Girls Only," *Chicago Sun-Times*, Aug. 22, 2000, at 6 (quoting a fourteen-year-old student at a Chicago charter school for girls explaining the distraction sexuality poses to girls in school: " 'When you're in high school with boys, it's a distraction. Girls try to look good instead of trying to do well in school' "). Similarly, in his dissent in *Mississippi University for Women v. Hogan*, Justice Powell expressed his belief that students' focus on their sexual development necessarily detracts from their focus on their intellectual development in school. Powell opined that a single-sex school "can free its students of the burden of playing the mating game while attending classes, thus giving academic rather than sexual emphasis." 458 U.S. 718, 739 n.5 (1982) (Powell, J., dissenting).

60. Barbara L. Fredrickson & Tomi-Ann Roberts, "Objectification Theory: Toward Understanding Women's Lived Experiences and Mental Health Risks," 21 *Psychology of Women Quarterly*, 173, 173–206 (1997). According to Fredrickson and Roberts, a woman is sexually objectified "whenever a woman's body, body parts, or sexual functions are separated out from her person, reduced to the status of mere instruments, or regarded as if they were capable of representing her. In other words, when objectified, women are treated as bodies—and in particular, as bodies that exist for the use and pleasure of others." Ibid., 175 (citation omitted).

61. Fredrickson & Roberts, "Objectification Theory," 177.

62. Fredrickson & Roberts, "Objectification Theory," 177.

63. Fredrickson & Roberts, "Objectification Theory," 177.

64. Fredrickson & Roberts, "Objectification Theory," 180, 184.

65. Fredrickson et al., "That Swimsuit Becomes You: Sex Differences in Self-Objectification, Restrained Eating, and Math Performance," 75 *Journal of Personality and Social Psychology* 269 (July 1998).

66. Fredrickson et al., "That Swimsuit Becomes You," 269.

67. Fredrickson et al., "That Swimsuit Becomes You," 269–71. The researchers describe self-objectification as a preoccupation with physical appearance.

68. Body shame was measured based on participants' degree of endorsement of such statements as "I wish I were invisible," "I feel like covering my body," and "I wish I could disappear," and on participants' ratings of how much they would like to change specific attributes of their bodies. Fredrickson et al., "That Swimsuit Becomes You," 273.

69. Fredrickson et al., "That Swimsuit Becomes You," 279.

70. Fredrickson et al., "That Swimsuit Becomes You," 280.

71. Michelle R. Hebl et al., "The Swimsuit Becomes Us All: Ethnicity, Gender, and Vulnerability to Self-Objectification," 30 *Personality & Social Psychology Bulletin*, 1322 (2004).

72. Hebl et al., "The Swimsuit Becomes Us All," 1324.

73. Hebl et al., "The Swimsuit Becomes Us All," 1329 ("All participants tended to perform worse when they were in a self-objectifying situation than when they were in the control condition."). The researchers also found a general increase in body shame among women and men in the swimsuit as opposed to the sweater. Ibid., 1327.

74. Diane M. Quinn et al., "The Disruptive Effect of Self-Objectification on Performance," 30 *Psychology of Women Quarterly*, 59 (2006).

75. Quinn et al., "The Disruptive Effect of Self-Objectification," 59. Moreover, the researchers found no racial and ethnic differences. All women were similarly affected by a state of self-objectification. Ibid., 62.

76. Hajo Adam & Adam D. Galinsky, "Enclothed Cognition," 48 *Journal of Experimental Social Psychology*, 918 (2012).

77. Adam & Galinsky, "Enclothed Cognition," 922.

78. See generally Barbara Ehrenreich, *Nickel and Dimed: On (Not) Getting By in America* (New York: Metropolitan Books/Henry Holt, 2001) (describing the pride many low-wage workers take in performing the craft aspects of their work well).

CHAPTER 6. EXPRESSIVE FREEDOM

1. See generally Katharine T. Bartlett, "Only Girls Wear Barrettes: Dress and Appearance Standards, Community Norms, and Workplace Equality," 92 *Michigan Law Review* 2541, 2543–44 (1994) (describing and explaining courts' frequent allowance of substantially different dress and appearance standards for female and male employees); Mary Anne Case, "Disaggregating Gender from Sex and Sexual Orientation: The Effeminate Man in the Law and Feminist Jurisprudence," 105 *Yale Law Journal* 1, 66–68 (1995) (arguing that sex-specific dress codes constitute sex discrimination under Title VII); Karen Engle, "The Persistence of Neutrality: The Failure of the Religious Accommodation Provision to Redeem Title VII," 76 *Texas Law Review* 317, 340 (1997) ("Courts have found that it is legal for employers to rely on what they see as dominant societal rules about how men and women should dress. Although courts have long held that Title VII prohibits employers from relying on stereotypes about men and women, courts in these cases overtly and unapologetically have allowed them to do just that."). With regard to race see generally Kenji Yoshino, *Covering: The Hidden Assault on Our Civil Rights* (New York: Random House, 2006), 131 (describing the racial covering demands imposed on minority workers in order to conform to white assimilationist workplace norms); Devon W. Carbado & Mitu Gulati, "Working Identity," 85 *Cornell Law Review* 1259, 1262, 1294 (2000) (describing the "identity work" that minority employees must do to comply with white cultural workplace norms); Barbara Flagg, "Fashioning a Title VII Remedy for Transparently White Subjective Decisionmaking," 104 *Yale Law Journal* 2009, 2029 (1995) (describing as "transparently white decisionmaking" the process by which employers define workplace rules and expectations according to white cultural norms); Tristin K. Green, "Work Culture and Discrimination," 93 *California Law Review* 623, 646 (2005) (questioning why workplace cultures "define acceptable and favored behavior along a white, male norm"); Camille Gear Rich, "Performing Racial and Ethnic Identity: Discrimination by Proxy and the Future of Title VII," 79 *New York University Law Review* 1134, 1194–95 (2004) (describing employer's shift from facially discriminatory policies to facially neutral ones that prohibit racially associated behaviors and attributes).

2. See, e.g., Devon Carbado, Mitu Gulati, & Gowri Ramachandran, "The Jespersen Story: Makeup and Women at Work," in *Employment*

Discrimination Stories, ed. Joel Wm. Friedman (New York: Foundation Press, 2006) 105, 132; Julie A. Greenberg, "The Gender Nonconformity Theory: A Comprehensive Approach to Break Down the Maternal Wall and End Discrimination against Gender Benders," 26 *Thomas Jefferson Law Review* 37 (2003); Colleen Keating, "Extending Title VII Protection to Non-Gender-Conforming Men," 4 *Modern American* 82 (2008).

3. Dylan Vade, "Expanding Gender and Expanding the Law: Toward a Social and Legal Conceptualization of Gender That Is More Inclusive of Transgender People," 11 *Michigan Journal of Gender & Law* 253, 264 (2005).

4. Franklin H. Romeo, "Beyond a Medical Model: Advocating for a New Conception of Gender Identity in the Law," 36 *Columbia Human Rights Law Review* 713, 753 (2005).

5. See Thomas Ling, "Smith v. City of Salem: Title VII Protects Contra-Gender Behavior," 40 *Harvard Civil Rights–Civil Liberties Law Review* 277, 285 (2005).

6. Johnny Lo, "Smith v. City of Salem, Ohio, 378 F.3d 566 (6th Cir. 2004)," 11 *Washington & Lee Race & Ethnic Ancestry Law Journal* 277, 282 (2005).

7. See, e.g., Tavora v. N.Y. Mercantile Exchange, 101 F.3d 907, 908 (2d Cir. 1996) (holding that a male employee fired for not complying with his employer's short-hair requirement for men could not state a claim for sex discrimination); Barker v. Taft Broadcasting Co., 549 F.2d 400, 401 (6th Cir. 1977); Longo v. Carlisle DeCoppet & Co., 537 F.2d 685, 685 (2d Cir. 1976) (holding that "requiring short hair on men and not on women does not violate Title VII"); Earwood v. Continental Southeastern Lines, Inc., 539 F.2d 1349, 1351 (4th Cir. 1976); Knott v. Missouri Pacific Railroad Co., 527 F.2d 1249, 1252 (8th Cir. 1975); Willingham v. Macon Telegraph Publishing Co., 507 F.2d 1084, 1091–92 (5th Cir. 1975); Baker v. California Land Title Co., 507 F.2d 895, 898 (9th Cir. 1974); Dodge v. Giant Food, Inc., 488 F.2d 1333, 1337 (D.C. Cir. 1973).

8. See, e.g., Kleinsorge v. Eyeland Corp., No. CIV. A. 99-5025, 2000 WL 124559, at *2 (E.D. Pa., Jan. 31, 2000) (holding that a grooming code allowing female but not male employees to wear earrings did not violate Title VII); Capaldo v. Pan American Federal Credit Union, No. 86 CV 1944, 1987 WL 9687, at *2 (E.D. N.Y., Mar. 30, 1987) (holding that a grooming code prohibiting men but not women from

wearing earrings did not constitute sex discrimination); Pecenka v. Fareway Stores, Inc., 672 N.W.2d 800, 804 (Iowa 2003) (holding in response to a sex discrimination claim brought by a male employee who was fired for refusing to stop wearing an earring that "personal grooming codes that reflect customary modes" of distinctly gendered grooming do not constitute sex discrimination); Macissac v. Remington Hospitality, Inc., No. 03-P-1015, 2004 WL 1541807, at *2 (Mass. App. Ct., July 9, 2004) (holding that enforcement of a grooming code prohibiting male but not female employees from wearing earrings did not constitute sex discrimination); Lockhart v. Louisiana-Pacific Corp., 795 P.2d 602, 604 (Or. Ct. App. 1990) (holding that a grooming code prohibiting male but not female employees from wearing facial jewelry did not constitute sex discrimination). See also Jespersen v. Harrah's Operating Co., 444 F.3d 1104, 1103 (9th Cir. 2006) (en banc).

9. Nichols v. Azteca Restaurant Enterprises, Inc., 256 F.3d 864, 874–75 (9th Cir. 2001).

10. *Nichols*, 256 F.3d at 875 n.7.

11. As Lucinda Finley asked more than twenty years ago: "Rather than blaming women and their nature for their underrepresentation in the high paying jobs, why not reexamine the jobs and their values?" Lucinda M. Finley, "Choice and Freedom: Elusive Issues in the Search for Gender Justice," 96 *Yale Law Journal* 914, 939 (1987) (reviewing David L. Kirp, Mark G. Yudof, and Marlene Strong Franks, *Gender Justice* (Chicago: University of Chicago Press, 1986)). See also Kathryn Abrams, "Gender Discrimination and the Transformation of Workplace Norms," 42 *Vanderbilt Law Review* 1183, 1223–25 (1989) ("If women with children are to attain equality in the workplace, then we must challenge the notion of a natural or pre-ordained line dividing work and family. . . . Employers will have to determine which jobs or tasks can be shared or accomplished through flexible scheduling, granting fringe benefits to part-time workers, and re-educate clients to greater confidence in the new arrangements."); Laura T. Kessler, "The Attachment Gap: Employment Discrimination Law; Women's Cultural Caregiving, and the Limits of Economic and Liberal Legal Theory," 34 *University of Michigan Journal of Law Reform* 371, 372–73 (2001) ("Women, more so than men, perform the unpaid family caregiving work within our society. . . . The American workplace and discrimination laws governing

employment have yet to address seriously this profound existential difference between men and women with regard to caregiving, despite women's substantial presence in the paid labor force for more than two decades."); Case, "Disaggregating Gender from Sex and Sexual Orientation," 4 ("Discrimination against the feminine is likely to have a disparate impact on women, who are disproportionately likely to be feminine and not masculine; it should be permitted only if job-related and justified by business necessity.").

12. See Abrams, "Gender Discrimination and the Transformation of Workplace Norms," 223–25; Kessler, "The Attachment Gap," 372–73.

13. Case, "Disaggregating Gender from Sex and Sexual Orientation," 4.

14. EEOC v. Sears, Roebuck & Co., 628 F. Supp. 1264 (N.D. Ill. 1986).

15. *Sears, Roebuck & Co.*, 628 F. Supp. at 1295.

16. *Sears, Roebuck & Co.*, 628 F. Supp. at 1290.

17. *Sears, Roebuck & Co.*, 628 F. Supp. at 1290. In addition, Sears gave most candidates a test that asked such questions as: "Do you have a low pitched voice?" "Do you swear often?" "Have you played on a football team?" Ibid. at 1300 n.29.

18. *Sears, Roebuck & Co.*, 628 F. Supp. at 1324.

19. Wislocki-Goin v. Mears, 831 F.2d 1374, 1376–77 (7th Cir. 1987).

20. *Wislocki-Goin*, 831 F.2d at 1379–80.

21. Case, "Disaggregating Gender from Sex and Sexual Orientation," 3.

22. Chi v. Age Group, Ltd, No. 94 CIV. 5253 (AGS), 1996 WL 627580 (S.D. N.Y., Oct. 29, 1996).

23. *Chi*, 1996 WL 627580, at *5.

24. Kessler, "The Attachment Gap," 404.

25. See *Smith*, 378 F.3d at 571 (asserting that *Price Waterhouse* "held that Title VII's prohibition of discrimination 'because of . . . sex' bars gender discrimination"); Balance v. City of Springfield, 424 F.3d 614, 617 (7th Cir. 2005) ("Title VII prohibits employers from discriminating against employees on the basis of sex or gender").

26. See 100 *Cong. Rec.* 7213 (1964) (explaining the limitations of Title VII to prohibit difference in treatment or favor based on race, color, religion, sex, and national origin and noting that employers' use

of other criteria or qualifications for employment is not affected). See also Hill v. St. Louis University, 123 F.3d 1114, 1120 (8th Cir. 1997) ("[The ADEA and Title VII] serve the narrow purpose of prohibiting discrimination based on certain, discreet [*sic*] classifications such as age, gender, or race. These statutes do not prohibit employment decisions based upon poor job performance, erroneous evaluations, personal conflicts between employees, or even unsound business practices.")

27. See, e.g., Juan Perea, "Ethnicity and Prejudice: Reevaluating 'National Origin' Discrimination under Title VII," 35 *William & Mary Law Review* 805, 833 (1994) (proposing that Title VII protect against discrimination based on ethnicity meaning protection of the "physical and cultural characteristics that make a social group distinctive, either in group members' eyes or in the view of outsiders"); Gowri Ramachandran, "Freedom of Dress: State and Private Regulation of Clothing, Hairstyle, Jewelry, Makeup, Tattoos, and Piercings," 66 *Maryland Law Review* 11, 19 (2006) ("Personal appearance choices play a unique and crucial role in the development and revision of a simultaneously public and personal identity . . . [and the] law can create a zone in which to better empower individuals to form and reform identity promoting a dynamic rather than static culture and society.").

28. For a discussion of different definitions of the antidiscrimination norm, see Mark Kelman, "Defining the Antidiscrimination Norm to Defend It," 43 *San Diego Law Review* 735, 736 (2006).

29. For instances in which sex is job relevant, see Kimberly A. Yuracko, "Private Nurses and Playboy Bunnies: Explaining Permissible Sex Discrimination," 92 *California Law Review* 147 (2004).

30. See Arlie Russell Hochschild, *The Managed Heart: Commercialization of Human Feelings* (Berkeley: University of California Press, 1983), 8 ("For the flight attendant, the smiles are a *part of her work*."); Jennifer L. Pierce, *Gender Trials: Emotional Lives in Contemporary Law Firms* (Berkeley: University of California Press, 1995), 52 ("Flight attendants' friendliness takes the form of deference: their relationship to passengers is supporting and subordinate.").

31. See Jim Allan, "Male Elementary Teachers: Experiences and Perspectives," in *Doing "Women's Work": Men in Nontraditional Occupations*, ed. Christine L. Williams (Thousand Oaks, CA: Sage Publications, 1993), 123–26.

32. See Allan, "Male Elementary Teachers," 119.

33. See Pierce, *Gender Trials*, 86.

34. See Pierce, *Gender Trials*, 2. As Pierce describes, the lawyers in her study "boast about 'destroying witnesses,' 'playing hard-ball,' and 'taking no prisoners' and about the size and amount of their 'win.'" Ibid. at 60.

35. See Hochschild, *The Managed Heart*, 1146 (indicating that "open aggression was the official policy for wringing money out of debtors").

36. See Christine L. Williams, *Gender Differences at Work: Women and Men in Nontraditional Occupations* (Berkeley: University of California Press, 1989), 1.

37. Rosemary Pringle, "Male Secretaries," in *Doing "Women's Work": Men in Nontraditional Occupations*, ed. Christine L. Williams (Thousand Oaks, CA: Sage Publications, 1993), 133 (describing how secretaries came to be defined in the twentieth century in "familial and sexual terms"). See also Rosabeth Moss Kanter, *Men and Women of the Corporation* (New York: Basic Books, 1977), 69 ("The secretarial job involved the most routine of tasks in the white-collar world, yet the most personal of relationships.").

38. Such preclusion was primarily by gender—the requirement of feminine deference weeding out the more traditionally masculine—and only to a lesser degree by sex—to the extent that sexual titillation was also being demanded.

39. It certainly may be, however, that the gendered aspects of the role are reaction qualifications rather than technical qualifications. See Alan Wertheimer, "Jobs, Qualifications, and Preferences," 94 *Ethics* 99, 100 (1983) (explaining that "reaction qualifications refer to those abilities or characteristics which contribute to job effectiveness by causing or serving as the basis of the appropriate reaction in the recipients. Technical qualifications refer to all other qualifications (of an ordinary sort)"). It may be, in other words, that being soft of voice and touch is important for elementary school teachers only because of the positive response such treatment elicits from young subjects. Yet for teachers of young children, being able to elicit happy and positive student reactions may be the most important qualification for the job.

CHAPTER 7. THE RACE PARADOX

1. Price Waterhouse v. Hopkins, 490 U.S. 228 (1989).

2. Title VII includes an exception to its general antidiscrimination mandate, which permits discrimination on the basis of religion, sex, or national origin in "instances where religion, sex, or national origin is a bona fide occupational qualification [(BFOQ)] reasonably necessary to the normal operation of that particular business or enterprise." 42 U.S.C. § 2000e-2(e)(1). Title VII does not include a BFOQ exception for race. Moreover, while race receives strict scrutiny under the Equal Protection Clause, sex receives the lower intermediate scrutiny. See United States v. Virginia, 518 U.S. 515, 533 (1996) (noting that strict scrutiny has not been extended to a classification other than race or national origin).

3. Barbara Flagg, "Fashioning a Title VII Remedy for Transparently White Subjective Decisionmaking," 104 *Yale Law Journal* 2009, 2029 (1995).

4. Flagg, "Fashioning a Title VII Remedy," 2013–15.

5. Juan Perea, "Ethnicity and Prejudice: Reevaluating 'National Origin' Discrimination under Title VII," 35 *William & Mary Law Review* 805, 833, 839 (1994).

6. Perea, "Ethnicity and Prejudice," 839.

7. Perea, "Ethnicity and Prejudice," 833. Perea describes such characteristics as including, but not limited to, "race, national origin, ancestry, language, religion, shared history, traditions, values, and symbols, all of which contribute to a sense of distinctiveness among members of the group." Ibid. *See also* Christopher David Ruiz Cameron, "How the García Cousins Lost Their Accents: Understanding the Language of Title VII Decisions Approving English-Only Rules as the Product of Rational Dualism, Latino Invisibility, and Legal Indeterminacy," 85 *California Law Review* 1347, 1367–72 (1997) (arguing that courts fail to treat Spanish-language discrimination as national origin discrimination because they do not appreciate the centrality of Spanish language in constructing a Latino identity); Drucilla Cornell & William W. Bratton, "Deadweight Costs and Intrinsic Wrongs of Nativism: Economics, Freedom, and Legal Suppression of Spanish," 84 *Cornell Law Review* 595, 604 (1999) (arguing that Title VII should be extended to prohibit workplace rules that penalize employees for speaking a language other than English because "the legal system should treat language as a fundamental identification encompassed by each

person's right of personhood"); Cristina M. Rodriguez, "Language Diversity in the Workplace," 100 *Northwestern University Law Review* 1689, 1694 (2006) (arguing for a presumption of invalidity of English-only rules in the workplace).

8. Perea, "Ethnicity and Prejudice," 833.

9. Richard T. Ford, *Racial Culture: A Critique* (Princeton: Princeton University Press, 2005), 185–86.

10. See Richard T. Ford, "Beyond 'Difference': A Reluctant Critique of Legal Identity Politics," in *Left Legalism/Left Critique*, ed. Wendy Brown & Janet Halley (Durham, N.C.: Duke University Press, 2002), 55–56.

11. See generally John J. Donohue, "The Law and Economics of Antidiscrimination Law," in *Handbook of Law and Economics*, ed. A. M. Polinsky and Steven Shavell (London: Elsevier, 2007); John J. Donohue III & James Heckman, "Continuous versus Episodic Change: The Impact of Civil Rights Policy on the Economic Status of Blacks," 29 *Journal of Economics and Literature* 1603 (1991).

12. Rogers v. American Airlines, Inc., 527 F. Supp. 229 (S.D. N.Y. 1981).

13. *Rogers*, 527 F. Supp. at 231.

14. Garcia v. Spun Steak Co., 998 F.2d 1480 (9th Cir. 1993).

15. *Spun Steak Co.*, 998 F.2d at 1484.

16. Griggs v. Duke Power Co., 401 U.S. 424, 426–28 (1971).

17. *Rogers*, 527 F. Supp. at 232.

18. *Spun Steak Co.*, 998 F.2d at 1480.

19. *Spun Steak Co.*, 998 F.2d at 1488.

20. See Devon W. Carbado & Mitu Gulati, "The Fifth Black Woman," 11 *Journal of Contemporary Legal Issues* 701, 717–18 (2001) (describing how racially loaded workplace norms may disadvantage minority employees); Devon W. Carbado & Mitu Gulati, "Working Identity," 85 *Cornell Law Review* 1259, 1269–70 (2000) (explaining that minority workers must do extra work to overcome expectations of a poor fit).

21. See generally Kenji Yoshino, *Covering: The Hidden Assault on Our Civil Rights* (New York: Random House, 2006), 131 (describing the racial covering demands imposed on minority workers in order to conform to white assimilationist workplace norms); Carbado and Gulati, "Working Identity," 1262, 1294 (describing the "identity work" that

minority employees must do to comply with white cultural workplace norms); Flagg, "Fashioning a Title VII Remedy," 2029 (describing as "transparently white decisionmaking" the process by which employers define workplace rules and expectations according to white cultural norms); Tristin K. Green, "Work Culture and Discrimination," 93 *California Law Review* 623, 646 (2005) (questioning why workplace cultures "define acceptable and favored behavior along a white, male norm"); Camille Gear Rich, "Performing Racial and Ethnic Identity: Discrimination by Proxy and the Future of Title VII," 79 *New York University Law Review* 1134, 1194–95 (2004) (describing employers' shift from facially discriminatory policies to facially neutral ones that prohibit racially associated behaviors and attributes).

22. See Charles R. Lawrence III, "The Id, the Ego, and Equal Protection: Reckoning with Unconscious Racism," 39 *Stanford Law Review* 317, 342, 356–57 (1987).

23. *Rogers*, 527 F. Supp. at 232. The *Rogers* court has not been alone in its thinking that a no-Afro/bush hair policy would be contrary to the nondiscrimination demands of Title VII. See E.E.O.C. Decision No. 72-979, 1972 WL 3999, at *1, 4 Fair Empl. Prac. Cas. (BNA) 840 (1972) (holding that employer's no-Afro/bush hair policy could not survive challenge under the disparate impact doctrine unless it could be justified by business necessity, because such hairstyles are worn "sometimes as an appropriate expression of [their] heritage, culture and racial pride as black [men]" (internal quotation omitted)); E.E.O.C. Decision No. 71-2444, 1971 WL 3898, at *1, 4 Fair Empl. Prac. Cas. (BNA) 18 (1971) (ruling in plaintiff's challenge to employer's no "bushy" hair requirement that even if the employer had applied the policy consistently against white and black workers, which it had not, the policy would constitute impermissible race discrimination because "the wearing of an Afro-American hair style by a Negro has been so appropriated as a cultural symbol by members of the Negro race as to make its suppression either an automatic badge of racial prejudice or a necessary abridgment of First Amendment rights").

24. Garcia v. Gloor, 618 F.2d 264 (5th Cir. 1980).

25. *Gloor*, 618 F.2d at 270.

26. See Hopkins v. Price Waterhouse, 618 F. Supp. 1109, 1117–19 (D.D.C. 1985).

27. They would be actionable not only because of their subordinating effect but also because race-specific demands, unlike sex-specific demands, are always illegal—formal neutrality being a real requirement in the race context. See, e.g., Amy L. Wax, "The Discriminating Mind: Define It, Prove It," 40 *Connecticut Law Review* 979, 982–83 (2008) (noting that "if a person treats someone differently—and adversely—because of that person's race, then that would violate the plain terms of Title VI").

28. See, e.g., Arlie Russell Hochschild, *The Managed Heart: Commercialization of Human Feelings* (Berkeley: University of California Press, 1983), 8 (explaining that "for the flight attendant, the smiles are a *part of her work*"); Jennifer L. Pierce, *Gender Trials: Emotional Lives in Contemporary Law Firms* (Berkeley: University of California Press, 1995), 114 (noting that "women lawyers are placed in a constant double bind between the requirements of the role of the 'good woman' and the role of the adversary"); Rosemary Pringle, "Male Secretaries," in *Doing "Women's Work": Men in Nontraditional Occupations*, ed. Christine L. Williams (Thousand Oaks, CA: Sage Publications, 1993), 132–33 (describing how secretaries came to be defined in the twentieth century in "family and sexual terms"); Peter Glick et al., "Evaluations of Sexy Women in Low- and High-Status Jobs," 29 *Psychology of Women Quarterly* 389, 392–93 (2005) (finding that sexy dressing diminished perceptions of competence for women in traditionally male but not traditionally female occupations).

29. As the court explained in Richardson v. Quik Trip Corp.: "Pseudofolliculitis barbae . . . is a facial skin condition that afflicts certain persons with curly or kinky hair follicles. After shaving, the curved hair follicles cause the already curly hair to curve back into contact with the skin surface, and pierce and re-enter the skin, forming a pseudofollicle. The pseudofollicle becomes inflamed, and painful papules and pustules result. In severe cases, abscesses develop around the pseudofollicles and, if untreated, cause scarring, hyperpigmentation, and disfigurement." 591 F. Supp. 1151, 1153–54 (S.D. Iowa 1984); see also University of Maryland at Baltimore v. Boyd, 612 A.2d 305, 311 (Md. Ct. Spec. App. 1992) (referring to expert testimony in the record that PFB makes shaving very uncomfortable). PFB affects a significant proportion of black men and affects almost exclusively black men. See *Richardson*, 591 F. Supp. at

1154 ("PFB is an immutable condition that, with few exceptions, afflicts only male blacks."); EEOC v. Trailways, Inc., 530 F. Supp. 54, 56 (D. Colo. 1981) ("Of the total black male population, 25% are unable to shave regularly without serious, painful disorders of the skin of the face."); *Boyd*, 612 A.2d at 311 ("PFB is predominately found in the African American male population and . . . the wearing of a beard is the most common cure.").

30. The fact that the burden imposed is both physical and race related is critical to the success of these claims. See Woods v. Safeway Stores, Inc., 420 F. Supp. 35, 42 (E.D. Va. 1976) (noting that "[t]he evidence adduced in the instant case does establish that the 'no beard' policy can act to disqualify an otherwise qualified black from employment solely on the basis of a genetic characteristic peculiar to his race").

31. *Richardson*, 591 F. Supp. at 1152.

32. *Richardson*, 591 F. Supp. at 1155.

33. *Boyd*, 612 A.2d at 307. The plaintiff in *Boyd* filed his claim under Maryland state law, though, as the court notes, Maryland's relevant antidiscrimination statute "is modeled on Title VII of the Civil Rights Act of 1964." Ibid. at 311 (internal quotation marks and citation omitted).

34. *Boyd*, 612 A.2d at 311 (noting that "[e]xpert witnesses testified that the symptoms of PFB, skin irritation, pus and blood filled sores, and scarring, are brought on by shaving and that some sufferers of PFB must abstain from shaving"). The court further noted that the Maryland Commission on Human Relations found that "Mr. Boyd's PFB condition impaired his appearance, scarred his face and created an externally visible disfigurement unless he wore a beard." Ibid. at 312 (internal quotation marks omitted). Moreover, the court concluded that "there is substantial evidence to prove that the severity of Mr. Boyd's PFB condition significantly impairs his ability to socialize, considered to be a major life activity, and, therefore, is physically handicapping to him." Ibid. at 313. Although the court discussed this particular evidence in the part of the case addressing the plaintiff's disability discrimination claim rather than his race discrimination claim it seems likely that the evidence also influenced the court's analysis of the plaintiff's race discrimination claim.

35. As a doctrinal matter, courts ground their protection for PFB plaintiffs in a disparate impact framework rather than in the disparate treatment framework used to protect effeminate men and transsexuals

in the sex context. It would be a mistake, however, to conclude that this different doctrinal framework, rather than the same substantive concern with status discrimination, is driving the results. In fact, courts stretch traditional disparate impact doctrine considerably in order to find for plaintiffs in these cases. First, courts allow plaintiffs to establish their prima facie case by pointing to general population data rather than to qualified labor pool data. In other words, instead of showing the proportion of blacks and whites in the relevant qualified labor pool who are harmed by the hiring requirement, plaintiffs present only the more general evidence of the proportion of blacks and whites in the population at large who would be harmed by the hiring requirement. See *Boyd*, 612 A.2d at 311 (finding disparate impact from no-beard policy by looking at general population data regarding PFB); Johnson v. Memphis Police Dept., 713 F. Supp. 244, 247 (W.D. Tenn. 1989) (finding disparate impact based on general population data of race-based impact of PFB and noting that "there is no way of determining how many, if any, black officers failed to apply or left the Department because they had folliculitis"); *Trailways*, 530 F. Supp. at 56–59 (finding prima facie case of disparate impact by looking at general population data and noting that "it is scientifically proven that PFB is a disease unique or at least almost unique to blacks"). Second, and more important, courts allow plaintiffs to establish a disparate impact without any evidence, and indeed despite contrary evidence, that the hiring requirement is leading to a lower proportion of blacks in the relevant position than would be expected absent the challenged criteria. See *Boyd*, 619 A.2d at 311 (finding disparate impact despite defendant's argument that "the evidence did not prove that the University's policy has affected any African American male other than Mr. Boyd" and defendant's argument that "the University employment statistics show that the University employs a higher percentage of African Americans than is found in the labor pool or in other similar agency positions"); *Trailways*, 530 F. Supp. at 56 (rejecting defendant's argument that plaintiff failed to make a prima facie case of disparate impact because the defendant's "employment of black drivers and other public contact employees exceeds percentagewise the overall Denver or Colorado population percentage of blacks").

36. Bradley v. Pizzaco of Nebraska, 7 F.3d 795, 796 (8th Cir. 1993).

37. *Bradley*, 7 F.3d at 796.

38. *Bradley,* 7 F.3d at 796.

39. The court "remand[ed] to the District Court for entry of an injunction granting the EEOC the narrow prospective relief it seeks. The injunction shall be carefully tailored to place Domino's under the minimal burden of recognizing a limited exception to its no-beard policy for African American males who suffer from PFB and as a result of this medical condition are unable to shave." *Bradley,* 7 F.3d at 799.

40. *Bradley,* 7 F.3d at 796. The court "affirmed the District Court's finding that Bradley suffers only a mild case of PFB and can appear clean-shaven as not clearly erroneous. Bradley thus was not entitled to relief and is no longer a party to the litigation." Ibid.

41. Not surprisingly, courts also view compliance costs as low when noncompliance is due to a sense of racial or personal identity rather than physical pain. Employees do not have success challenging employers' no-beard policies when the challenge is grounded in a personal preference rather than a physical need. See, e.g., Wofford v. Safeway Stores, Inc., 78 F.R.D. 460, 469 (N.D. Cal. 1978) (holding that a no-beard policy was not racially discriminatory when applied to an employee whose beard was an important part of his racial identity); Keys v. Continental Illinois National Bank and Trust Company of Chicago, 357 F. Supp. 376, 380 (N.D. Ill. 1973) (same); In re Pacific Southwest Airlines and Southwest Flight Crew Association, 77 LA (BNA) 320, 1981 WL 27140 (Lab. Arb. Rep., July 31, 1981) (Jones, Jr., Arb.) (holding that employer could enforce its no-beard policy against a pilot who "had become rather attached to [his] beard" and did not want to shave it).

42. *Rogers,* 527 F. Supp. at 233.

43. *Spun Steak Co.,* 998 F.2d at 1487–88.

44. See Gary Peller, "Race Consciousness," 1990 *Duke Law Journal* 758, 823 (1990) (explaining that "the clash between nationalism and integrationism extended from the period starting in 1966—when the 'Black Power' slogan first gained national prominence—and lasted until the marginalization of black nationalists was complete in the mid-1970s").

45. See Peller, "Race Consciousness," 771.

46. Peller, "Race Consciousness," 792 (explaining that "the idea of race as the organizing basis for group consciousness asserts that blacks and whites are different, in the sense of coming from different

communities, neighborhoods, churches, families, and histories, and of being in various ways foreigners to each other").

47. Peller, "Race Consciousness," 789.

48. Peller, "Race Consciousness," 791, 797.

49. See Ford, *Racial Culture,* 33 (observing that "opposition to integration in the name of tradition and racial difference, while a competing position of the 'nationalist' left, was also and most notably the position of the racist right"); Peller, "Race Consciousness," 761 (explaining that "most white liberals and progressives, protecting themselves as the enlightened avant garde of the white community, automatically associated race nationalism with the repressive history of white supremacy").

50. Peller, "Race Consciousness," 760.

51. See Ford, *Racial Culture,* 33 (noting that "integration (especially colorblindness and assimilation) became the ideals of the mainstream in the late 1960s and 1970s"); Peller, "Race Consciousness," 790 (describing the "centering of integrationism as the mainstream ideology of American good sense" and the marginalization of nationalism). Certainly the split between integrationist and nationalist ideology was not as simple or stark as my description suggests, nor was the victory of integration over nationalism as complete. A number of policies begun in the civil rights era refute any rigid commitment to colorblindness and reflect the country's continued race consciousness. See Andrew Kull, *The Color-Blind Constitution* (Cambridge, MA: Harvard University Press, 1992), 190 (describing race balancing of public schools, affirmative action policies in business, and race-based voting rights legislation).

52. *Rogers,* 527 F. Supp. at 232.

53. *Rogers,* 527 F. Supp. at 232 (citation and internal quotation marks omitted).

54. *Rogers,* 527 F. Supp. at 232; see also McBride v. Lawstaf, Inc., No. 1:96-cv-0196-cc, 1996 WL 755779, at *1–2 (N.D. Ga., Sept. 19, 1996) (holding that "as a matter of law, an employer's grooming policy prohibiting a braided hair style is not 'an unlawful employment practice' as defined by 42 U.S.C. § 2000e-2"); Carswell v. Peachford Hospital, No. C80-222A, 1981 WL 224, at *2 (N.D. Ga., May 26, 1981) (holding that the employer did not engage in race discrimination when it terminated the plaintiff for wearing to work her hair in braids with beads at the end of each braid).

55. See, e.g., *Wofford*, 78 F.R.D. at 469 (dismissing the race discrimination claim of a male employee who refused to shave his beard, which he claimed was part of his racial identity, by explaining that "where easily changed physical characteristics are made the basis for an individual's racial identity, it is simply not the law that 'an *asserted* racial or cultural identity cannot legally be the basis for denial of employment' "); *Keys*, 357 F. Supp. at 380 (denying Title VII protection to a plaintiff challenging his employer's no-beard rule by arguing that beards and long sideburns were critical to his racial identity).

56. *Spun Steak Co.*, 998 F.2d at 1483.

57. *Spun Steak Co.*, 998 F.2d at 1486–87.

58. *Spun Steak Co.*, 998 F.2d at 1487.

Index

Abrams, Kathryn, 140
Adams, Hajo, 134
addiction, 91–92
affirmative action, 80, 188n1;
  voluntary plans, 198n87
African Americans. *See* race
Afro/bush hairstyle, 158
aggression, gender norms and, 1, 6, 7,
  13–18, 44, 47, 48, 50, 64, 66, 67,
  109, 140, 142, 161
airlines. *See* flight attendants
anticlassification principle, 180n1
antidiscrimination law. *See*
  Title VII
antisubordination, 9, 27, 54–88, 120,
  205n42; BFOQ cases and, 71–78,
  115–16, 119; burden-shifting
  framework and, 96–98; disparate
  treatment and, 87–88; 156, 172;
  double bind and, 64–71; impact of,
  88; race discrimination and, 155–63,
  169; unequal burdens test and,
  56–64, 156–57
appearance: double bind and, 64–65,
  68, 71; female self-objectification
  and, 130, 131–33; nonconformists
  and, 45–46; transsexual legal claim
  and, 208n18; unequal burdens and,
  56–64, 68, 189–90nn9,10; white

middle-class norms and, 138, 157.
  See also dress; grooming codes; hair;
  makeup
ascriptive status, definition of,
  90–91
Austin v. Wal-Mart Stores, Inc.
  (1998), 98
autonomy. *See* self-agency
Avery, Dianne, 65

Backus v. Baptist Medical Center (1982),
  215–16n23
Barnes v. City of Cincinnati (2005),
  22–23, 92–93
bartending, 2, 24–25, 59; feminization
  of, 65–66, 88, 104
bathroom access, 76, 96–98,
  128–29n34, 204n37
beard bans, 58, 60; black PFB
  exemption, 163–64
BFOQ (bona fide occupational
  qualification), 71–87, 115–24, 136,
  230n2; degrading vs. widely shared
  gender norms and, 63, 68–69,
  146–47, 193n48; privacy job
  continuum and, 72–73, 74–76, 84,
  87, 116–17, 193n48; slippery slope
  and, 77, 84, 85, 86–87
Bicentennial uniform, 68, 121

stigmatization and, 61–63; unequal
burdens test and, 57–64, 67, 156,
157; worker challenges to, 1–2,
14–18, 23–26, 104–5, 145
gender stereotypical jobs, 4, 5, 12–18,
28, 77, 82–87, 108–9, 147;
antisubordination impact on, 88;
education and, 93–94, 146–47;
equal access vs., 32; professional
demands and, 64, 65, 67, 159, 160;
reconceptions of, 24–26, 88, 104–5,
139; sales as, 141–42; soft jobs and,
78–79, 82–84; women's
stigmatization and, 62–63. *See also*
BFOQ; plus-sex jobs; workplace fit
demands
General Electric Co. v. Gilbert (1976),
35, 36
Gerdom v. Continental Airlines (1981),
57, 68–69
GID. *See* gender identity disorder
Glick, Peter, 65, 129
Green, Edith, 30, 31
Griggs v. Duke Power Co. (1971), 55,
155, 189nn2,4
grooming codes: burden-shifting and,
96–98; compliance costs of, 164;
court protection of, 6, 44–45,
57–58, 65–66, 104–5, 138–39, 141,
142; employer's business image and,
190–91n21, 192n32; gender bending
and, 51–52, 98, 188n58; race and,
154, 158, 163–64, 165, 167; sex
stereotyping ruling in conflict with,
23–26, 44–46, 48–49, 208n65;
unequal burdens and, 25, 57–60, 68,
190n10. *See also* beard bans; hair;
makeup
group equality, 71–88, 89; disparate
treatment and, 56, 172; expressive
rights and, 139–43, 149, 167–68
*Guardian Capital v. N.Y. State Division
of Human Rights* (1974), 70, 120–21
Gurung, Regan, 129–30

hair: female options, 51, 57–58, 155;
feminine styling of, 1, 2, 15, 65; male
length restrictions, 6, 19, 50–51, 57,
60, 64–65, 98, 139, 141, 190–91n21,

192n31; racial identity and, 154–55,
158, 165, 167; social meaning of, 47,
48–50, 158; strict neutrality and,
48–50, 154–55
Hardin v. Stynchcomb (1982), 75
*Harper v. Edgewood Board of
Education* (1987), 94
Haskar, Vinit, 213n2
health-care privacy, 71–76, 118
Hebl, Michelle, 133
Hispanic workers, 152–53, 155, 156, 157,
158–59, 165, 167–68
homosexuality, 18, 20, 49, 77, 101,
206n53; workplace neutrality and,
36–37. *See also* effeminate men
Hooters Girls, 127, 128, 196n69
Hopkins, Ann. *See Price Waterhouse
vs. Hopkins*
hospital workers, 72, 75–76
human flourishing, 10, 113–15, 116, 126
Hurka, Thomas, 113, 114, 214n10

immutabile traits. *See* status
intellectual development, 10, 113–15,
125–26, 135; sexualization threat to,
70–71, 112, 125–36, 220–21n56
intrinsic values, 113–14
involuntary actions, 91–95
Iowa Supreme Court, 98

James v. Ranch Mart Hardware
(1995), 38
*Jespersen v. Harrah's Operating
Company* (2006), 2, 23–26, 44–45,
58, 59–60, 104–5, 108, 139; court's
reasoning and, 65–66, 98–99, 141,
208n65; dissenting judges and,
25–26, 59; gender expression
hypothetical and, 145, 146; unequal
burdens test and, 190n10
*Johnson v. Transportation Agency, Santa
Clara County, California, et al.*
(1987), 198n87
Jones v. Hinds General Hospital (1987),
75–76
Justice Department, 48–49

Kelly, Edith, 31
Kelman, Mark, 92

status, 9, 89–110, 149, 163–65; broad
conception of, 92; dangers of
expansion of, 102–9; effeminate
men harassment cases and, 206n53;
gender and, 89–102, 168; immutable
traits and, 7, 98, 109–10, 158, 159,
199n1; meaning of, 90–92;
sex-neutral soft qualifications
and, 81
stigmatic burden, 62, 63, 157–58, 159
strippers, 73, 122, 123
strip searches, 116
Supreme Court, U.S.: affirmative
action and, 198n87; disparate
impact claims and, 55; neutrality
conception of, 35–36; same-sex
harassment ruling, 19–20; sex-blind
workplace ruling, 31; sex
stereotyping precedent (*see* sex
stereotyping); status conception
of, 91–92

technical job qualifications, 78
television news anchor, 40–42,
58–59, 63
Tenth Circuit Court of Appeals,
96–97
Title VII, 1–27, 182n11;
antisubordination and, 9, 27, 54–55,
87–88; basic commitments of, 11;
BFOQ exceptions (*see* BFOQ);
burden-shifting and, 97–98;
congressional intent and, 29–30,
182n11; core value of, 8–9 (*see also*
neutrality); disparate impact test,
55–71, 155, 172, 188n56; double-bind
principle, 64–71, 159–63;
Employment Non-Discrimination
Act (2007) and, 100–102; equal
opportunity underlying, 32, 77,
182n11, 208n42; expanded scope of
(*see* gender nonconformity
protection); expressive freedom
exempted from, 10, 68, 138, 139,
144–49, 167–68; female
discrimination as last-minute
inclusion, 29–30, 151, 170;
gender-based exemptions from, 2,
6, 8, 23–26, 51, 101–3, 188n58; group

focus of, 71–88, 89, 172; judicial
perfectionism and, 111–36; national
origin discrimination and, 152–53,
167; racial/ethnic protection limits,
150–59, 162, 165–69, 233n27; sex
stereotyping precedent and (*see* sex
stereotyping); status-based
application of, 9, 89, 90, 106–7,
109–10, 149
trait neutrality. *See* neutrality
Transgender Law Center, 104
transsexuals, 1–2, 5–9, 45–46, 92–95,
150, 151, 178n28, 203n18; bathroom
access and, 96–98, 178–79n34,
204n17; biological sex vs. gender
identity of, 101, 209n67, 210–
11nn69–72; case example, 21–23;
clinical threshold for, 212n85; courts'
distinctions between gender benders
and, 101–2; disparate treatment
framework and, 234n35;
Employment Non-Discrimination
Act and, 100–101; gender identity
disorder diagnosis and, 21, 91, 103–4;
medicalized concept of, 94, 105,
106–7, 172, 173, 208–9n66; opposite-
sex gender norms and, 2, 47, 93, 105,
107–8; sex stereotyping precedent
and, 21–23, 93; Title II extension to
(*see* gender nonconformity
protection); traditional gender script
and, 103–4; trait neutrality
comparator problem, 37–38

Ulane v. Eastern Airlines (1984), 21
unequal burdens test, 56–64;
burden-shifting framework and,
96–98; case examples of, 60–61,
156, 194n56; double bind vs., 67,
156, 196n54; male vs. female
appearance and, 25, 57–60, 68,
189–90nn9,10; narrower conception
of, 60–63; race cases and, 156, 157;
sex-specific grooming codes upheld
despite, 57–60, 68; stigmatization
of women and, 62, 63, 157;
workplace neutrality and, 60, 63–64
*University of Maryland at Baltimore v.
Boyd* (1992), 163–64